HOMELESSNESS IN THE UNITED STATES

Recent Titles in Contributions in Sociology

Homelessness in the United States

Volume I:
STATE SURVEYS

EDITED BY
JAMSHID A. MOMENI

FOREWORD BY
BRUCE WIEGAND

Contributions in Sociology, Number 73

GREENWOOD PRESS
New York
Westport, Connecticut
London

Library of Congress Cataloging-in-Publication Data

Homelessness in the United States / edited by Jamshid A. Momeni ;
  foreword by Bruce Wiegand.
       p.   cm. — (Contributions in sociology, ISSN 0084-9278 ; no.
  73)
     Includes index.
     Contents: v. 1. State surveys.
     ISBN 0-313-25566-0 (lib. bdg. : v. 1 : alk. paper)
     1. Homelessness—United States. 2. Homeless persons—Services
  for—United States. I. Momeni, Jamshid A., 1938- . II. Series:
  Contributions in sociology ; no. 73, etc.
  HV4505.H656   1989
  362.5'0973—dc19   88-10964

British Library Cataloguing in Publication Data is available.

A paperback edition entitled *Homelessness in the
United States—State Surveys* is available from
Praeger Publishers (ISBN 0-275-93603-1).

Library of Congress Catalog Card Number: 88-10964
ISBN: 0-313-25566-0
ISSN: 0084-9278

First published in 1989

Greenwood Press, 88 Post Road West, Westport, CT 06881
An imprint of Greenwood Publishing Group, Inc.

Printed in the United States of America

∞

The paper used in this book complies with the
Permanent Paper Standard issued by the National
Information Standards Organization (Z39.48-1984).

10 9 8 7 6 5 4 3 2

To All Homeless People in the World

Contents

Figures and Tables

Foreword

As Americans were rediscovering the homeless in the early years of this decade, there emerged a set of popular myths, which were accepted on face value. For example, at that time it was believed that the size of the homeless population was between 2 and 3 million. It was also widely held that women and children made up a growing portion of the population, and that the loss of factory jobs and the premature release of mental patients into communities were the most important explanations for the apparently sudden outbreak of the problem.

In contrast to these myths, another set of beliefs also arose and gained popular support. Drawing upon assumptions of personal responsibility and moral righteousness, these beliefs recalled earlier stereotypes of the ''skid-row bum.'' The claim here was that today's homeless are nothing more than the latest manifestation of the age-old problem of broken men, alcoholism, and failed dreams. An even earlier conception—the myth of the hobo or carefree vagabond—appears to be inconsequential to present-day debates over the causes and cures of homelessness. Thus, for the past seven or eight years, we have witnessed an ideological contest with conflicting stereotypes—the myth of the ''new homeless'' versus the myth of the ''skid-row bum''—at its base. And as the contest to determine which of the myths will provide the blueprint for domestic national policy as it relates to the homeless continues, I am troubled by the inflated language and unsubstantiated claims on both sides.

The success of Jamshid Momeni's volume is that it is one of the first attempts to deflate the hyperbole that has come to be associated with homelessness. The material he has selected for this book does not favor one ideological position or another, but instead calls upon established social science methods to strip away the myth and rhetoric that have limited our knowledge and treatment of the problem. The conclusions that the researchers draw in these 14 chapters do not stray irresponsibly from the empirical data that they provide to the reader. What their data suggest to me is the complex and perhaps even paradoxical nature of homelessness.

Consider these three findings, which are covered in much more detail in the text. First, the homeless live a mobile, itinerant life-style. Unfortunately, researchers have not mapped out their migration routes, which would be a tremendous help in administering public policy. Yet, surveys and enumerations in Illinois, New Jersey, Ohio, and Tennessee, among other states, show that the homeless orbit locally. In other words, their drifting is not as aimless as one might suspect, but rather exhibits a distinct "homing sense." Second, research in such diverse corners of the country as Alabama, Massachusetts, Missouri, New York, Utah, and Virginia has highlighted the fact that the homeless are cut off or disaffiliated from social institutions such as family or church. But, curiously, many of these same people profess to have friends and primary networks that they can count on. Thus, we start to perceive homelessness as being a shared cultural experience, in addition to being an economic and a psychological deprivation. Third, research shows that the demographic composition of the populations seems to vary by state and region of the country. For example, in Texas, Tennessee, and Utah, the homeless population seems to be largely unmarried, white males. But in New Jersey, New York, and the Northwest, there are more homeless families, war veterans, young males, and blacks and other minorities. Nonetheless, despite such differences, researchers from every region of the country are quick to agree on the need for an integrated federal policy to solve the problem of homelessness.

This brings me to the greatest paradox of all. For whatever combination of reasons, the fact is that we are all confronted by the problem nearly every day of our lives. We are appalled, and even threatened, that the homeless have become so visible in our cities. Yet, despite public recognition of the problem, we have a very poor understanding of its causes, consequences, and magnitude. This creates a climate, such as we have now, in which stereotypes and misinformation are popularly distributed and consumed. This volume of research does much to debunk the unfounded myths that surround homelessness and thereby permits our powers of analysis to be turned toward the great social problem of the 1980s.

—Bruce Wiegand
School of Justice
American University

Preface

This is the first of two volumes in the work *Homelessness in the United States*. Volume I concentrates on the statewide distribution, variations, trends, and characteristics of homelessness in America—a major and growing socioeconomic and health problem. In view of the eloquent and extensive descriptions of this book by Professor Wiegand, the author of the Foreword, and by Professor Bahr, a leading authority on skid-row and homelessness research and the author of the Introduction that follows, I will limit my comments to only one point. Many still generally believe in the myth that homeless people primarily consist of a group of deinstitutionalized, mentally ill persons who wander the streets of America. By implication, of course, it is thought that very little can be done for them. The prime objective of this book is to substantiate the fact that this characterization of the homeless in America is simply wrong. The data in several chapters of this volume show that on the average only about 25 to 30 percent of the homeless suffer varying degrees of mental illness (in some cases a consequence of homelessness itself). The remaining 75 percent are perfectly normal, average people, including young and innocent children, the elderly, family members, and victims of eviction and family violence, who have suddenly and unexpectedly fallen to the lowest social stratum. In addition, this volume documents the fact that a large segment of the population is "homeless-vulnerable," who do not fit the mentally ill stereotype. It may be pointed out that irrespective of its cause—mental illness or other—the homeless should be viewed from a sociological perspective. Such a perspective views them as a social group entitled to all rights and privileges of membership in the society and to respectable treatment by the society at large. If the essays and empirical data presented here—free from biases, philosophical orientations, or political affiliations and commitments—change the views of some, especially of policymakers, in the direction of adopting a sociological perspective of the homeless, it has achieved its goal.

Regrettably, we were unable to obtain a suitable chapter on homelessness in California for this volume. Substantial discussion of California is presented in Volume II.

The second volume examines topical issues such as homelessness and drug problems, housing, and economic survival strategies. In addition, it contains a notable survey entitled "No Place to Go: A National Picture of Homelessness." The data for this particular chapter were collected with the support I received from some 90 U.S. senators, 45 state governors, and hundreds of mayors of cities with populations of 40,000 and over.

—Jamshid A. Momeni

Acknowledgments

I wish to express my gratitude to Dr. James T. Sabin, executive vice president of Greenwood Press/Praeger Publishers, who accepted the initial proposal for this two-volume project. The project's success will be due in part to Dr. Sabin's foresight and commitment. The trust placed in me acted as a major energizer for the completion of this work as scheduled. I must also thank the authors for their timely contributions and for their patience and cooperation in revising their manuscripts to meet the review and editorial requirements. Howard University's institutional support is appreciated.

Finally, I am greatly indebted to my wife, Dr. Mahvash Momeni, and my children, who provided most necessary moral support for this project.

Introduction

Perusing Professor Momeni's ambitious *Homelessness in the United States*, I am reminded of a reviewer's comment about Alfred Kinsey's *Sexual Behavior in the Human Male*. The book is like a Russian dancing bear. The wonder is that the bear dances at all, and one does not criticize the beast for not keeping strict time. *Homelessness in the United States* may not be all that the purists—pragmatic, theoretical, or methodological—might wish. Even so, it represents a noteworthy advance over most of the existing literature on homelessness. In an area of inquiry marked by a multitude of local studies and innumerable bureaucratic reports, a field of study in which systematic attention to the regional or national context is notably lacking, Professor Momeni aims to correlate and to integrate via a state-by-state assessment of contemporary homelessness.

The essays in this first volume represent the work of more than a score of scholarly specialists in homelessness and cover approximately one-third of the nation. They reflect a variety of perspectives on homelessness, draw upon different sources of data, and sometimes produce findings that are at odds with each other. Occasional inconsistencies are to be expected in studies by different people in different locales using different methods. What is remarkable in this volume is the general uniformity of findings and the repetition of a few familiar themes. While there are local variations, these essays dramatize the national uniformity of the problem of homelessness. It doesn't seem to matter whether we examine Florida or the Frostbelt, Massachusetts or Missouri; we confront the same syndrome.

Among the dominant themes is the finding that in most ways, the "new" homelessness is much like the old. Most homeless people are still multiproblem men. There are many kinds or subtypes of the homeless, but compared to the general population they are apt to be disabled, diseased, or mentally ill; they have attenuated kinship and friendship networks; they tend to be long-term unemployed or unemployable; and they are more likely to have histories of drug use, alcoholism, arrest, and incarceration. Much of the research, both in this volume and elsewhere, shows that true homelessness—what some of the best methodological studies call "literal homelessness" (Rossi et al., 1987)—is a long-term condition, a more or less permanent situation not readily treatable by a bureaucratic "quick fix" (cf. Freeman and Hall, 1987).

Another dominant theme, evident in every essay in this book, is that what is "new" about today's homelessness in the United States is an unprecedented shortage of low-income housing. There are virtually millions of the "near homeless," and the higher percentages of women and children among today's shelter populations are one manifestation of that housing crunch. But most of the "near homeless" manage to double up, to cooperate with friends and relatives, to combine income and private or government aid in ways that enable them to have a "home" and avoid the use of emergency shelters. The homeless people described in the essays of this book come closer to the "traditional" homeless than to that vast urban underclass who might be eligible for low-income housing.

One of the marks of a useful book is that it provokes discussion and reexamination of issues. My own examination of Professor Momeni's useful work prompted reconsideration of three aspects of the literature on homelessness as it relates to today's "crisis" and the issues of public policy. There is the matter of defining homelessness, the relevance of the past, and the problem of policy.

First, let us consider the problem of definition. Not all authors are explicit about their definitions of homelessness, and so sometimes the literal homeless and the near homeless, as well as a multitude of related populations, are combined or at least not distinguished for the reader. This ambiguity of definition is one of the problems in the entire vast literature on the subject and is especially troublesome when researchers turn to matters of public policy.

Sometimes homelessness is defined as the simple absence of shelter; sometimes it refers to people who are trapped in or have chosen a deviant life-style. Social service agencies and government researchers tend to define homelessness in line with their own objectives, political orientations, or traditions. Most of the definitions, or the elaborations of them, point to the homeless as dislodged, marginal, multiproblem people. Some definitions seem designed to minimize the scale of the problem of homelessness, as in estimates on counts of how many people are homeless in a given night. Other definitions maximize the size of the population, as in projections of how many people are homeless (that is living in streets, in emergency shelters, or in certain designated low-level accommodations) at least once in a given year. Thus the size of the population "moves," depending upon an author's intent. If our purpose is to show how serious an emergency we face, perhaps the number of homeless should include those without appropriate shelter at least once in the past two, three, or five years.

The point is that with a slight change in definition, we can transform a veritable epidemic into a minor, regrettable consequence of a changing national economy; or we can make of ordinary circumstance an emergency. The authors of Chapter 2, "Homelessness in Colorado," illustrate the problems of conflicting definitions when they explicitly include "more people than just those without shelter" in their approach to homelessness and then lament a state government approach that minimizes, rather than maximizes, the population deserving assistance.

As for the relevance of the past, in the vast contemporary literature on homelessness and in the essays in this book there are frequent references to how little we know, how much research is needed, and how scanty the store of knowledge. According to one lengthy report (80 pages, buttressed by 156 separate works cited in the reference section): "To begin with, there is scant information . . . on the scale of the problem. Homeless people cannot be tagged like geese and their patterns of migration charted" (Hopper and Hamberg, 1984: 7). Of course, homeless people *can* be tagged, or could be if doing so were as efficient with people as with geese. In fact, homeless people are much easier to study than geese, and for more than a century the homeless population—the "new" homeless, the old guard, the temporary and the long-term, the mentally unfit and the sharp predators, the winos and the retired seamen, the bag ladies, the bottle gangs, the displaced families, the runaway children, and the newly released ex-convicts—have been studied, counted, interviewed, observed, accompanied, photographed, human-interest storied, enumerated, given projective tests, life-history interviewed, captured on application and eligibility forms—in short have been analyzed and interrogated more than any population of comparable size— I want to say anywhere but don't *know* that for sure and so will hedge—more than any population of comparable size *almost* anywhere.

The bibliographies of *directly* relevant research, limited primarily to homelessness in the United States, now fill two inch-thick volumes. More than a decade ago, before the outpouring of print on the so-called "new" homelessness, Theodore Caplow summarized the literature this way:

Every field of scientific or scholarly investigation has certain topics that fascinate the professional investigator and that are studied more often and more closely than their importance may warrant. Hamlet is such a topic for literary scholars; the fruitfly has occupied such a place in genetics. The study of homeless men . . . has attracted sociologists since the earliest days of social research for reasons that have nothing to do with the relative urgency of homelessness as a social problem. (Caplow, 1971: 3)

And, may I add, not merely sociologists but journalists (*especially* journalists), physicians, nurses, clergymen, psychologists (both social and clinical), social workers, political scientists, psychiatrists, family specialists, demographers, urbanologists, geographers, and human ecologists—the range of disciplines represented and the scope, both geographic and topical, of the inquiries into the lives and minds of homeless people are enormous. If anything, there is information overload—too much rather than too little—and, overwhelmed by the literature to be digested, the practitioner or new analyst turns away and does some focused, manageable study directly and superficially relevant rather than think about and interpret a century of work.

Bear in mind that much of the accumulated research *can* be rendered obsolete by the touch of the definitional wand. If we cast our problem in terms of "true magnitude" of the homeless population and include new populations such as the "prehomeless" (defined in one report as "large numbers of people—making do under barely tolerable living circumstances" [Hopper and Hamberg, 1984: 8], an apt description, I believe, for all human life in all societies in all of history) then it is possible to lament the dearth of relevant information—possible but not convincing. It is not information we lack.

It turns out on inspection that the past *is* relevant after all, although from the typical report on contemporary homelessness one would be led to believe that we confront a totally new situation. Many of the recommendations made in the essays collected by Dr. Momeni—the call for coordination among agencies, the need for a comprehensive program providing a variety of rehabilitative services, the pleas for special services for homeless women and children, the frustration with local and private officialdom and the hope for well-designed programs mandated at the federal level, and the recognition that homelessness is a special case of the larger problem of poverty—are recurrent themes in the homelessness literature of the 1930s and the 1950s.

Turning now to the question of public policy, we must again refer to definitions. Many advocates for the homeless seem to think that by defining the population as broadly as possible—by making as much of the population homeless as they can manage—they increase their chances for getting funds to help homeless people. I believe this strategy is politically and historically naive. The larger the potential client population, the wider the variation among the homeless, and the fewer resources will trickle down to the most abject, the most powerless. That brings us to a sociological truism, a phrase credited to Robert Merton, among others. It is called the Matthew Principle and, in its roughest form, reads like this: Them that has, gets.

The Matthew Principle, more than any other, dooms the comprehensive treatment of literal homelessness. Resources are always limited; there are always too many good causes and too little time and money to do all the good we would. People, organizations, and governments must establish priorities, and the less powerful—however you measure power—generally end up getting the short end of things. And it is power, more than anything else, that the homeless lack, for in human society, power stems from affiliations—from belonging to families, schools, companies, interest groups, political units, churches, voluntary associations of all kinds—groups that provide sustenance, that multiply one's cry of pain in times of need, that exert check-and-balance power or threaten establishments with sufficient clout to shake loose benefits of various kinds.

Homelessness, narrowly defined as literal homelessness, is a condition of disaffiliation, a lack of bonds, a pathology of connectedness, and not an absence of proper housing, or a necessary concomitant of abject poverty or of deviant life-styles. One recent summary of the subpopulations that comprise the homeless poor today—victims of domestic violence, single men and women, single-parent households, the psychiatrically disturbed, the unemployed and undocumented immigrants—explains the common thread tying them all together this way: "They have one thing in common: owing to the brute reality of having nowhere else to turn, they have been forced to resort to the kindness of strangers to survive" (Hopper and Hamberg, 1984: 11). It is disaffiliation that leaves one at the mercy of strangers.

Affiliations generate significant others for us, they affirm our identities, and they create means for controlling our environments. As long as one has viable social ties, that is, has other persons bound to him or her by reciprocal rights and obligations, one's defectiveness is, at worst, only partial. But the more disaffiliated and the more powerless one becomes, the less "needed" or "expected" or "obligated" he or she is and the easier it is for the adjectives "lost," "forgotten," "passed by," and "surplus" to be applied. With the passing of obligations go also rights, and the new self-definition is imprinted via stigmatization, victimization and discrimination in interaction with others. If one has visible stigma—marks of being "damaged goods" which are visible to all—the impact on the self of powerlessness and disaffiliation may be even greater. With the collapse of one's affiliations goes what little power the homeless individual can command. The stranger, especially the aged, scarred, alcoholic, mentally ill, or deformed stranger, has no social margin. He or she may be free to come and go, subject always to the approval of the others—the powerful affiliated ones.

Sometimes, as (one would hope) in the present time of high visibility of the homeless, the needs and wishes of the more powerful affiliated ones may coincide with those of the homeless. But always the homeless one is vulnerable and on the outside; organizations and programs of the affiliated represent *their* interests, first and foremost, and not the interests of the homeless. Typically the disaffiliate has little voice in others' decisions about his or her treatment and future.

This absence of power does not apply to the near or prehomeless. For one thing, there are many more of them. For another, they retain affiliations and can muster some political power by virtue of those affiliations. The powerlessness of the "truly homeless" means that, by and of themselves, they can never generate sufficient public interest or political influence to satisfy their needs.

Let us take a specific illustration. The federal Committee on Government Operations formally recommended to President Ronald Reagan in 1985 that, by executive order, he "direct all Federal agencies to give top priority to and expand their current efforts on behalf of the homeless." Subsequent reports criticized the president for ignoring this recommendation. Yet, from the standpoint of political reality, the recommendation was doomed from the start. How many "top priorities" can there be? Was the committee seriously suggesting that the welfare of the powerless, unorganized homeless be given priority over the needs of Democrats for a strong defense, or of the nation's schoolchildren, or of the shuttle program, or of AIDS research, or of the country's deteriorating highway system, or more than a hundred other more pressing needs from the standpoint of maintaining a stable and apparently responsive government? The homeless population may be experiencing personal crises, but that in itself is neither new nor exceptional. In fact, it is business as usual for the bottom of the underclass. The best predictor of future behavior is past behavior, and the historical record, massively documented, shows that the literally homeless have *never* been adequately served by government or by private charity. Indeed, the more complex and costly the programs demanded by the advocates for the homeless, the less likely it is that anything workable will come to be.

The existing research literature on homelessness in America suggests that literal homelessness—the syndrome of disaffiliation and deviance that we may think of as "traditional" homelessness and which seems to characterize a majority of the homeless populations described in the following essays—has never been successfully confronted and treated in American society. Moreover, there is no clear evidence that we know *how* to treat it successfully, whatever the cost, and there is quite clear evidence that neither public nor private institutions have been willing to bear the necessary costs even to apply the techniques deemed most successful at any particular time. This past failure does not mean we should not continue to try. It does, however, suggest that we be cautious in adopting the expensive and intrusive procedures urged by those who would "medicalize" the problem of homelessness.

To argue, with the author of the essay on "Homelessness in New Jersey," that contemporary homelessness is a problem of the social structure—is simply an exercise in terminology, a matter of assigning a label, and does not automatically dictate a structural solution. A structural problem it may be, but it manifests itself in individual terms, and resolution of literal homelessness requires rehabilitation of individual homeless persons, a process only partially understood and a social technology still to be perfected. Similarly, when the authors of "Homelessness in Alabama" assert that "the development of a comprehensive program is required," they affirm a truism but neglect a history in which no such comprehensive program has been enacted and shown to be feasible, effective, and acceptable.

It is not only that the homeless lack power. Even if we had sufficient resources, there are serious questions about what *should* be done. The burden of the research literature on program evaluation and therapy of various kinds for the literal homeless is that (1) with reference to "rehabilitation," doing nothing works almost as well as doing anything at all, from group singing through psychiatric therapy; and (2) the best cost-benefit ratios derive from programs that provide essential protection—inexpensive food, shelter, and not much else—and do not attempt to change the lives or attitudes of homeless clients who do not actively seek personal change. Here the operative distinction is between help and rehabilitation. "Help" is acceptable; attempts to remake the homeless person typically are not. In practice, this means that a successful program for the homeless would permit them to vegetate, if they wish, in a more or less secure environment.

The evidence at hand suggest that, as a practical matter, simply providing enough warm places for the homeless to rest, reconnoiter, or vegetate seems to be beyond the capacity of our communities and governments. Our cities are vast reservoirs of unmet needs. Them that has, gets, and the literal homeless do not have.

The situation is much different for the near homeless, or the prehomeless. They are not the target population of the present volume, although they are included in some of the essays. There are millions of them; they are the victims of a decline in the stock of low-income housing, and their homelessness is remediable. Here the historical record justifies hope, because the solution to the current crisis, the "explosion" of homelessness, is low-income housing. And that is something that we know how to do, if the necessary political clout can be put together. We are not talking here of "comprehensive programs" or massive rehabilitation schemes, but simply the construction of houses and apartments. The technology is known, and no breakthroughs of psychiatry, counseling, or welfare management are needed.

Here, then, some of the assertions about policy by authors of these essays deserve discussion. The authors of "Homelessness in Texas" state that "the principal implication of such findings is straighforward: intervention efforts cannot stop with the provision of emergency food and shelter." For the literal homeless, this may be true; for the prevention of increases in family homelessness, it may be precisely the *wrong* conclusion. Writing in *Social Policy*, James Wright and Julie Lam take a contrasting position:

In a hypothetical world where there are no alcoholics, no drug addicts, no mentally ill, no deinstitutionalization movement, indeed, no personal or social pathologies at all, there would still be a formidable homelessness problem, simply because at this stage in American history, there is not enough low-income housing to accommodate the poverty population. (Wright and Lam, 1987: 53)

Homelessness in the United States is not intended to be a definitive treatment of policy matters. The authors are researchers, and the primary focus is on estimating the number and characteristics of the homeless. The estimates, however, derive from contacts with the homeless or with agencies that attempt to serve them, and the authors do not hesitate to incorporate their values and policy positions into their essays.

The reader cannot help but get involved in weighing alternative actions, agreeing or disagreeing, or in simply being motivated to elaborate and extend the assumptions made and the proposals offered. Some parts of this book are provocative, and my own response includes these thoughts on public policy and "treating" contemporary homelessness:

1. To go looking for unmet needs may be good political strategy, but is poor resource management strategy.

2. Charity, grounded in humanistic or religious values, is admirable but is a poor substitute for political clout. The historical record amply demonstrates the severe human costs of relying on charity as the basis for ameliorating homelessness. Effective national, state, and local programs must be grounded in sterner stuff.

3. Being appalled, offended, or shocked is similarly of little practical use. Nothing is surer than that the homeless will continue to be underserved. One approach might be to find ways to increase the benefits that organizations and persons receive for serving the homeless.

4. The fractions of national, regional, state, and local resources devoted to a given problem are so much the products of historical evolution, and intergroup conflict, compromise over priorities, and similar forces that major reapportioning is very difficult to create and sustain. Those who would serve the homeless should recognize that even slight increases in available funding represent remarkable success or good fortune.

5. Delivering more and better services to the homeless will require marked changes in the attitudes and priorities of the public. The high visibility of the homeless in the national media in the past year or two has helped to create a favorable climate as is documented in the essay on "Homelessness in Virginia." There must be a way to generate political power on behalf of the homeless. Such changes are difficult to sustain, although modern media can create an "instant" and short-lived "social problem" before the public's attention span is exceeded.

    There are perils and unanticipated consequences of crisis rhetoric, of comparisons with ideals as opposed to real comparisons with past or present performance. Remember that to ignore the political reality, which in the end is an affiliational relativity, is self-defeating. Appeals to virtue and humanity are not enough.

6. We must not expect too much, for governments and bureaucracies are by nature inept and often out of control. To expect a systematic, well-integrated federal program, coordinated with state and local efforts, is to indulge in utopian thinking. A quick review of existing federal programs suggests the absence of a consistent, integrated approach to *any* contemporary social problem.

7. Probably the more complex a proposed program, the higher its likelihood of failure, from the standpoint of meaningful "trickle down" to the literally homeless.

8. It is virtually certain that there will continue to be cycles of homelessness. The experience of a century suggests that homelessness is tied to economic factors far more than to direct government action, and it will continue to wax and wane.

9. If the past is at all useful as a predictor of the future, we must expect even well-intentioned, apparently well-designed private and government programs to serve the near homeless and the partially homeless—the relatively more powerful and "better connected" among the homeless—better than the truly abject and disaffiliated.

10. As far as we can tell from the record, the processes that create literal homelessness and the associated syndrome of problems are only partially reversible, if they are reversible if at all. Given the difficulties inherent in serving the truly homeless, success is often hard to distinguish from failure.

As is by now apparent, Professor Momeni's book generates response. I believe that the process of response, discussion, and reassessment of "facts," perspectives, and potential actions that this book encourages will be beneficial to those who would understand homelessness and, ultimately, to the homeless themselves.

Homelessness in the United States represents an essential stage in the process of understanding contemporary homelessness. Its effort to integrate different kinds of information from many sources goes well beyond most available work. If it falls short of the ideal, it certainly moves us ahead. If it is less than we will ultimately need, it nevertheless represents more than we had before. Its conclusions and recommendations are certain to foster debate, and the consistency of its findings on the characteristics of the homeless will surely increase recognition of homelessness as a national problem deserving effective national response.

—Howard M. Bahr
Brigham Young University

REFERENCES

Caplow, Theodore. 1970. The Sociologist and the Homeless Man. In *Disaffiliated Man: Essays and Bibliography on Skid Row, Vagrancy, and Outsiders*, edited by H. M. Bahr, 3–12. Toronto: University of Toronto Press.

Freeman, Richard B., and Brian Hall. 1987. Permanent Homeless in America? *Population Research and Policy Review* 6: 3–27.

Hopper, Kim, and Jill Hamberg. 1984. *The Making of America's Homeless: From Skid Row to New Poor*. New York: Housing and Urban Policy Unit and Institute for Social Welfare Research, Department of Public Policy.

Rossi, Peter H., et al. 1987. The Urban Homeless: Estimating Composition and Size. *Science* 235 (March 13): 1336–1341.

Wright, James D., and Julie A. Lam. 1987. Homelessness and the Low-Income Housing Supply. *Social Policy* 17 (Spring): 48–53.

HOMELESSNESS IN THE UNITED STATES

1

Homelessness in Alabama: A Variety of People and Experiences

Mark La Gory, Ferris J. Ritchey,
Timothy O'Donoghue, and Jeffrey Mullis

Homelessness is no longer assumed to be a problem confined to large, aging cities in the northern industrial states. Clearly, it is prevalent in both the Sunbelt and Frostbelt regions, but the variation in numbers by region, state, and local area is virtually unknown (Snow and Anderson, 1987; U.S. General Accounting Office, 1985). Alabama could be expected to have a particularly severe problem, because it is a relatively poor state even by southern standards. It ranks forty-seventh in the nation in terms of median family income (U.S. Bureau of the Census, 1983). The state has the nation's highest infant mortality rate, and only two states have more serious poverty. Nearly 19 percent of all persons in Alabama live below the poverty line compared to 12.4 percent nationally. With regard to housing, Alabama residents are more likely to live in crowded quarters with less than adequate plumbing: 5.4 percent of Alabamians live in units with two or more persons per room, and 4.2 percent lack complete plumbing as compared to 4.5 percent and 2.2 percent, respectively, for the nation as a whole.

While these data suggest a socioeconomic environment conducive to a serious homeless problem, as of 1986 there were no accurate statewide indicators of homelessness. The little available published information either involved educated guesses about Birmingham's total homeless problem (Gleghorn, 1983) or agency-specific data for a few shelters in the state such as the Salvation Army and a network of shelters for victims of domestic abuse. No effort had been mounted to coordinate data-gathering procedures at local or state levels. Many shelters were not staffed sufficiently to keep a simple count, let alone maintain client record files. Nonetheless, it was recognized that such data were essential in order to assess local needs adequately and to gain the necessary financial resources to address those needs.

Recognizing the importance of objective baseline data, a coalition of Birmingham shelter providers, city officials, and health care personnel, under the title of Metropolitan Birmingham Services for the Homeless, requested that the authors develop more accurate information on the state's homeless problem. The intent of the research was twofold: (1) to make Alabamians aware of the housing crisis in the state, and (2) to develop a reliable data source to assess the needs of homeless persons and service providers in the various communities of the state. The project involved a three-phase effort that included:

Phase 1. A count of sheltered homeless persons in the eight areas of Alabama designated as Standard Metropolitan Statistical Areas (SMSAs) in the 1980 U.S. Census of Population.

Phase 2. A simultaneous count of homeless persons in a 300-square-block area of downtown Birmingham.

Phase 3. A survey of 150 systematically sampled street-and shelter-based homeless people in Birmingham.

The purpose of Phases 1 and 2 was to develop reliable, conservative figures on the size and basic demographic characteristics of the homeless population, while Phase 3 was to provide detailed information on the nature and consequences of homelessness. This paper reports on the salient aspects of all three phases.

Several critical issues are examined here: What is the size of the homeless population in Alabama's eight metropolitan areas? What is the demographic makeup of this population and does it fit descriptions of the pre-urban-renewal, skid-row population that characterized homelessness before the late 1970s? What are the causes of homelessness in Alabama, and what do these causes suggest about possible solutions? Are Alabama's homeless disaffiliated from the community or, alternatively, do they maintain essential social ties through informal social networks?

DEVELOPING RELIABLE COUNTS OF THE HOMELESS POPULATION

A census of any population requires that several critical methodological issues be addressed including who is to be counted, where and when the count is to take place, and what methods are to be used to establish population figures. These issues present peculiar methodological challenges with regard to a social condition such as homelessness.

Who Is to Be Counted?

Just exactly what constitutes homelessness? To be homeless obviously means to be without a home, but *home* is a complex social and psychological construct, not simply a physical structure. The literature on homelessness reflects the difficulty of defining it. In the last 20 years a variety of criteria have been used to distinguish the homeless from the homed. These include:

1. *transiency*, "itinerant persons using accommodations provided for transients" (Leigh, 1979: 95)

2. *frequency*, "persons . . . who are chronically homeless or in danger of becoming so" (Tiller, 1980: 3)

3. *ecology*, "those whose primary nighttime residence is either in the publicly or privately operated shelters or in the streets, in doorways, parks, subways, abandoned buildings, loading docks, and other well-hidden sites known only to their users" (Baxter and Hopper, 1981: 7)

4. *spatial marginality*, "[The homeless are those who occupy marginal space.] Marginal space includes alleys, dumps, space under bridges, behind hedgerows, on the roofs of buildings, . . . around railroad yards . . . [and] very poor residential or commercial areas" (Duncan, 1983: 92)

5. *social marginality*, "Homelessness is a human condition of disaffiliation and detachment from the primary agents of social structure" (Larew, 1980: 107)

Obviously these definitions vary significantly and are likely to yield quite different counts. The definitions centering on transiency, frequency and social marginality are value-laden, and their use is likely to exclude large numbers of people who lack basic shelter. The spatial-marginality definition, on the other hand, is too inclusive relative to current usage. It suggests that all marginally sheltered persons are homeless. Under its criteria, people living in dilapidated housing would be counted because they have no "real home" as defined by prevailing cultural standards.

Given these considerations and an interest in developing a conservative but accurate count, we opted for the more straightforward ecological criteria with some consideration given to spatial marginality. Our census included only persons whose nighttime residence was either in a shelter, on the street, or in other public sites. A list of such sites is given below. This definition was similar to that used in recent enumerations in Chicago (Rossi, Fisher, and Willis, 1986) and Nashville (Cuoto, Lawrence, and Lee, 1985).

Enumeration Timing, Location, and Procedures

Following our previously stated philosophy of developing a conservative count, we used enumeration procedures developed by Barrett A. Lee (cited in Cuoto, 1985) in his census of homeless in Nashville, Tennessee. Because of the limited resources available for our count, both Phase 1 and Phase 2 censuses were geographically restricted. Phase 1, the statewide shelter count, was restricted to shelters in the eight SMSAs defined by the 1980 United States Census of Population, that is: Birmingham, Anniston, Florence, Gadsden, Huntsville,

Mobile, Montgomery, and Tuscaloosa. In so doing, homelessness was assumed to be predominantly an urban problem. A master list of shelters was developed for each SMSA based on information gathered from local Salvation Army officers, Traveler's Aid Societies, statewide United Way Volunteer and Information Services, and other local service providers. The resulting list of 54 shelters ranged from traditional missions serving the needs of chronically homeless men or women, to domestic violence shelters, shelters for runaway children, halfway houses (for people released from substance abuse treatment programs, prisons, or mental institutions), and "intermediate housing facilities," which provided extensive housing and employment counseling. Entree was established with all shelter providers; they were mailed census forms and instructed to fill them out for the night of February 11, 1987. The results were transferred to us by phone the following morning. Every shelter completed the forms on the assigned night.

Phase 2, which was conducted the same night as Phase 1, involved an enumeration of street-based homeless people, those who for one reason or another were not sheltered on the census night. This street count was limited to downtown Birmingham because of the extensive energy and resources necessary to maintain eligibility. Fourteen teams of trained enumerators, ranging from two to eight persons, combed a 300-square-block area between the hours of 3:00 and 5:00 A.M.

The date of the enumeration was chosen to coincide with typical winter nighttime temperatures. Homeless enumerations generally face a serious problem in that the population to be enumerated is not highly visible or readily accessible. People without shelter are exposed to the environment in all its complexity and are vulnerable to predation and constant surveillance. This forces them to seek privacy and limited visibility. A cold night was likely to encourage a more accurate count, as persons who might often use the street or an abandoned building in warmer temperatures sought the more predictable surroundings of a shelter. The low temperature for the enumeration night was 24 degrees Fahrenheit.

The issue of visibility also prompted the selection of the enumeration hours. It was presumed that from 3:00 to 5:00 A.M. (1) people were likely to be at rest, reducing the possibility of double-counting those walking through more than one enumeration area; (2) people in public areas downtown would be more visible and accessible because of reduced congestion; and (3) persons encountered in the downtown area were likely to be there because they had nowhere else to go. That is, they were homeless.

Because the count of homeless street people was thus restricted geographically and temporally, it should be noted that this count yields information on only the most visible portions of a population that has been characterized by its invisibility. It is important to denote not only those places where we searched, but those places we could not or did not look. The public places scrutinized in this count included: (a) streets, alleys, passageways; (b) parking decks and garages; (c) parks and thickets; (d) under bridges and overpasses; and (e) in railroad box cars, abandoned vehicles, and trailers. In addition, using the conservative judgment of professionals who work with the homeless, some people in the following places were counted: (f) lobbies of public buildings such as post offices, city hall, night courts, and accessible hospital waiting rooms; (g) all-night restaurants; (h) bus stations, and (i) city jails (for people jailed on the census night who had no legal place of residence).

The enumeration did not include people residing in abandoned buildings, houses, mines, or single-room occupancy (SRO) hotels; individuals admitted to hospital emergency rooms; or homeless persons residing outside the downtown area in the residential areas of the city, suburbs, or small towns of the metropolitan counties. In addition, our definition of the homeless was restricted. We did not, as noted before, include the marginally housed, nor did we consider those families or individuals who were "living in" with friends or relatives on a temporary basis. Thus, the count provides a very conservative figure on what is without question a much larger problem. Our figures must be used cautiously and with the recognition that they significantly undercount the homeless population in Alabama.

THE CENSUS COUNT: RESULTS OF PHASES 1 AND 2

The following data indicate the number of homeless persons actually counted in the eight metropolitan areas of Alabama on February 11, 1987.[1]

Area	Number	Percentage of Total Statewide
Birmingham		
Shelters	495	39
Downtown streets	77	6
Other sites	26	2
Shelters of other Alabama SMSAs		
Anniston	48	4
Florence	22	2
Gadsden	33	3
Huntsville	203	16
Mobile	259	20
Montgomery	88	7
Tuscaloosa	16	1
Total	1,267	100

As the data show, a total of 1,267 persons were counted. This figure represented a significant undercount of Alabama's metropolitan homeless, because it excluded street-based homeless persons other than those in downtown Birmingham. It also excluded a count of individuals using the three single-room occupancy hotels in Birmingham, as well as SRO users in the other SMSAs. To

Table 1.1
Estimates of Sheltered, Street, and Single-Room Occupancy (SRO) Homeless
Populations for Alabama SMSAs on February 11, 1987

Metro-Area	Frequencies			Rates	
	(A) Estimated Street Population[a]	(B) Estimated SRO Residents[b]	(C) Total Including Shelters	(D) Central City Population	(E) Homeless per 1000 Population
Anniston	10	10	68	29,553	2.30
Birmingham	103[c]	100	698	284,413	2.45
Florence	5	5	32	37,029	0.86
Gadsden	7	7	47	47,565	0.99
Huntsville	43	41	287	142,513	2.01
Mobile	55	52	366	200,452	1.82
Montgomery	19	18	125	177,857	0.70
Tuscaloosa	3	3	22	75,211	0.29
Total	245	236	1,645	994,593	1.65

a: These estimates are conservative because they were computed on the basis of the Birmingham street count, which was limited to the nonresidential, downtown business district. Estimates were based on the assumption that the ratio of street to sheltered homeless found in Birmingham would be identical in all SMSAs. This ratio was 0.213.

b: These estimates are derived from SRO occupancy figures for Birmingham. While no SRO censuses were taken in these SMSAs it was assumed that Birmingham ratio of SRO occupancy to sheltered homeless would be identical in all SMSAs. This ratio was 0.202.

c: Actual count.

adjust for these two critical missing pieces of information, simple estimation procedures were used. To assess the SRO population, data on the number of available SRO beds in Birmingham were compiled. Then, based on estimates used by the Metropolitan Birmingham Services for the Homeless, an average daily occupancy rate of 85 percent was assumed. This assumption yielded an estimate of 100 persons in Birmingham's SROs on an average night. Since neither street counts nor SRO counts were available for the other SMSAs, estimates for them were based on the Birmingham figures. The estimation procedure assumed that the ratio of street- to shelter-based homeless and SRO- to shelter-based homeless would be similar to Birmingham's. Table 1.1 presents estimates of the total homeless adjusting for the lack of direct SRO and street counts in SMSAs other than Birmingham. From these estimates, rates per 1,000 (central city) population are computed.

As can be seen from Table 1.1, the largest number of persons per 1,000 population (2.45) were found in Birmingham; the smallest (0.29), in Tuscaloosa. Birmingham also had the greatest number of shelters (22) while Anniston and Florence had the fewest. This variation by place could not be totally attributed to population differences (Table 1.1, Column E), as there was no straightforward relationship between central city size and estimated daily homeless rates.

Estimating a Statewide Total

Since cities are the major sites for social services and employment for homeless people, implicit in our counting procedure was an assumption that homelessness is primarily an urban problem. We did not, therefore, attempt to count persons in the nonmetropolitan areas of the state. Nonetheless, about 40 percent of the state's population lives outside its metropolitan areas. Thus, to obtain a statewide figure depicting homelessness in Alabama, it is appropriate to estimate the extent of the problem of homelessness outside SMSAs.

The U.S. Department of Housing and Urban Development (HUD) (U.S. Department of Housing and Urban Development, 1984), in a controversial report on homelessness, suggested that homelessness in rural areas and small towns would approximate the rates of the average small SMSA (those ranging from 50,000 to 250,000 persons). Using that assumption, 960 homeless persons could be expected in the nonmetropolitan areas of Alabama, giving a total of 2,605 homeless persons in Alabama on any given day. This estimation procedure, however, is somewhat suspect. Our belief is that the nonmetropolitan rate is not as close to that of small SMSAs as HUD has assumed. A more conservative strategy would be to assume that the rate was no higher than that of the lowest metropolitan rate. If that assumption is made, the nonmetropolitan homeless would number 256 persons for a statewide total of 1,901 persons. That estimate, however, is probably low, since the metropolitan area with the lowest rate is a rather prosperous and homogeneous university town. Therefore, we believe the best conservative estimate of the total number of homeless persons in Alabama on a given day falls somewhere between these extremes of 1,901 and 2,605.

Demographic Characteristics of Alabama's Sheltered Homeless

Table 1.2 provides information on the basic population characteristics of shelter users by metropolitan area. These results were striking; most of those counted were young, male, and white. While there were slight deviations in these patterns for a few smaller places, the total shelter count figures revealed 61 percent to be under 40, 75 percent to be male, and 70 percent to be white.

The data for age were of interest because the pre–1970s literature on homelessness focused on the skid-row population, which was comprised predominantly of older males. More recent studies reveal the new homeless to be younger. Table 1.3 provides a comparison of earlier with more recent findings on the age distribution of the homeless. Clearly, the age structure of Alabama's homeless fits this description of a more youthful population. Indeed, in our shelter census, 18 percent were actually children, and as the street figures for Birmingham show (Table 1.4), a few children were not sheltered but were found sleeping on the streets.

Shelter data by race and sex were also informative. The racial distribution of *sheltered* homeless in Table 1.2 was proportional to the actual distribution of

Table 1.2
Sheltered Populations of Alabama Metropolitan Areas by Estimated Age, Sex, and Race, February 11, 1987[a]

Characteristics	Anniston % (N)	Birmingham % (N)	Florence % (N)	Gadsden % (N)	Huntsville % (N)	Mobile % (N)	Montgomery % (N)	Tuscaloosa % (N)	Total % (N)
AGE									
Under 20	12 (6)	15 (73)	64 (14)	58 (19)	15 (30)	17 (44)	27 (24)	19 (3)	18 (213)
20-39	40 (19)	47 (231)	27 (6)	21 (7)	37 (76)	50 (126)	35 (31)	37 (6)	43 (502)
40-59	40 (19)	32 (159)	9 (2)	15 (5)	41 (83)	29 (74)	30 (26)	37 (6)	32 (374)
60+	8 (4)	6 (31)	0 (0)	6 (2)	7 (14)	4 (10)	8 (7)	6 (1)	6 (69)
Total	100 (48)	100 (494)[b]	100 (22)	100 (33)	100 (203)	100 (254)[b]	100 (88)	100 (16)	100 (1158)[b]
SEX									
Male	90 (43)	76 (374)	27 (6)	48 (16)	87 (177)	70 (181)	70 (62)	81 (13)	75 (872)
Female	10 (5)	24 (121)	73 (16)	52 (17)	13 (26)	30 (78)	30 (26)	19 (3)	25 (292)
Total	100 (48)	100 (495)	100 (22)	100 (33)	100 (203)	100 (259)	100 (88)	100 (16)	100 (1164)
RACE									
White	88 (42)	65 (320)	68 (15)	79 (26)	84 (170)	67 (173)	69 (61)	44 (7)	70 (814)
Nonwhite	12 (6)	35 (175)	32 (7)	21 (7)	16 (33)	33 (86)	31 (27)	56 (9)	30 (350)
Total	100 (48)	100 (495)	100 (22)	100 (33)	100 (203)	100 (259)	100 (88)	100 (16)	100 (1164)

a: These numbers include persons who reported a legal residence but who were unable or unwilling to return home on the census night.

b: The ages of 1 person in Birmingham and 5 in Mobile were not reported.

Table 1.3

Mean Age of the Homeless Found in Selected Research by Study and by Year in Chronological Order

City	Study Author(s)	Study Year[a]	Mean Age Found
41 cities	D. Bogue	1963	45-74
Philadelphia	J. Rooney	1964	55
New York	H. M. Bahr and T. Caplow	Mid-1960s	55
London	G. Edwards, V. Williamson, A. Hawker, C. Hensman, and S. Postoyan	1968	46
New York	State Democratic Taskforce[b]	1969	43
London	I. C. Patch	1971	47
Seattle	B. A. Lee	1975	55
New York	State Democratic Taskforce[b]	1975	38
New York	State Office of Mental Health[b]	1981	36
New York	E. Baxter and K. Hopper	1982	40
Boston	E. Bassuk, L. Rubin, and A. Lauriat	1983	34
Portland (OR)	Multnomah County Social Services[c]	1983	38
Los Angeles	M. Robertson, R. Ropers, and R. Boyer	1984	37
Unnamed city in the Northwest	M. Whitney, O. Osborne, M. Godfrey, and K. Johnston	1985	36

a: The study years cited are the actual years in which the surveys were done. These years may be slightly different from the bibliographic citations, which lists the years in which results were published.

b: Study data contained in House Subcommittee on Housing and Community Development report, 1982, " Homelessness in America."

c: Study data contained in House subcommittee on Housing and Community Development report, 1984, "Homelessness in America II."

the races in Alabama. In absolute terms, many more whites than blacks used the state's publicly and privately supported shelters. At the same time, the sex ratio of the shelter population was far different from that of Alabama's general population. Males used shelters disproportionately more than their numbers in the state's population.

What do these figures mean? Is homelessness less likely to be a problem for blacks and females? The answer to this question is undoubtedly "no." Certainly women and blacks have held weak economic positions in American society, and this economic weakness has been reproduced, even exaggerated, in Alabama's cities. Single or divorced women and blacks are more likely to be living on the edge of poverty. Such impoverishment in turn yields a higher probability of homelessness. Yet these groups are clearly minorities in the shelters. The statistics on the Birmingham street-based homeless (Table 1.4) were instructive. Only 33 percent of this population was white, while of the residents in the Birmingham shelters 65 percent were white. It appeared that blacks in Birmingham were less likely to be sheltered or to seek shelter. While the reasons for this have not been demonstrated, a similar pattern may hold for other Alabama metropolitan areas.

Table 1.4
Birmingham Shelter and Street Populations by Estimated Age, Sex, and Race, February 11, 1987

Characteristics	Shelters[a] Percent	N	Street[b] Percent	N	Total Percent	N
AGE:						
Under 20 years	15	73	3	3	13	76
20-39 years	47	231	37	38	45	269
40-59years	32	159	38	39	33	198
60 +years	6	31	2	2	5	33
Not discernable	0	1	20	21	4	22
Total	100	495	100	103	100	598
SEX:						
Male	76	374	85	88	77	462
Female	24	121	3	3	21	124
Not discernable	0	0	12	12	2	12
Total	100	495	100	103	100	598
RACE:						
White	65	320	33	34	59	354
Nonwhite	35	175	50	52	38	227
Not discernable	0	0	17	17	3	17
Total	100	495	100	103	100	598

a: These numbers include 84 persons who reported a legal residence but who were unable or unwilling to return home on the census night. An abused woman and her children residing in a family violence shelter is a case in point.

b: Includes 17 persons in jail without permanent addresses, 7 abandoned buildings occupied by at least one person, and 2 persons sighted outside the downtown area.

Apparently black homelessness is less likely to be addressed by formal institutions; thus, it is also less visible and more susceptible to underenumeration. A lot of evidence has been presented in recent years indicating that the black extended family is more likely to provide mutual aid to its members in crisis situations (Hill and Shackleford, 1975; Willie, 1976). This often includes allowing relatives or friends to stay over for an indefinite period of time. Such informal sheltering could not be detected in the February 11 census. If such sheltering is taking place, while it may be the preferable option for the homeless individual, it puts strains on an already economically burdened social structure. What the economic and social costs of such mutual aid may be for black families is not clear.

Just as homeless blacks are less likely to use formal sources of aid for shelter, it may be that women are underrepresented in this census because of their ability to garner informally provided shelter. Given the traditional gender roles in American society, women may be more likely to be taken in by a relative or friend if a housing problem arises, or they may remain in an unhealthy domestic environment because of their economic vulnerability.

In spite of these qualifications, two conclusions can be drawn from these census data. First, Alabama has a significant homeless problem, although the severity of the problem here may not be as great as it is in large urban states in the Northeast and West (U.S. General Accounting Office, 1985). Second, Alabama's homeless are diverse—a varied population of young and old, men and women, whites and blacks. This demography more closely fits the profile of the "new homeless" of whom much has recently been written.

THE INTERVIEW SURVEY: RESULTS OF PHASE 3

While the census yielded a simple sketch of Alabama's homeless problem, the Birmingham survey was designed to provide more specific information on the population and their experiences. The interviews averaged about one hour in length and furnished a range of data including: (a) detailed demographic profiles of homeless persons, along with housing and employment histories; (b) the circumstances that led to homelessness; (c) the incidence of additional life crises among the homeless; and (d) the extent of family and friendship networks and instrumental supports available to this segment of the population.

The Sample

The distribution of homeless found in the February enumeration, according to location (shelter versus street), sex, and race, were used as the basis to obtain a stratified random sample of 150 persons. The response rate was 99.3 percent. Population estimates had an error range of ±8 percentage points at the 95 percent level of confidence.

The demographic makeup of the sample is presented in Table 1.5. The sample differed from the enumeration in that the former was restricted to those 18 years of age and older. It also underrepresented black males who were homeless but resided outside shelters on the streets. Thus, generalizations and statistical associations must be qualified.

Sex, Race, Age, Education, Marital Status. Survey results yielded a fine-grained demographic portrait of Alabama's homeless. Homelessness, as already established in the enumeration, was overwhelmingly a male problem, a finding at odds with recently cited national trends showing that the fastest growing segments of the homeless are women and children. Sheltered respondents were proportionate to the population with respect to race, but street-based homeless were disproportionately black and male. As was the case nationally, the mean age of the sample (39.7 years) was lower than that found in earlier studies. Additionally, educational levels of the homeless were identical to the general Alabama population. About 57 percent of the sample had at least a high school diploma, compared to 56.5 percent for the state. Clearly, the homeless are a reasonably well-educated group.

The data revealed a statistically significant association between age and sex.

Table 1.5
Sample Representation Relative to the Birmingham Enumeration (Adults Only)

Respondents Characteristics	Enumeration Population Percent	N	Survey Sample Percent	N	Significance
AGE:					
20-39	53.8	269	54.0	81[a]	N.S.
40-59	39.6	198	40.0	60	N.S.
60+	6.6	33	6.0	9	
Total	100.0	500[b]	100.0	150	
SEX:					
Male	78.8	462	76.7	115	N.S.
Female	21.2	124	23.3	35	N.S.
Total	100.0	586[c]	100.0	150	
RACE					
White	60.9	354	68.7	103	$p < .05$[e]
Nonwhite	39.1	227	31.3	47	$p < .05$
Total	100.0	581[d]	100.0	150	
SHELTER STATUS					
Sheltered	82.8	495	80.7	121	N.S.
Street	17.2	103	19.3	29	N.S.
Total	100.0	598	100.0	150	

a: Includes two between 18 and 20 years of age.

b: Excludes 76 under 20 years old and 22 individuals for whom age was not discernable.

c: Excludes 12 for whom sex was not discernable.

d: Excludes 17 for whom race was not discernable.

e: Reflects underrepresentation of blacks in street interviews; significance level is for a one-tail test.

On average, males tended to be 8.2 years older (41.6 years versus 33.4 years), and whites 4.3 years older than blacks. Females tended to be better educated.

Marital status dramatically distinguished the homeless from the "homed." Only 7 percent of respondents were currently married. Thirty-five percent were divorced, 21 percent were separated, 6 percent were widowed, and 31 percent had never married. The low percentage of married couples precluded establishing the effects of marital status on other variables. Apparently, the conditions causing homelessness, or the situation itself, were not conducive to maintaining a spousal relationship.

Nativity and Transience. An examination of data on residential history strongly rejects the stereotypical portrait of the homeless as transients who have come from afar to exploit the local community. Of the respondents 9 percent had never lived outside the five-county Birmingham metropolitan area, 35.3 percent had lived in the Birmingham area most of their lives, and 6 percent called Birmingham their home. Using these criteria, 50.7 percent of the sample may be considered natives of the Birmingham area. An additional 14.6 percent were native to other parts of Alabama. In sum, 65.3 percent of respondents considered Alabama home. Nativity was significantly related to race. Blacks were slightly overrepresented among the native homeless.

For this research, a transient was defined as someone who had migrated at least twice in the last two years, and 32 percent of all respondents fit the criterion. But one third of these transients were Birmingham natives, "prodigal sons" who had left and returned. Thus, of the total sample, only 21 percent were nonnative transients. Statistically significant differences among demographic variables were not found for transience. This analysis of nativity and transience made it clear that homelessness in Birmingham was not an "outsiders' problem."

Duration of Homelessness. The survey included items on how long respondents had been without their own residence (that is, a house, apartment, or trailer), and on how long they had lived there. Chronic, or long-term, homelessness was defined as (*a*) not having had one's one place for over a year, and/or (*b*) not having had one's own place for over six months and prior to that not having stayed in one's own place for at least one year. Acute homelessness, then, was characterized by a recent, short-term housing instability. Of the total sample, 39 percent were chronically homeless, and 61 percent acutely so. Those who were Birmingham natives tended to be represented disproportionately in the chronic group. The data also suggested that older respondents were more likely to be chronically homeless.

In summary, homelessness was predominantly a local problem. Most homeless persons had encountered this situation only recently, and few were transients. They were also young and reasonably well educated. Despite these common threads, the population was diverse. Females were disproportionately young and better educated, and blacks were more likely to be Alabama natives. Overall, a very small proportion of the homeless were married.

Causes of Homelessness in Alabama

Why are these people homeless? Clearly this condition is in part an economic problem. When asked what one thing could change their current situation, 86 percent cited some financial change (pension, job, more money, and so on). The homeless consist of the unemployed and the underemployed. Of the total sample, only 30 percent had worked during the previous seven days. The average work week consisted of 26.4 hours with a mean hourly pay scale of $3.69, or $97.42 per week. Not surprisingly, most of those currently holding jobs had experienced considerable downward occupational mobility. The mean occupational prestige score as measured by the Hodge-Siegel-Rossi scale (National Opinion Research Center, 1986: 481–496) was 23.3 compared to 30.8 for prior jobs. Of those currently working, 69 percent were employed in jobs with lower prestige than past employment. Age was the only variable related to current employment;

those under 40 were twice as likely to have worked in the past week than those over 40.

While only one third of respondents worked in the seven days before the interview, 46 percent said that work was still their main source of income. Another 17 percent said that selling blood, plasma, personal items, or recyclable cans was their main source, and 15 percent indicated government assistance (Social Security, Aid to Families with Dependent Children, disability payments). Private support from relatives or friends was cited by 9 percent, and 13 percent said they had no income. The median income of the sample for the past month was $122, but transients and the chronically homeless averaged only $55 and $41, respectively. Men were more likely to state work as their main support, while women were more likely not to have any income, or to rely on public or private support. Blacks disproportionately relied on government assistance, while not a single black listed friends or relatives as their main source of income. Transients were also unlikely to get most of their income from private sources. Those with the least education relied on work, those with moderate education depended on government assistance, and those highly educated used private sources.

The homeless are clearly underemployed or unemployed, indicating that their condition can be defined as an economic crisis. Yet homelessness is not just a matter of economics. The causes of homelessness are complex and varied. We cannot hope to unravel this complexity here, but we can attempt to get some sense of how the homeless themselves explain their problem. To accomplish this, we asked respondents why they no longer had a place of their won. Each respondent was permitted to give up to three reasons; hence, the results sum-marized below show percentages totaling more than 100.

Reason	Number	Percentage
1. Personal crises (divorce, separation, abuse)	49	32.7
2. Financial (lost job, rent went up)	47	31.3
3. Spatial change (evicted, place condemned, lease ran out)	19	12.7
4. Drinking problem	18	12.0
5. Migrated for work	17	11.3
6. Boredom, tired of place	12	8.0
7. Other reasons	28	18.6

The modal response category was personal crises (nearly 33 percent). A sig-nificantly higher proportion of those interviewed on the street explained their condition in these terms. Thirty-two percent of the sample gave financial reasons, and 11 percent left home to migrate for work, with nonnatives disproportionately represented in this category. Spatial changes, events often out of the control of the respondent (such as eviction, place condemned, lease ran out) were cited by 13 percent; Birmingham natives were most likely to give this reason. Twelve percent attributed the loss of their residence to alcoholism, with whites more likely to state this cause. Eight percent simply stated that they were ready for a change.

At a minimum it is apparent that the reasons for a homeless condition are varied. It is likely that for some, homelessness may be solely a matter of being unable to afford a place. For others it may be due to interpersonal problems, or to problems beyond their control. It is possible, however, that for a good many people, several of these factors are intertwined to create an even more complex problem. Poverty is a structural condition that fosters a number of individual crises.

Stressful Life Events among the Homeless

Homelessness is clearly a stressful situation in and of itself. Our data reveal this condition to be preceded or accompanied by a series of life crises or stressful life events. Of the sample 65 percent had previously lost a job, and 60 percent of all respondents, and 86 percent of ever-marrieds, had had marital problems. Twenty-nine percent had been evicted from a house or an apartment. Fifty-five percent had been jailed or imprisoned, 33 percent had had trouble getting along with the people around them, and 25 percent had been kicked out of school. Thirty-five percent had been physically abused and 11 percent sexually abused. Sixty-four percent had a problem with alcohol or drugs, and 17 percent had spent some time in a mental hospital. A count of these life crises revealed that only three respondents had experienced none of them. About two-thirds (65 percent) had experienced three or more crises, with job loss, marital problems, and alcoholism being the most common. There were no statistically significant differences in the mean number of stressful life events by age, sex, race, education, nativity, or transience status. The chronically homeless, however, averaged about one more of these events than the acutely homeless.

Social Networks and Supports: Homelessness and Social Isolation

Generally, multiple life crises characterize homelessness. Such a state of severe social, economic, and psychological deprivation requires access to formal and informal support systems for mere survival. Informal social supports may be especially important for those undergoing such a critical life event (Kahn, 1979). Theoretically, informal supports should provide for emotional needs such as affection (a sense of being loved) and affirmation (self-worth and esteem), as well as for material needs. To what extent does this population have access to a variety of informal social ties, and do these ties fulfill social support functions?

Are there sociodemographic differences among the homeless in terms of social networks and supports?

The literature on homelessness contains conflicting views on the degree to which this socially disadvantaged population is detached or disaffiliated from society (Lee, 1987). What Lee terms the "isolation perspective" (Bahr, 1973; Bogue, 1963; Rossi, Fisher, and Willis, 1986) contends that homelessness by its very nature involves detachment from society's institutions. The homeless are seen as a subpopulation without community, a condition viewed both as a cause and consequence of homelessness. In short, homeless people are portrayed as having failed to nurture or maintain social ties, who consequently find themselves in their present deplorable condition. Running counter to this view is the "integration perspective" (Anderson, 1923; Snow and Anderson, 1987; Wallace, 1965) that describes the homeless as having strong social ties and a sense of commitment to a community of others. As Lee (1987) observes, each perspective tends to be associated with a particular research methodology—isolation with survey research, and integration with participation observation. We are thus left with a less than clear picture of the social networks of the homeless—a situation that represents a critical gap in our knowledge.

It appears that the Alabama sample of homeless was not comprised of social isolates. Based on the findings of this study, almost every respondent had at least one individual who might be sought for social support, and most had extensive contacts. Although only 6.7 percent of respondents were still married, 66.6 percent had living children, 95 percent had at least one other living relative, and only two respondents (1.3 percent) claimed no relatives at all. Overall, 79 percent of respondents had close friends—"persons they could ask for help or advice." Fifty-eight percent had at least one close friend in the Birmingham area, and 69 percent had relatives or friends there. Only one respondent, a 74-year-old widower, claimed to have neither friends nor relatives anywhere. Regarding frequency of contact, 52 percent of respondents had talked to or seen a relative in the last two weeks; while 71 percent visited, talked to, or wrote to relatives every two or three months.

Respondents used these social ties in a number of ways. Six of seven respondents (85.3 percent) had received some form of aid from their informal social networks over the past year. On the average, respondents received three of eight types of aid listed. Material support (money, food, clothing, transportation, or shelter) was received by 84 percent, and emotional support (love, advice/counsel, and sick care) by 77 percent. Shelter (67 percent) and advice (75 percent) were the single most frequently received material and emotional supports, respectively.

An examination of the data revealed some consistent demographic patterns. Blacks and women were more likely to have relatives and friends in the area and to have seen them recently. These stronger social contacts for blacks and females supported our earlier explanation of the underrepresentation of these two groups in the February census. Simply put, blacks and women had stronger social networks which they could tap in time of crisis. Further, those under 40, the nontransient, and the acutely homeless were more likely to have such support systems available. Given the interrelationships among these demographic variables, the key causal factor probably was chronicity. The percent of chronically homeless receiving some form of aid was significantly lower than other groups, though even this percentage (77 percent) was quite high. Perhaps to some extent the chronically homeless had exhausted their informal support networks or "overstayed their welcome" with friends and relatives.

While individuals without social support or contacts were rare (10 percent), it is difficult to characterize the homeless as socially affiliated. Clearly, the homeless, even those with significant social impairments such as alcoholism or mental illness, have not been totally abandoned by friends and relatives. Yet, in spite of such networks, their social condition persists. Indeed, the quality and intensity of these networks is somewhat suspect, for in spite of such attachments, 40 percent of our sample described themselves as lonely some or all of the time. Support systems exist and they are important in the everyday life of the homeless, but such systems can only supplement the professionally trained, relatively resource-rich, formal support structures in the local community.

SUMMARY

The data analyzed here suggest that Alabama has a significant homeless problem which touches a variety of people and has an assortment of causes. Furthermore, homelessness tends to be either preceded or accompanied by other life crises such as alcoholism, mental illness, job loss, imprisonment, or problems with significant others. At least in Alabama, it is a problem that tends to affect its native sons and daughters, rather than transients from other states. Alabama's homeless are not loners or social isolates, and their present problem cannot be traced to antisocial tendencies. These people maintain social supports, but these supports are incapable of providing for the complex needs of a homeless person.

Despite assertions in the popular press and the mental health literature, Alabama's homeless include only a small portion of deinstitutionalized mentally ill. Nonetheless, our sample does experience severely stressful conditions, which could lead to mental illness. In fact, a majority of respondents can be classified as chronically depressed based on their responses to the Center for Epidemiological Studies Depression (CES-D) scale incorporated in our study (Lin, Dean, and Ensel, 1986).

In a simplistic sense, homelessness is an economic problem. Certainly Alabama consists of a disproportionate number of economically deprived persons. But poverty is not simply a matter of low income. It is a condition that breeds a variety of other problems. It is a way of life, a complex weave of deprivations. Homelessness represents the greatest depths of this system of crisis called poverty.

The policy implications of these findings are clear. It is unlikely that simple solutions can even begin to solve such a complex problem as homelessness. It cannot be solved by simply providing temporary shelter or by a policy addressed simply at finding permanent homes for all. While homelessness is a housing problem, it is much more. To address the needs of the homeless, the development of a comprehensive program is required. It should include job training and career counseling, the availability of alcohol and drug abuse detoxification programs and counselors, medical and psychological services, legal and welfare assistance services, as well as the temporary provision of shelter. Though such comprehensive programs are at present nonexistent, there has been an increased awareness of the need for them. For example, Metropolitan Birmingham Services for the Homeless is working to develop a network of agencies that could provide this complex set of services in an efficient manner. To stimulate this effort, Governor Hunt recently provided the Birmingham Housing Authority with seed money for a computer network to coordinate activities among shelters and other agencies providing services to the homeless. Additionally, United Way has funded an organizational study of local service provision efforts. That study, along with the results of the census and survey reported here, will assist policymakers in meeting the diverse needs of the homeless.

ACKNOWLEDGMENT

The authors gratefully acknowledge the assistance of Barrett Lee, Max Michael, Karen Carney, and a host of local service providers. This research was funded by a grant from the Birmingham Healthcare for the Homeless Program.

NOTE

1. These numbers include persons who reported a legal residence but who were unable or unwilling to return home on the census night. Examples would include some persons in domestic abuse shelters, halfway houses for alcohol or drug users, and shelters for ex-offenders or runaways. The number of these persons in each metropolitan area are: Anniston (22), Birmingham (84), Florence (11), Gadsden (7), Huntsville (0), Mobile (94), Montgomery (8), and Tuscaloosa (0). The total for all areas was 226.

REFERENCES

Anderson, Nels. 1923. *The Hobo: The Sociology of the Homeless Man*. Chicago: University of Chicago Press.
Bahr, Howard. 1973. *Skid Row: An Introduction to Disaffiliation*. New York: Oxford University Press.
Bahr, Howard, and Ted Caplow. 1973. *Old Men Drunk and Sober*. New York: New York University Press.
Bassuk, Ellen, Lenore Rubin, and Alison Lauriat. 1984. Is Homelessness a Mental Health Problem? *The American Journal of Psychiatry* 141: 1546–1550.
Baxter, Ellen, and Kim Hopper. 1981. *Private Lives/Public Spaces*. New York: Community Service Society.

Bogue, Donald. 1963. *Skid Row in American Cities*. Chicago: Community and Family Study Center, University of Chicago.

Cleghorn, James S. 1983. *Residents Without Residences: A Study of Homelessness in Birmingham, Alabama*. Unpublished Master's Thesis, University of Alabama at Birmingham.

Cuoto, Richard A., Risley P. Lawrence, and Barrett A. Lee. 1985. Healthcare and the Homeless of Nashville: Dealing With a Problem Without a Definition. *Urban Resources* 2 (2): 17–23.

Duncan, James S. 1983. Men Without Property: The Tramp's Classification and Use of Urban Space. In *Readings in Urban Analysis: Perspectives on Urban Form and Structure*, edited by Robert W. Lake. New Brunswick, N.J.: Rutgers University Press.

Edwards, Griffith, Valerie Williamson, Ann Hawker, Celia Hensman, and Seta Postoyan. 1968. Census of a Reception Centre. *British Journal of Psychiatry* 114: 1031–1039.

Hill, Robert, and Lawrence Shackleford. 1975. The Black Extended Family Revisited. *The Urban League Review* 1: 18–24.

House Subcommittee on Housing and Community Development. 1982. *Homelessness in America*. H241–17, December 17. Washington, D.C.: Congressional Information Service.

———. 1984. *Homelessness in America II*. H241–24, January 25. Washington, D.C.: Congressional Information Service.

Kahn, Robert. 1979. Aging and Social Support. In *Aging from Birth to Death: Interdisciplinary Perspectives*, edited by Matilda Riley. Boulder, Colo.: Westview Press.

Larew, Barbara. 1980. Strange Strangers: Serving Transients. *Social Casework* 61: 107–113.

Lee, Barrett A. 1978. Residential Mobility on Skid Row: Disaffiliation, Powerlessness and Decision Making. *Demography* 15: 285–300.

———. 1987. Homelessness and Community. Unpublished paper presented at the annual meeting of the American Sociological Association. Chicago, Ill.

Leigh, Leonard. 1979. Vagrancy and the Criminal Law. In *Vagrancy: Some New Perspectives*, edited by Timothy Cook. London: Academic Press.

Lin, Nan, Alfred Dean, and Walter Ensel. 1986. *Life Events, Social Support and Depression*. New York: Academic Press.

National Opinion Research Center (NORC). 1986. *General Social Surveys: 1972–1986: Cumulative Codebook*. Storrs, Conn.: The Roper Center for Public Opinion Research, University of Connecticut.

Patch, I. C. Lodge. 1971. Homeless Men in London I: Demographic Findings in a Lodging House Sample. *British Journal of Psychiatry* 118: 313–317.

Robertson, Marjorie, Richard Ropers, and Richard Boyer. 1984. *The Homeless of Los Angeles County: An Empirical Evaluation*. Los Angeles: Basic Shelter Research Project, University of California at Los Angeles.

Rooney, James. 1976. Friendship and Disaffiliation among the Skid Row Population. *Journal of Gerontology* 31: 82–88.

Rossi, Peter, Gene A. Fisher, and Georgianna Willis. 1986. *The Condition of the Homeless in Chicago*. Amherst, Mass.: Social and Demographic Research Institute.

Snow, David A., and Leon Anderson. 1987. Identity Work among the Homeless: The Verbal Construction and Avowal of Personal Identities. *American Journal of Sociology* 92 (6): 1336–1371.

Tiller, Elaine. 1980. *Research Paper on the Homeless*. Washington, D.C.: The Interfaith Conference on Metropolitan Washington.

U.S. Bureau of the Census. 1983. *County and City Data Book*. Washington, D.C.: U.S. Government Printing Office.

U.S. Department of Housing and Urban Development. 1984. *A Report to the Secretary on the Homeless and Emergency Shelters*. Washington, D.C.: Office of Policy Development and Research, U.S. Department of Housing and Urban Development.

U.S. General Accounting Office. 1985. *Homelessness: A Complex Problem and the Federal Response*. Gaithersberg, Md.: U.S. General Accounting Office.

Wallace, Samuel. 1965. *Skid Row as a Way of Life*. Totowa, N.J.: Bedminster.

Whitley, Marilyn P., Oliver H. Osborne, Mary A. Godfrey, and Karen Johnston. 1985. A Point Prevalence Study of Alcoholism and Mental Illness Among Downtown Migrants. *Social Science and Medicine* 20: 579–583.

Willie, Charles. 1976. *A New Look at Black Families*. Bayside, N.Y.: General Hall.

2

Homelessness in Colorado

Hazel A. Morrow-Jones and
Willem van Vliet—

In many ways, a discussion of homelessness in Colorado puts artificially restrictive boundaries on the analysis of a problem with roots that transcend unique regional and local manifestations. Homelessness in Colorado is significantly affected by federal housing polices (and the lack thereof) and trends in the national economy, which in turn reflect global developments involving increased mobility of capital and a restructuring of employment opportunities. Effective intervention requires insight into the ways and the extent that homelessness is anchored in this broader context. While space limitations in this chapter do not permit much more than a cursory analysis of the homelessness problem, we want to emphasize this wider framework as critical background for the information that follows.

Our discussion first offers a profile of the homeless population in Colorado. This profile contains data on such basic characteristics as estimated size, composition, and spatial distribution—data that we try to compare with those in other parts of the country. We then examine emergency shelters as well as programs and legislation intended to alleviate the problem. Next, we consider aspects of low-income housing, economic developments, and demographic trends that we view as significant contextual dimensions of the problem. The final part summarizes our conclusions.

CHARACTERISTICS OF THE HOMELESS POPULATION

Size

According to the 1980 Census, the western region of the United States contained approximately 19 percent of the nation's population, but in 1984, according to estimates by the U.S. Department of Housing and Urban Development (HUD), 34 percent of the homeless population. HUD also found that for cities of over 1 million (of which Denver is one) the rate of homelessness was 13 per 10,000. Using 1980 census data for the total population of the Denver metropolitan area and the low and high estimates of the number of homeless in the area, we find a rate of homelessness for Denver that ranges between 10.5 and 24.5 per 10,000 population. It seems likely that Denver has a higher rate of homelessness than many other large cities. This situation may be explained by the positive correlation, discussed by Redburn and Buss (1986), between the growth rate of a city and the size of its homeless population.

However, in Colorado, as elsewhere, counting the homeless is a controversial activity. The outcome is very much a function of the way homelessness is defined and measured, which is in turn greatly influenced by ideological leanings and institutional biases of those who do the counting. Official government estimates, for example, are typically on the low side, whereas figures from service providers in the field tend to be much higher.

For Colorado, both types of data are available. Using a narrow definition of the homeless as those without shelter at one point in time, the total homeless population in Colorado has been estimated to be between 5,000 and 6,000 (Homeless Action Group, 1987:11). The homeless are particularly concentrated in metropolitan Denver, a five-county area where their number is estimated to be between 1,500 and 3,500 (Comprehensive Home Assistance Plan, 1987, Colorado Coalition for the Homeless, 1986). Numbers for other cities are: Colorado Springs, 95–100 (U.S. Department of Housing and Urban Development, 1984) or 200–300 (Comprehensive Home Assistance Plan, 1987), Pueblo, 45–50 (U.S. Department of Housing and Urban Development, 1984), and Boulder, 105.[1] These figures exclude the "hidden" homeless, that is, people in temporary accommodations or doubling up with friends or relatives.

When counting the homeless as people who have experienced homelessness for at least some time during a year, the numbers are much higher: between 15,000 and 20,000 according to the state's Comprehensive Homeless Assistance Plan, or CHAP (1987). About 10,000 of these people are in Denver, and about 6,000 are in Colorado Springs.

The disparate outcomes of the different definitions and measures of homelessness are clearly illustrated by records from the Boulder Shelter for the Homeless, which suggest about 70 homeless people during any given night during the six months of its operation in 1987, but about 500 homeless individuals during that entire period. These figures do not include families who experienced homelessness, of which there were about 300 in 1987 in Boulder County alone. Nor is a much larger residentially vulnerable population included, including households sharing apartments, living in cars, or existing under otherwise inadequate circumstances.

Trends for Colorado show that its homeless population is growing. According to information from a 25-city survey carried out for the U.S. Conference of

Mayors (1986), the number of homeless people in the Denver area increased in 1985, and it continued to grow in 1986 (Homeless Action Group, 1987) when demand for emergency shelter rose by 20 percent (U.S. Conference of Mayors, 1986). Data for Boulder County show a 25 percent increase in 1986 (O'Keefe, 1987). A recent report by the National Partnership for the Homeless (1987) found a 25 percent increase in Denver's homeless population, the second highest increase in the nation.

Composition

Eleven-year-old Maurice Sharp sleeps in a bunk bed in a room shared with 20 strangers. During his two months in Denver, he and his family have been evicted from two homes, and he has had to switch schools once. His mother can't afford a tube of toothpaste—or a home (Enda, 1987). The situation of Maurice and his family is characteristic of an increasing proportion of Colorado's homeless population. Women and children are the fastest growing segment of Denver's homeless population, accounting, in 1987, for 35 percent of those without shelter, up from 13 percent in 1985 (Homeless Action Group, 1987; U.S. Conference of Mayors, 1986a).

Recent reports prepared for the U.S. Conference of Mayors (1986a, 1986b) show several basic characteristics of the homeless population in Metropolitan Denver:

	1985	1986
Families	13%	20%
Single men	73	45
Single women	14	37
Mentally ill	60	35
Substance abusers	41	10
Transient	20	NA

The figures (exceeding 100 percent because of overlapping categories) reveal rather dramatic changes from 1985 to 1986. While single men still make up nearly half of all the homeless people, their proportion has declined sharply from 73 percent in 1985. In addition to the steep drop in the proportion of single homeless men, the last year has also seen significant decreases in the proportion of substance abusers and the mentally ill. Coupled with these changes, there has been a considerable increase in homelessness among families and women. The proportion of the former rose from 13 percent in 1985, to 20 percent in 1986, to 35 percent in 1987, while the proportion of the latter increased from 14 percent in 1985, to 37 percent in 1986. These changes reflect a shift away from what has long been considered a typical profile of the homeless population to what the literature now calls "the new homeless" (e.g., Stefl, 1987; Sullivan and Damrosch, 1987), a new homeless population that is, if anything, more like the rest of the population, more like us.

What the data do not reveal are the factors that precipitated the lack of shelter among these new homeless. While more research is needed to identify these factors and to establish how they vary in significance from one region to another, we will briefly return to this point in our discussion of the context of homelessness later in this chapter.

Spatial Distribution

It is clear that the homeless population varies geographically, both in numbers and in characteristics. This is true at the national scale, for urban and rural areas, for urban areas of different sizes, for states, and within local communities. Unfortunately, while all our information about the homeless is sketchy, data on the geographic distribution and on spatial variations in the characteristics of this population are especially hard to obtain. However, since most planning and funding are carried out on the basis of political subdivisions, it is critical that we grapple with the geographic characteristics of the homeless population.

In 1987, the Homeless Action Group (HAG), sponsored by the Denver Mayor's Office, the Piton Foundation, and the Colorado Coalition for the Homeless reported, "The homeless population is clearly clustered *most visibly* in Denver" (HAG, 1987: 11; emphasis in the original). However, in the opinion of the group, the issue must be recognized as one of statewide importance (HAG, 1987). While the homeless are most visible in the front-range cities (Pueblo, Colorado Springs, the Denver Metropolitan Area, Fort Collins, and Greeley), and most of the estimates that we have of the homeless come from these cities, especially Denver, the problem is broader than that and varies by region of the state. For example, the southeastern portion of the state has a migrant farm labor population, the majority of which spends part of the year homeless (usually doubled up) and moves about between Pueblo and the farming communities, while more of the Northeast's migrant farm labor population leaves the state when the farm work is done (Don Krasniewski, at a meeting of the Advisory Group to the CCH, Oct. 16, 1987, and in a telephone conversation on Oct. 27, 1987).

Within the cities, the homeless have traditionally congregated in certain zones that offer the most shelters and services and also the least visibility for the homeless population. (Redburn and Buss, 1986; Peroff, 1987.) In part, this is a response to zoning and other local pressures on shelter location and service providers. The CCH notes that:

The result of this is that shelters tend to be very concentrated geographically in a few neighborhoods. While the rest of the city escapes awareness of and any sense of responsibility for the issue, the few affected neighborhoods feel they are bearing an unreasonable share of the responsibility and become understandably resistant to any new proposed shelter. (CCH, 1986)

The Housing Action Group suggested that Denver adopt a "fair share" ordinance to spread shelters out in a more equitable manner, but such an action seems politically unlikely.

Wolch and Akita (1987: 28) argue that the homeless are dispersing to the suburbs, partly as a result of gentrification and redevelopment in core city areas. Services in these outlying communities are more limited, and the homeless are creating "invisible favelas" as they take advantage of whatever shelter they can find. It is difficult to ascertain whether this is happening in Colorado. There are some shelters in suburban areas around the city of Denver, for example, in Jefferson County, and in the city of Boulder, but it is not clear whether these are examples of needs that have been created by the displacement of the homeless out of Denver, by overall increases in the number of homeless, or by other factors. Boulder, for example, has had a transient or homeless population of its own at least since the 1960s (Boulder study, 1984).

While statistics on homelessness in Denver's suburbs are difficult to find, we can examine information on the poverty levels of the different areas to get some sense of the relative populations vulnerable to homelessness. Unfortunately much of this recent information is from 1980 and will not show recent growth in poverty in the suburban ring, the symptom we might expect if Wolch and Akita are correct about the suburbanization of homelessness. Information from a Piton Foundation (1987: 22) report on poverty in Denver illustrates the distribution of the below-poverty population between the central city and the suburbs in 1980:

	Percent in Suburban Ring
Percent of total population below poverty level	50.9
Percent of <18 poverty level population	48.3
Percent of <5 poverty level population	45.4
Percent of 5–17 poverty level population	49.7
Percent of 18–59 poverty level population	52.9
Percent of 60+ poverty level population	42.3

For the overall poverty level population, the split is nearly 50–50, but Denver has a larger proportion of children and the elderly, while the suburbs have more of the 18- to 59-year-old population (this group also makes up the majority of the homeless population). Data on the geographic distribution of cases within several aid programs for 1982–1983 appear below:

Program	Denver	Suburban Counties
AFDC percent of metropolitan cases	57.8	42.2
Average $ per case	$289.90	$284.04
OAP percent of metropolitan cases	58.2	41.8
Average $ per case	$108.44	$113.95
AND percent of metropolitan cases	54.7	45.3
Average $ per case	$ 66.13	$ 73.76
Food stamps percent of metropolitan cases	59.5	40.5
Average $ per case	$ 47.28	$ 48.42

For these four programs (reported by the Piton Foundation, 1987) Denver has the largest percentage of cases but provides less money per case than the suburbs for all except Aid to Families with Dependent Children (AFDC). It is also worth noting that the Denver metropolitan region experienced an economic downturn after these statistics were collected.

If we compare the 1980 data on poverty with the 1982–1983 data on program participation, we see that although the suburbs have 48 percent of below-poverty level children, they have only 42 percent of the AFDC cases and provide less money per case than Denver. On the other hand, they have 42 percent of the elderly poor population, nearly 42 percent of the Old-Age Pension (OAP) program, and they provide more dollars per case. Suburbs seem to be more likely to shoulder their share of the burden of care for the elderly than for children. Food Stamps are by far the largest form of aid (almost 92,000 cases compared to almost 12,500 cases for the second largest aid program, AFDC). They are available to a wide range of age groups. The suburbs served 40 percent of these clients, but have 50 percent of the below-poverty population. In the early 1980s, the Denver suburbs do not seem to have undertaken their fair share of the programs aimed at helping the poor, considering the proportion of the poverty-level population they contained. This supports Wolch and Akita's contention that fewer services for the poor are available in suburban communities.

We might expect that this lack of assistance would push more people into homelessness and that the suburban communities would display the same reluctance to provide shelter that they display toward provision of other services for the poor. Wolch and Akita extend this argument to say that the suburbs can be expected to attempt to exclude the homeless as such people become more apparent in the suburban communities and that many local administrations will attempt to shift the burden of providing for the homeless to other levels of government. The perception of homelessness as a Denver central city problem will contribute to those efforts within Colorado.

Spatial Variations in the Characteristics of the Homeless

As mentioned, we know little about the spatial variations of the characteristics of the homeless and have access to few sources of information. Consequently,

Table 2.1
Characteristics of Clients Seen in the Health Care for the Homeless Project
(Figures in %)

Characteristics	National Thru Feb. 1986[a]	Denver Nov. 1985 - Feb. 1986[b]
AGE:		
Under 20	13.9	7.6
20-24	10.0	11.6
25-34	28.6	26.1
35-44	21.6	24.1
45-54	13.5	16.5
55-64	9.1	9.6
65+	3.3	4.4
N	8,269	249
GENDER:		
Male	68.7	68.3
Female	31.3	31.7
N	15,305	249
RACE/ETHNICITY:		
White	46.0	56.5
Black	38.7	11.8
Hispanic	11.2	28.6
Asian	1.1	0
American Indian	2.0	2.4
Other	0.9	0.8
N	14,986	255

Sources: (a)Wright, James D. (1987). Health Care for the Homeless. In *The Homeless in Contemporary Society*. Beverly Hills, CA Sage Publications; and, (b) Health Care for the Homeless Clinic Summary made available by the Colorado Coalition for the Homeless.

we need to use whatever sources are available, while keeping in mind their limitations. Table 2.1 combines published data about the characteristics of clients nationwide seen in the Health Care for the Homeless Project through February 1986, and information from the Denver Health Care for the Homeless clinic summary for November 1985 through April 1986 (made available by the Colorado Coalition for the Homeless). The table offers some insight into how comparable Denver's homeless population is to the national homeless population using the program. The Denver client age distribution appears to be somewhat older with fewer people under 20 being seen in the clinic. Denver clients are more likely to be white, much more likely to be Hispanic, and less likely to be black than the national averages. There is not much difference in the proportions of male and female between the two samples.

Within the state, we can make a comparison of numbers from the Denver homeless population and those from the Boulder shelter. According to the U.S. Conference of Mayor's estimates (1986: 28), 10 percent of Denver's homeless population are substance abusers. In Boulder, according to a shelter newsletter, 48 percent are substance abusers. Even this limited comparison indicates that the homeless population's characteristics may vary widely within as well as between states, and may vary in ways that are important to our ability to provide assistance to the homeless.

Mobility Characteristics

What we know about the mobility characteristics of Colorado's homeless comes from two sources. The first is a 1984 study conducted by the Colorado Coalition for the Homeless (CCH) that focused on shelter clients in the Denver area. The second is a study by the Colorado Children's Campaign done in 1987 across the state, but concentrating entirely on families. One part of the latter study involved in-depth interviews with 49 families in six urban shelters.

The CCH study found that of those in the shelters, 47 percent had lived in a car, in a shelter, or on the street. Twenty-eight percent had had their own apartments, 7.4 percent had lived in hotels, and 17 percent had stayed with friends or relatives. Thirty-six percent called themselves transients. Nineteen percent said they were homeless because of migration or resettlement and 17 percent because of eviction or foreclosure. Seventy-seven percent of those interviewed had lived in the city and county of Denver during the three months prior to the interview, and 75 percent had not used any area shelters in 1983. Of the families interviewed by the Children's Campaign, 75 percent were from Colorado and 25 percent were from other states. These results indicate that many of the homeless are local residents, or at least people who have lived in the state for awhile. The implication is that homelessness is not entirely a problem imported by migrants. It also happens to significant numbers of local people in their own communities.

EMERGENCY SHELTERS

"Shelters provide the spatial focus" of the network of caregivers for the homeless (Redburn and Buss, 1986: 116). In Colorado, as in other places, the network is concentrated in the larger urban areas, but it extends to some rural parts of the state as well. Figure 2.1 shows the counties in the state in which there is at least one shelter provider known to the Colorado Coalition for the Homeless, as well as the counties that provide other kinds of emergency assistance to the homeless. The shelters described in this section include all those emergency shelters and transitional housing units that actually provide beds or

Figure 2.1
Counties in Which Some Form of Emergency Shelter and/or Other Services for the Homeless Are Available

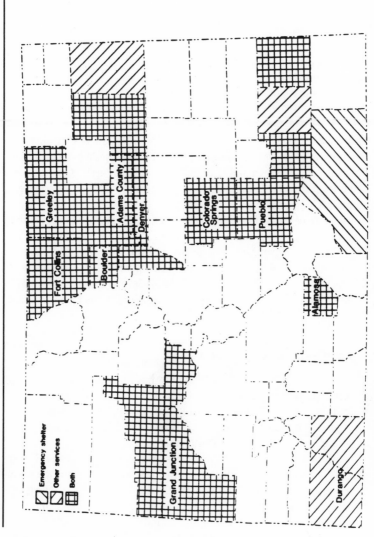

Source: Information has been taken from a list prepared for the Colorado Coalition for the Homeless and from conversations with Don Krasniewski, the list's compiler. Places/names referred to in the text are placed in the correct counties.

shelter for homeless people. While safehouses for battered women could be counted in this category, they have not all been included because of their specialized function. Those that are included also provide emergency shelter for women who are not battered, on a space-available basis. Homes strictly for the chronically mentally ill have not been counted.

Colorado's CHAP (1987) estimates that there are 1,500 emergency shelter beds in the state (not counting transitional housing or safehouses), including about 800 in the Denver metropolitan area, 275 in Colorado Springs, 105 in Boulder, 32 in Alamosa, 30 in Pueblo, and 30 in Grand Junction (see Figure 2.1). In addition, there are 89 transitional housing units in Colorado Springs, 72 in Denver, and 37 in Grand Junction, and the city of Denver can provide vouchers for up to 100 units on a one-time basis.

The shelters' ability to provide beds and other services varies from place to place as well. The form of the available "shelter" ranges from apartments to hotel/motel vouchers, to beds, cots, or mats in a shelter, to tents and blankets. Most of the shelters around the state remain open all year (Boulder's is a major exception). Most will accept men, women, and families, though there are some for men only, women only, or women with children. Other services offered range from travel assistance to food, counseling, and job assistance (Don Krasniewski, CCH, 1987).

The Denver-based Colorado Coalition for the Homeless works with two paid staff members as well as volunteers and, in 1985, had an internal budget of $45,600. This organization performs a coordinating function for a variety of service agencies including (but not limited to) the Salvation Army, the Denver Emergency Housing Coalition, and the Volunteers of America. They are able to provide most of the services mentioned above, and they operate the Stout Street Clinic (CCH Fact Sheet).

PROGRAMS AND LEGISLATION

Federal assistance to the homeless has been meager and has operated through a variety of federal agencies. The role of the states was to pass funds through to local governments (U.S. Housing and Urban Development, 1984: 47), and local governments often had the choice of whether certain kinds of funds were to be used for the homeless or for other needs.

The Stewart B. McKinney Homeless Assistance Act, passed in the summer of 1987, provides $355 million nationwide in federal aid for the homeless. This money will be disbursed through HUD, the Department of Health and Human Services, Federal Emergency Management Agency (FEMA), the Department of Education, and the Veterans Administration (VA). At the state level in Colorado, the primary outcome of this plan is the required development of a plan and the provision of some coordination among agencies. Local areas will still have primary decision-making power.

The required Comprehensive Homeless Assistance Plan (see the Federal Register, 1987) has been submitted to HUD and approved. Among other strategies, it calls for a governor's task force on the homeless with local government representation and an emphasis on coordination among governments and agencies. Existing Colorado state statutes deal with social services in general, not with homelessness specifically. The problem of homelessness has been viewed as a local issue. The proposed governor's task force may help provide some coordination, but essentially the strategy will still remain one of funneling federal dollars to the local areas that feel a need to do something about the homeless.

It is estimated that the state of Colorado will receive $2,212,000 (0.6% of the total authorized by the bill) through the various programs of the McKinney Act. Of this, $244,000 comes to the state for emergency shelters, and another $194,000 will be divided among three local governments for emergency shelters. The city and county of Denver is expected to receive the lion's share of this money ($133,000). Colorado Springs should receive $34,000 and Adams County $27,000 (Federal Funds Information for States, 1987). Twenty percent of the $2,212,000 will be used directly for emergency shelters.

Nationwide, the $355 million will be disbursed by several different agencies. (The following is taken from an Action Letter of the National Governor's Association, Aug. 1987.) The Department of Housing and Urban Development will receive $180 million, about 28 percent ($50 million) of which will go directly to Emergency Shelter Grants for government entities that meet community development block grant standards. Colorado contains three such entities: the city and county of Denver, the city of Colorado Springs, and Adams County in the Denver metro area. The other HUD money will go to permanent housing for the handicapped (a minimum of $15 million), transitional housing (probably $65 million), other services to the homeless ($15 million), and Section 8 assistance to single-room occupancy dwellings ($35 million).

Health and Human Services will disburse about $133 million dollars primarily for community health centers. The Department of Education has $4.6 million to provide to state education departments for educating homeless children. FEMA will grant $10 million for shelters, and the VA will provide $20 million for domicilary care beds and chronically mentally ill veterans.

Redburn and Buss (1986: 139–140) say that local responses to the problem of homelessness are needed but that "the very uneven geographic distribution of the homeless population and variations in local capacity and willingness to address the needs of that population suggest a role for higher levels of government . . . centralization at the local level is a virtual prerequisite." The states should lead in developing coordination in the system of services and demonstration projects, and it is this coordination role that Colorado's CHAP (1987) emphasizes.

HUD (1984) notes that city and county governments can undertake a variety of programs to aid the homeless. In Colorado, those actions have primarily taken the form of helping private operators of shelters. All shelters in the city and county of Denver, for example, are run by nonprofit or religious organizations

(CCH Briefing Paper, 1986). The city expends approximately $9,000 a month on vouchers, $15,000 a year on emergency food coupons, $22,000 for assisted housing, and $282,301 for battered and homeless women's shelters. In addition, the city funded one half of the renovations for a new shelter ($185,000), leases the building for the shelter, provides an emergency social worker for eviction assistance, and provides assistance and backup through the Department of Health and Hospitals to the Health Care for the Homeless Program (CCH Briefing Paper, 1986). In 1986–1987, the Boulder Shelter for the Homeless received 6 percent of its funding from FEMA and 11 percent from the city government. The remaining 83 percent came from private contributions (Boulder Shelter Newsletter, 1987). ECHO House in Boulder, a facility accommodating homeless families with children, gets support from the city in the form of five apartments (the facility is owned by the city and leased for one dollar per year). ECHO House also receives 49 percent of its cash operating revenue from the City of Boulder. In contrast, the City of Longmont provides no operating funds for the Atwood Shelter, a similar facility, which must rely on the United Way, Boulder County, and private donations to cover expenses. In both cases, Community Development Block Grants from each city were used to assist in the original purchase of the shelter facilities.[2]

In May 1987, a "Shelter the Homeless" initiative appeared on the ballot in the city of Denver. This effort, had it passed, would have required Denver to provide "adequate overnight shelter to all homeless persons in Denver unable to be housed in existing shelters" (informational brochure produced by the Citizens Committee to Shelter the Homeless, 1987). In spite of the wide range of support for this initiative from service groups, it did not pass.

There is no question that the available shelters are inadequate. Using the state's CHAP figures of emergency beds available in different locations and various estimates of the number of homeless in different areas, we arrive at the following figures:

Area	Number of Emergency Beds	Number of Estimated Single-Night Homeless	Persons per Bed
Denver Metropolitan Area	800	1,500–3,500	1.9–4.4
Colorado Springs	275	90–300	.3–1.1
Pueblo	30	45–50	1.5–1.7
Boulder	105	105	1.0

Granting that these numbers are estimates, it still appears that in general there is an insufficient number of emergency beds and that the degree of sufficiency or insufficiency varies around the state. Colorado Springs either has more beds than needed (though HUD's estimates have been criticized as too low) or about the right amount if the CHAP estimates are accurate. Pueblo has 50 percent fewer beds than needed according to HUD's estimate, and Denver has only half of the beds needed under the rosiest estimate of the number of homeless in the metro area. When the figures were compiled, the Boulder shelter could accommodate only one third of the demand, but a new facility that opened in December 1987 tripled the previous capacity.

THE CONTEXT OF HOMELESSNESS

The context of homelessness has a horizontal and a vertical dimension. The horizontal dimension refers to a cluster of problems of which being homeless is one. Homelessness does not occur in isolation. It is typically part of a broader syndrome of hardships experienced by those affected. For example, while their proportions are declining, in 1987 there are still substantial numbers of homeless people in Colorado who suffer from substance abuse (10 percent) and mental illness (35 percent). Many experience hunger. In 1986, the demand for emergency food in Denver increased by 55 percent, and even more among the elderly and families with children (respectively, 64 percent and 70 percent), more than in any other of 25 cities across the country included in the most recent survey of the U.S. Conference of Mayors (1986b).

The vertical dimension of the context of homelessness refers to a broader set of processes and conditions that combine to generate homelessness among vulnerable population groups. Homelessness does not come out of the blue and occur in a vacuum. Political ideologies regarding government responsibilities for the welfare of disenfranchised population groups as well as economic resources play an important role in preventing or permitting homelessness. For example, East European countries face many serious housing problems, but homelessness is not among them. However, their prosperity is much lower than that of the United States where homelessness *is* a problem.

Most salient in the policies of the Reagan administration has been the approach called the "New Federalism." This approach has several defining elements, but dominant among them are the devolution of traditionally federal responsibilities to lower levels of government and their shift to the private sector. Recent research has assessed the effects of this approach for assisted housing in Colorado (Hero and Sullivan, 1986). Based on questionnaire responses from and interviews with directors of 73.5 percent of all public housing authorities in the state, this study found a negative impact, particularly among the larger authorities.

Funding cuts were seen as an abandonment of federal commitment and a smokescreen to dismantle housing programs (Hero and Sullivan, 1986: 174). Forced greater reliance of the authorities on nonfederal funds has also changed their programmatic goals. It has become harder to serve the neediest low-income households. The need to make a profit has meant greater program orientation to moderate-income families and homeowners, and less to renters. In addition, the outcome of joint public/private efforts, encouraged by Reagan's policies, has resulted in less low-income housing because of pressures to allow profit margins to private participants (Hero and Sullivan, 1986: 174).

Another factor behind the diminished low-income housing market has been the extensive demolition in Denver of old low-rent hotels and apartments as a result of office space construction which, between 1970 and 1978, proceeded at the highest rate among 31 major cities (Klein, Marine, Wilensky, and Yantz, 1987: 9). In addition, gentrification of central urban areas has displaced low-income residents (Klein et al., 1987: 9). Furthermore, many cities, including Denver, have stopped accepting applications for assisted housing, even though demand has increased (U.S. Conference of Mayors, 1986b). From these data it would appear that diminished opportunities for low-income housing have contributed to homelessness in Colorado.

During the recent period, economic conditions in the state have worsened. This is especially evident in the unemployment rate which, expressed as a percentage of the civilian labor force, increased from 5 percent in August 1984 (when it was among the lowest in the nation) to 9.3 percent in January 1987 (among the highest in the country). Not only has unemployment gone up, but the employment structure has also changed as jobs in the construction and manufacturing sectors have declined, a trend that affects people often ill equipped to cope with joblessness and the attendant loss of income. In 1980, median monthly homeowner costs in Colorado were $422.00 or 115 percent of the figure of the country as a whole, while mean hourly wages for production workers were only marginally higher than the national average, making housing in Colorado relatively expensive (Business Research Division, 1987: 227, 403).

CONCLUSIONS

In a general sense, the conclusions that can be drawn from this brief analysis of the problem of homelessness in Colorado are similar to those from comparable analyses of other states. In Colorado, homelessness is a growing problem that affects more people than just those without shelter. And it should be viewed in a broader economic and political context (cf. Teich Adams, 1986). However, there are certain aspects that are more specific to Colorado. Among these aspects is the rapid population growth in the state, a condition that appears to have a correlation with homelessness, at least in the United States (Redburn and Buss, 1986). While the state is currently going through an economic downturn, the expectation is that further demographic shifts will characterize future development in the state. From 1980 to 1984, the state's population rose by 10 percent, the seventh largest increase in the nation (BRD, 1987), and current projections by the Colorado Department of Local Affairs suggest an increase of 15% since 1980 (Klein et al., 1987: 13).

A second important distinguishing feature of Colorado with respect to the problem of homelessness is that the state government has a tradition of minimal participation in federal programs (such as Medicaid) and has often reacted negatively to federal controls. Data on fiscal 1984 (Business Research Division, 1987: 655–659) permit calculations showing that the state of Colorado consistently allocated proportionately less money in its budget for public housing, Section 8, low-rent operating assistance, and direct housing payments to individuals than did the federal government. As a rule, Colorado is not generous in its public programs for the poor, according to a recent report on poverty in metropolitan Denver (Klein et al., 1987). This "philosophical heritage of pioneer times and independent spirit" (Klein et al., 1987: 9) undermines further the limited federal initiatives regarding homelessness and shifts more of the burden of responsibility for the problem to the private and nonprofit sector, to the local level, and to the homeless themselves.

The current situation is reflected well in the observation of the Homeless Action Group (1987: 16) that homelessness is a problem in many communities throughout Colorado, but that there is virtually no acknowledgment and no commensurate commitment of resources. The future of aid to the homeless around the state seems to depend on the extent to which nonprofit service groups can continue to meet the needs of the growing numbers of homeless and the extent to which the McKinney Act is enforced to insure needed federal funding and requisite statewide cooperation.

NOTES

The authors would like to thank the following people and organizations for giving generously of their time and knowledge: Don Krasniewski and John Parvensky of the Colorado Coalition for the Homeless; Terry Benjamin of Boulder's Emergency Family Assistance Organization; Meri Lou Johnson of the governor's office; Marsha Gould of the Colorado Children's Campaign; Mary Resh of the Boulder Shelter for the Homeless; Katie Tynan of Congresswoman Pat Schroeder's office; Bill Verbeten of the Colorado State Division of Local Governments; and Peg Wadman of the Boulder Emergency Family Assistance.

1. Personal Communication, November 18, 1987; Mary Resh, Boulder Shelter for the Homeless.

2. Personal Communication, November 18, 1987; Peg Wadman, Boulder Emergency Family Assistance.

REFERENCES

Adams, Carolyn Teich. 1986. Homelessness in the Postindustrial City: Views from London and Philadelphia. *Urban Affairs Quarterly* 21 (4): 527–549.

Boulder Shelter Newsletter. 1987. Spring. Boulder Shelter, 4545 N. Broadway, Boulder, CO.

Business Research Division (BRD). 1987. *Statistical Abstract of Colorado: 1987*. Boulder, Colo: BRD, College of Business Administration, University of Colorado.

Citizens Committee to Shelter the Homeless. 1987. Homeless Shelter Initiative pamphlet
for election held on May 19, 1987.

City of Boulder, Community Development Program. 1984. Emergency Shelter: Homelessness in Boulder. By Robert G. Cornwell with Julie Nelson Davis, in association
with the Division of Research and Evaluation, Department of Community Planning
and Development. Produced for the city of Boulder and Boulder County United
Way.

Colorado Children's Campaign. 1987. No Room at the Inn. Executive summary of study
funded by the Colorado Trust. Colorado Children's Campaign, 1750 Gilpin St.,
Denver, CO 80218.

Colorado Coalition for the Homeless. 1986. Briefing Paper on the Homeless in Denver.
Colorado Coalition for the Homeless, 2100 Stout St., Denver, CO 80205.

Colorado Coalition for the Homeless "Fact Sheet."

Colorado Coalition for the Homeless. 1984. Summary Analysis of the 1984 Emergency
Shelter Survey.

Enda. 1987. Denver Becoming Home for Homeless. Rocky Mountain News 7.

Federal Funds Information for States. 1987. Issue Brief 87–14. Information on Federal
Aid for the Homeless. (August 7). Suite 295, 400 North Capitol St., NW, Washington, DC 20001.

Federal Register. 1987. Vol. 52, no. 157 (August 14).

Hero, Rodney E. and Richard Sullivan. Assisted Housing and Reagan's New Federalism:
The Colorado Experience. The Journal of Federalism 16 (Winter, 1986): 167–
179.

Homeless Action Group. 1987. Report of the Homeless Action Group. Sponsored by the
Office of the Mayor, City, and County of Denver; the Piton Foundation, 511 16th
St., Denver, CO 80202; and the Colorado Coaliton for the Homeless.

Krasniewski, Don. 1987. Personal and telephone conversations. Staff member, Colorado
Coalition for the Homeless.

National Partnership for the Homeless. 1987. National Growth in Homelessness: Winter
1987. Broken Promises/Broken Lives. National Partnership for the Homeless. 6
East 30th St., New York, NY 10016.

O'Keefe, M. 1987. Homelessness Up in Boulder. Colorado Daily 94 (145) (April 13):
1, 13.

Peroff, Kathleen. 1987. Who are the Homeless and How Many are There? In The Homeless
in Contemporary Society, edited by Richard D. Bingham, Roy E. Green, and
Sammis B. White. Newbury Park, Calif.: Sage Publications.

Piton Foundation. 1987. A Profile of Poverty in Metropolitan Denver. Denver: Piton
Foundation.

Redburn, F. Stevens, and Terry F. Buss. 1986. Responding to America's Homeless;
Public Policy Alternatives. NY: Praeger Publishers.

Stefl, M. Z. 1987. The New Homelessness: A National Perspective. In The Homeless in
Contemporary Society, edited by R. D. Bingham, R. E. Green, and S. B. White.
Newbury Park, Calif.: Sage.

Sullivan, P. A., and S. P. Demrosch. 1987. Homeless Women and Children. In The
Homeless in Contemporary Society, edited by R. D. Bingham, R. E. Green, and
S. B. White. Newbury Park, Calif.: Sage.

U.S. Conference of Mayors. 1986a. The Growth of Hunger, Homelessness and Poverty in America's Cities in 1985: A Twenty-Five City Survey. U.S. Conference of Mayors, 1620 Bye St. NW, Washington, DC 20006.

U.S. Conference of Mayors. 1986b. The Continued Growth of Hunger, Homelessness and Poverty in America's Cities: 1986. U.S. Conference of Mayors, 1620 Bye St., NW, Washington, DC 20006.

U.S. Department of Housing and Urban Development. 1984. A Report to the Secretary on the Homeless and Emergency Shelters. Division of Policy Studies in the Office of Policy Development and Research.

Wolch, Jennifer R., and Anchea Akita. 1987. Hear No Evil, See No Evil: The Federal Response to Homelessness and Its Implications for American Cities. Paper presented at the national meetings of the Association of American Geographers. Portland, Ore.

Wright, James D. 1987. The National Health Care for the Homeless Program. In *The Homeless in Contemporary Society*, edited by Richard D. Bingham, Roy E. Green, and Sammis B. White. Newbury Park, Calif.: Sage Publications.

3

Homelessness in Florida

Doug A. Timmer and
J. David Knottnerus

By 1984 population estimates, Florida had become the sixth largest state (University of Florida/Bureau of Economic and Business Research, 1984). Since then it may well have become the fifth largest. Media accounts have recently reported a significant homeless population in this rapidly growing Sunbelt state.

The purpose of this paper is to ascertain, as well as possible, the answers to four questions: (1) How many homeless are there in Florida? (2) What is the composition of the Florida homeless population and what are their sociological and demographic characteristics? (3) What are the primary sources of Florida homelessness? (4) What is being done, both publicly and privately, to address the problem of homelessness in Florida and what more needs to be done to combat it?

Due to the nature of homelessness itself, answers to questions like these have been difficult to come by throughout the United States. (Rossi et al., 1987). But they have been even more difficult to answer in Florida, for, we believe, at least two reasons. First of all, a very conservative political climate prevails in Florida, which creates a tendency for state and local officials, busily hustling developers, and investors from outside the state to deny the reality of serious social problems like homelessness. In the official chamber of commerce promotion of Florida as a Sunbelt utopia, there is no room for the homeless. Second, in regard to all manner of public service expenditures, Florida consistently ranks at or near the bottom of all 50 states. Thus, the public dollars that could support research on the homeless as well as services to them have been virtually nonexistent.

In short, although homelessness is undeniably a growing and serious problem in Florida, for political reasons official recognition of it has lagged behind many

other parts of the nation. It is within this context that we have attempted to find
the best available answers to the above questions. In many instances, the best
information is obviously limited by research design, reliability, validity, rep-
licability, and generalizations. Often the best information is only the best estimate, and in some cases, the "best" information available is the only information
available.

For the most part, the data in this report come from four sources: A Statewide
Task Force on the Homeless report of June 1985 (made up of 11 separate reports,
one from each of the districts of the State Social Service bureaucracy—the
Department of Health and Rehabilitative Services); reports and surveys of local
coalitions for the homeless (mostly completed between 1984 and the present);
interviews with state, county, and city officials; and interviews with "hands-
on" service providers and activists. All interviews were conducted on site between December 1986 and June 1987.

There is one final limitation to this description of homelessness in Florida.
We have limited our report to urban homelessness. We do not feel that this is
a serious shortcoming, since homelessness in the United States is clearly concentrated in cities. We have focused our Florida study on the six largest metropolitan areas. Moving from north to south through the state, the 1985 Florida
Statistical Abstract gives the following 1984 population estimates for these six
metropolitan statistical areas (MSAs): Jacksonville (788,000), Orlando (815,000),
Tampa–St. Petersburg–Clearwater (1.8 million), West Palm Beach–Boca Raton–
Delray Beach (683,000), Fort Lauderdale–Hollywood–Pompano Beach (1.1 million), and Miami-Hialeah (1.75 million). These six metropolitan areas represent
approximately 65 percent of Florida's total population of 10,930,000 (1984
estimate) and approximately 70 percent of the total Florida MSA population.

JACKSONVILLE

Most of the population of the Jacksonville MSA is in Jacksonville itself (over
600,000). The Statewide Task Force on the Homeless (1985) calculated that
there were 645 homeless persons in Health and Rehabilitative Services (HRS)
District 4. This district includes Jacksonville, three other counties in the MSA,
and another three small counties outside the MSA. This figure represents a one-
day estimate for March 26, 1985. It was devised by surveying shelters for the
homeless, counting homeless persons there, and multiplying that count by 2.73
(as the Federal Department of Housing and Urban Development had done in
some of its surveys in other cities) to estimate the number of unsheltered homeless
on the street. Adding the sheltered population to the estimate of the street population produced the numbers the task force reported as being homeless across
the state.

Across Florida, we found that people were very critical of this report. In
Jacksonville, an HRS administrator who headed the local committee that put the
report together in his district dismissed it as politically motivated. He believes

that Governor Bob Graham wanted it done to assist with his U.S. Senate campaign against Republican incumbent Paula Hawkins. He and other critics contend that the report was done much too fast (45 days), used far too narrow a definition of homelessness, and used research and statistical techniques that generated very low estimates of the numbers of homeless. These low numbers were then used politically to minimize the problem of homelessness and justify the failure of the state and cities to respond to it with money and programs. Because of all of this, the HRS administrator in Jacksonville did not disagree with a local Department of Housing and Urban Development (HUD) estimate of as many as 6,000 homeless in the city of Jacksonville alone. The task force had estimated only 10,000 to 13,000 in the entire state.

The HUD figure given to us in Jacksonville is, of course, based on a much broader definition of homelessness than that used by the statewide task force. For example, temporary kinds of housing, like "doubling up" with relatives or friends for a short period of time, are defined as homelessness. Other figures given to us by agencies providing services to the homeless in Jacksonville were much lower and used much stricter definitions. The Salvation Army estimates 300 to 400 persons with no place to go on a given night, and the City-County Welfare Department estimate fell in the range of 250 to 300. The welfare department, however, also reports giving housing and shelter assistance to between 4,000 and 5,000 people between October 1985 and September 1986. Many of these people, the department believes, are the "near homeless," persons and families who would be homeless if it weren't for the assistance provided. Traveler's Aid in Jacksonville estimates that in December 1986, each night there were roughly 200 people in local shelters and 400 on the city's streets with nowhere to go. From 1979 to late 1984 there was no real increase in the numbers of homeless persons that Traveler's Aid saw. In late 1984, the numbers shot upward. In 1985, each month had an increase over the corresponding month in 1984. In 1986, each month had an increase over the corresponding month in 1985—until the agency ran out of money (Traveler's Aid Society of Jacksonville, n.d., 1985, 1986).

Officials at both the Salvation Army and the City-County Welfare Department believe that no more than 10 percent of Jacksonville's homeless population is comprised of the deinstitutionalized mentally ill. This estimate is consistent with the recent research findings of Snow et al. (1986). HRS believes that the proportion of deinstitutionalized homeless in Jacksonville is somewhat greater than this because it is near the Northeast Florida State Hospital.

W. Godwin, director of social services at the Red Shield Lodge for the Salvation Army, contends that only about 10 percent of the Jacksonville homeless are families. She described the majority—about 70 percent—of the local homeless as transient, "professional hobos and vagrants." Virgil Green, director of the City-County Welfare Department, estimates that at least 60 percent of the local homeless population is transient and that only about 20 percent is families— with half of them transient, half of them local. Green estimates that 60 percent of the homeless individuals in Jacksonville are white, while 40 percent are black, and just a few are Hispanic. He believes homeless resident families to be about 50 percent black and 50 percent white. William Dunford, the director of the Jacksonville Traveler's Aid Society, agrees that 60 percent to 70 percent of Jacksonville's homeless are transient. Individuals and families with whom his agency has contact are 75 percent white and 25 percent black. Dunford also reports that significant numbers of industrial workers from West Virginia, New York, Pennsylvania, and Michigan, who have been laid off or had their plants close down are among the homeless. The recent oil bust in Texas and Louisiana has also brought workers from these states. Dunford also tells of migrant workers who are taken from shelters in Chicago and New York to Georgia to pick fruit; when their labor is no longer needed, some find their way to Jacksonville.

The transient character of the Jacksonville homeless is contradicted by Rudy Vaughn, a housing advisor specialist for HUD, who maintains that no more than 20 percent fit into this category. He believes that of those who are transient, nearly all are white. The HRS Aging and Adult Service Program supervisor, E. Lee McCubbin, argues that at least 40 percent of Jacksonville's homeless are families and that no more that 25 percent are the "traditional street derelict." He also believes that these homeless families are disproportionately white, as blacks have better developed kinship and support networks to cope with the crisis of homelessness.

The extent to which homelessness in Jacksonville is the transient homelessness of the "bum" or "derelict" has emerged as a real political issue. The city has essentially taken the position that there is no problem with homelessness in Jacksonville. The transients coming in constitute the problem. This quasi-official ideology maintains that since Jacksonville is the "gateway" to Florida from the north and the first stop on Interstate 95, it unfairly bears the brunt of this problem for other places. Attracted by the climate and the services provided for them, transients come from all over the northern United States, and they stay. The only study of the homeless completed to date in Jacksonville was business-initiated and motivated, and dealt with "The Downtown Derelict." It concluded that the Jacksonville homeless were transients and that the way to keep them out of the downtown area was not to provide them with any services there.

Service providers to the homeless agree that no one would stay in Jacksonville to take advantage of the services, since they are so limited. And many, as we have seen, point out that not all of the homeless are transients but the majority are local residents.

It may be that Jacksonville as the "gateway" city is a stopping place for homeless individuals and families on the move from one place to the next, but officials in Jacksonville do not understand that these are not always homeless "bums" or "derelicts" looking for sunshine and a free lunch. Often, they are homeless industrial workers, displaced by economic changes. In short, they characterize the homelessness of the "new poor" (Harrington, 1984). Often, they are homeless alcoholics and mentally ill abandoned by their families, their communities, and the state.

Homelessness and the Lack of Affordable Housing

Those attempting to respond to the real problem of homelessness in Jacksonville cite lack of affordable housing as its primary source. There are 4,000 people on Section 8 waiting lists in the city, and the waiting list itself has now been suspended. Other factors contributing to what is generally perceived as a growing homelessness in Jacksonville were cited by those we interviewed. These factors include: unemployment and the demise of federal job programs like the Job Corps and the Comprehensive Employment and Training Act (CETA); the failure of HRS to fund general assistance, emergency assistance, and specific assistance for the homeless programs; the lack of a strong mental health support system with adequate community mental health clinics and crisis stabilization units; the lack of accessible medical care for the poor; the unavailability of transition and shelter housing for single women; and the absence of long-term shelters where families and individuals can remain until they have accessed employment and community resources and have stabilized.

But as the assistant director of the Traveler's Aid Society in Jacksonville put it, "The people we see are not a political constituency and until they are there will be no solution to this problem." In the meantime, the Salvation Army's shelter, two other church-funded shelters (in December there were about 200 shelter beds in Jacksonville with the Salvation Army planning to add another 150), small amounts of eviction and housing assistance for residents from the City Welfare Department, and smaller amounts of travel and housing assistance offered transients at Traveler's Aid will not stem the tide of homelessness in Jacksonville. Of course, smaller amounts of federal dollars for housing, utilities, weatherization, and food available through the Northeast Florida Community Action Agency along with food and clothing from a handful of other private religious charities will not meet the needs of the homeless in this area.

It appears that the recognition of the problem of homelessness in Jacksonville lags behind that of other Florida cities. It is the only metropolitan area we studied that did not have an advocacy Coalition for the Homeless. Throughout the rest of our report we will be able to rely on at least some preliminary surveys and research done by these coalitions around the state. In Jacksonville, no one knows the extent and nature of the homeless problem. For the most part, our efforts could only produce the wide-ranging estimates of the various officials and service providers we visited. We believe that those concerned with the plight of the homeless in Jacksonville should begin to address this need for critical information.

ORLANDO

The Statewide Task Force (1985) estimated the homeless population in HRS District 7 at 1,440. This district includes the Orlando MSA plus one other adjoining county. None of the officials or service providers we talked to in Orlando had any real quarrel with this estimate.

A 1984 survey of local shelters carried out by the Christian Service Center interviewed 282 homeless persons. It found that 41 percent were families (couples with children, single parents with children, and couples with no children), 47 percent were single men, and 12 percent were single women. Seventy-seven percent of the 282 were white, 16 percent were black, and 6 percent were Hispanic. Twenty-four percent were employed (confirming the validity of the concept of the "working homeless"), 54 percent were unemployed, and 14 percent were on public assistance of some sort. Thirty-three percent of this sample reported physical health problems, 13 percent cited mental health problems, and 14 percent had an alcohol problem. In terms of length of stay in Orlando, 40 percent said they had been there less than one week, 10 percent had stayed between one week and one month, 15 percent had been there from one to six months, and 35 percent were permanent long-term residents. The survey also found that single women and families with children were most often permanent residents. Eighty-nine percent of female-headed families surveyed, for example, were permanent residents. Another survey of Orlando's homeless carried out by the city in the fall of 1986, basically confirms the findings of the Christian Service Center. It also found that when asked about their occupations, 58 percent of those surveyed were blue-collar workers, with 37 percent identifying themselves as laborers, and another 31 percent said that they were construction workers. That most were not successful in finding permanent work and adequate wages in the area was indicated by the 88 percent who said they had used labor pools, notorious for poor working conditions and low pay. The city survey also found that only 25 percent of its sample intended to leave Orlando in the near future and that the average age for males was 34, while for females it was 30. The racial composition of the city's sample was about 85 percent white and 14 percent black.

The Christian Service Center survey determined that 13 percent were homeless due to eviction, 8 percent left home due to domestic violence, 11 percent were homeless because of overcrowded living conditions, 4 percent were deinstitutionalized, and 3 percent had been living in uninhabitable homes. The largest response to this part of the survey on the causes of homelessness, however, was given by the 60 percent who attributed their situation to being nonresidents or being transient. In most cases, these people are northern individuals or families displaced by a deindustrializing economy. The Statewide Task Force (1985: 11) describes what appears to be the central dynamic of Orlando homelessness:

Officials of the Christian Service Center and the Salvation Army told the Task Force that Orlando experiences a high proportion of "new homeless" because of the lure of jobs in that area. Orlando businesses advertise around the nation, emphasizing job prospects. Many of the jobs are low-paying, often associated with hotels and restaurants. The low pay, coupled with high housing costs, can turn a dream into a nightmare for men and women, often accompanied by children, moving to the sunbelt in search of opportunity. Service industry wages usually will not provide for the front-end costs of procuring housing—first month's rent, security deposit, utility deposits, etc. When such funds are available, the critical shortage of low-cost housing often forces people into housing they cannot afford on marginal incomes. Even the slightest financial crisis can put them on the streets.

In January 1987, the following was available for various kinds of homeless persons in Orlando: Young Women's Community Club (working single women paying very minimal rent)—10 spaces; Salvation Army, Rescue Mission, and the First Methodist downtown shelter—a combined capacity of about 300, with most of the space used for single men and women; the Christian Service Center's Fresh Start (a longer-term shelter serving primarily single individuals—about 40 spaces); the CSC's Cold Night Program—providing 150 spots only on those nights when the temperature dips below a certain level; and another 150 spaces in residential mental health, drug, alcohol, and spouse abuse facilities, sheltering many who if not there, would have nowhere else to go.

Recently, the city has donated land for a "mixed" shelter that is to provide at least some of the badly needed shelter space for families. The shelter will then be privately run by a nonprofit church and civic group. This land donation appears to be the sum total of the city's efforts to assist its homeless. According to the director of the Christian Service Center, "the only other thing the city has done is put them in jail." Police statistics bear him out. From January to August 1985, the Orlando Police Department made 1,837 transient arrests. In 1985, transients accounted for 23 percent of all the arrests made by the Orlando Police Department. The downtown area in particular has not been friendly to the homeless. Downtown businesses, banks, and development interests have sought to rid the area of the homeless as well as the services provided for them. The First Methodist downtown shelter, for example, has faced stiff opposition. And, of course, there is no room for the homeless in Disney World.

In sum, it seems obvious that decent jobs and affordable housing are the keys to resolving the problem of homelessness in Orlando. In addition, the local Coalition for the Homeless has identified the immediate need for (1) long-term stabilizing shelters, (2) coordination and centralization of existing services for the homeless, (3) more research on the transient homeless population and more readily distributed information on the services for which they are eligible, (4) medical care for street people, and (5) public restrooms and showers for street people.

TAMPA–ST. PETERSBURG–CLEARWATER

This MSA includes two larger core cities. Tampa is only slightly larger than St. Petersburg, and together the two cities, connected by bridges over Tampa

Bay, have a population of a little over 500,000. The Statewide Task Force on the Homeless estimated 615 homeless persons in HRS District 5, which includes St. Petersburg, the rest of Pinellas County, and Pasco County (another county in the MSA). For HRS District 6, which is made up of Tampa and the rest of Hillsborough County, as well as four smaller counties not in the MSA, the task force estimated about 685 homeless people. The fourth and smallest county in the MSA, Hernando, is in yet another HRS District and therefore is not included in these estimates. The best statewide task force estimate of the number of homeless people in the Tampa–St. Petersburg–Clearwater MSA is therefore about 1,300.

Metropolitan Ministries in Tampa operates a family shelter, a soup kitchen, limited shelter for single males, and, in cooperation with the city, two emergency shelters on cold nights. Its executive director believes there are roughly 1,300 homeless individuals and 90 homeless families in the Bay area. Richard Brown, chairman of the Data Committee for the Hillsborough County Coalition for the Homeless, says that because Tampa is a "Sunbelt boom town," persons displaced through the loss of jobs and housing in other parts of the country are "in and out." This makes the homeless situation "fluid." The "chronic" or "traditional" homeless are visible, but the "newcomers" are not. Brown believes this makes an accurate count of the homeless in Tampa even more difficult than it is in other cities around the country. He reports the coalition's current estimate to be 1,400 to 3,000 homeless persons in Hillsborough County.

The research that has been done on the homeless in Tampa and Hillsborough Counties has tended to be limited to surveying particular kinds of people that make up part of the homeless population. No research that supports an overall estimate of the size and composition of the homeless population has been conducted. For example, the Hillsborough County Coalition for the Homeless reported the following studies and findings:

1. Every Saturday night in Tampa, the Food Line Ministry provides a free meal under a Cross Town Expressway overpass. On Saturday, September 13, 1986, 157 homeless persons were surveyed there. Among the findings: most were men, most were in their 30s and 40s, a large percentage had histories of substance abuse, most were receiving no services, almost 45 percent were at least temporarily employed, almost 20 percent identified unemployment as the cause of their homelessness (the most frequently occurring response to this question), and nearly 30 percent saw employment as the solution to their homelessness (again, the most frequent response to this question).

2. A survey of 146 homeless persons served by Metropolitan Ministries and Travelers Aid in February and March 1987 found that just over 25 percent were veterans; that 62 percent were white, 27 percent were black, and 7 percent were Hispanic; that 33 percent were from Florida and that more were from the Northeast and Midwest than from the rest of the South; that for nearly 45 percent, their homelessness was a "new experience"; that about 60 of them had graduated from high school and 10 from college; that 35 percent were with their families and 65 percent were alone; that over

120 had never been in a state mental hospital; that about 110 had never been in alcohol detox, and over 120 had never been in drug treatment.

The coalition also reported 116 homeless runaway adolescents at the Beach Place Runaway Center in March 1987. Ninety-one of these teens were permanent residents of Tampa, Hillsborough County, or elsewhere in Florida before becoming homeless.

In addition, the coalition found that Tampa has the busiest of Florida's state-funded spouse and child abuse programs. In the year that ended March 31, 1987, 954 victims of domestic violence, including 629 children who accompanied them, were sheltered. A further 612 homeless victims of domestic violence were denied entrance during the year because the shelter was full.

Between January 7 and 9, 1987, the Pinellas County Coalition for the homeless (the county which includes St. Petersburg and Clearwater) surveyed all but 10 to 15 shelter beds in the county. Based on this survey, the coalition estimated that there were 500 to 600 homeless persons. This figure includes all those who requested shelter and were housed, those who requested shelter but could not be accommodated, and a modest estimate of those who had not requested shelter and were homeless on the street. Thus, the available information on the size and composition of the homeless population in Pinellas County is much more systematic and comprehensive than what we found in Hillsborough County.

Based on this survey, the Pinellas County Coalition has reported that:

- The "new" and temporarily homeless make up 89 percent of the local homeless population.
- Families with children represent 46 percent of all the homeless.
- Single-parent, female-headed families are the largest single category of homeless, representing 29.7 percent of the entire homeless population.
- About 23 percent of the homeless were "nonchronic" single males. More than 10 percent were single females.
- The "chronic" or "traditional" homeless make up no more than 7 percent of the total homeless population.
- Thirty-eight percent of the homeless have been in the county more than one year and 62 percent have been there less than 2 years.
- Homeless individuals and families relocating in the county do so because of a lack of employment, poor paying jobs, and higher costs of living where they come from, not because of Florida's weather or the services provided homeless people in the state.
- The percentage of deinstitutionalized homeless in the county is reportedly very small.

Back in Tampa, the situation regarding the homeless is rife with contradictions. First of all, we believe that next to Miami, Tampa (and the rest of Hillsborough County) may have the largest homeless population in the state. In the face of this, the city (like Miami) has basically done nothing, abdicating any responsibility by claiming that it is essentially the country's role to assist the homeless (this is, indeed, a pattern typical of all Florida metropolitan areas). To our knowledge, to this date, specific assistance to the homeless by the city has been limited to the donation of an abandoned neighborhood firehouse for a private, nonprofit soup kitchen and the $40,000 rehabilitation of four HUD-donated houses, which were turned over to private, nonprofit shelter providers. The response of private agencies to the immediate needs of the homeless population in Tampa, however, appears to be greater than anywhere else in the state. Much of it is religiously sponsored, and food banks, souplines, clothing, medical care, and shelter appeared more available than what we found in other Florida cities. The Family Care Center, for example, built and run by Metropolitan Ministries, is the largest family shelter in Florida, and probably in the entire Southeast.

But, in the end, compared to the other Florida cities we have studied, Tampa knows very little about the size and composition of its homeless population, the causes of its homelessness, and the existing gaps in services provided for the homeless.

Across the bay in St. Petersburg and Pinellas County, the bulk of the response to the homeless population has also been primarily by the private, nonprofit organizations. The city and county have, however, provided some limited funding for shelters. The local Coalition for the Homeless presently reports a real shortage of shelter space, particularly for homeless families with children. For some in the coalition, the recent state funding of a secure facility for homeless alcoholics ''prone to commit crimes'' may not be what they had in mind (Tobin, 1987:1).

Nonetheless, the Pinellas County Coalition for the Homeless (1987), when compared to its Hillsborough County counterpart, is much more aware regarding where the homeless come from and what needs to be done to address the problem:

• Pinellas County has a critical shortage of low- to moderately-priced decent rental units for the low- to moderate-income families and individuals.

• The tourist-oriented economy of Pinellas County employs many low- to moderate-income people at a minimum wage; their incomes range from $6,000 to $9,000 per year. Due to the critical shortage of affordable rental units, these families are: (a) forced into occupancy of unsuitable rental units; (b) forced to live in units they cannot afford; (c) forced to move often due to eviction; (d) unable to provide a decent, stable living environment for their families and children.

• Competition for existing affordable rental units is fierce among low- to moderate-income families.

• Families with housing crises or emergencies are not transients, but have lived in Pinellas County for a minimum of one year (based on survey data).

• Most families who are homeless want to be independent and support themselves and their children. However, they are finding it almost impossible to do so with such a large gap between income and current housing costs. Many spend over half their monthly income on housing costs simply because they have no other choice. Obviously, their standard of living is drastically reduced to below minimum living standards.

• All subsidized housing programs (housing authorities) have waiting lists of up to two and one half years for family units.

• Subsidized housing program funding has been drastically reduced, and there is no expectation that such funding will be increased, but will likely be further reduced in the future.

WEST PALM BEACH–BOCA RATON–DELRAY BEACH

The cities of West Palm Beach, Boca Raton, and Delray Beach are all part of Palm Beach County, which is on the southeast coast of Florida. Little has been done in this area to obtain a systematic count of the homeless. Moreover, interviews with knowledgeable persons and a reading of the assessments that have been done suggest that the number of homeless far exceeds the estimates of the Statewide Task Force Report. According to this report, 96 people were served by shelters and a total of 135 homeless people were seeking some kind of service in March 1985 in HRS District 9, which is composed of Palm Beach County and four smaller counties. There are many more homeless in the area, according to Karen Deringer, research program director of Community Services for the United Way and chair for the report of the Needs Assessment Subcommittee of the Homeless Coalition, entitled "The Homeless Population in Palm Beach County" (1986). Indeed, she believes there were approximately 350 people in different shelters when the state report was conducted. Furthermore, Art Ellich, a FEMA staff worker and member of the Community Service Council for Broward County, suggested in a telephone interview that there may be up to 2,000 homeless in Palm Beach County. Finally, A. Thomas White, director of the Department of Community Services of the Division of Human Services for Palm Beach County, estimated in an interview that there are 3,000 to 5,000 homeless in Palm Beach County with the largest number in West Palm Beach. In sum, we estimate the number of homeless for this MSA to be at least 3,000.

According to "The Homeless Population in Palm Beach County" report (1986), a number of the homeless are among the lower-income county residents who face some financial or other crisis that causes them to lose their housing and become homeless. Nonresidents who come to this area with too few resources also contribute to the homeless population. It is projected that, due to the growing population of the area and lack of housing, these groups will continue to grow. Special population groups further contribute to the homeless problem. They include migrants and farmworkers, deinstitutionalized mentally ill, transients, runaways, abused and neglected women and children, and people with drug and alcohol dependencies. A point stressed by A. Thomas White was that there has been an influx of Haitians in recent years, along with Mexican and Cuban (for example, Merilitos) migrant workers; including men, women, and children. A common pattern for these people is to migrate, even if there is no work or shelter, between Homestead, Florida, and West Palm Beach. Consequently, many of these individuals who are in the country illegally are homeless. Their illegal status makes counting them even more difficult than counting other groups of homeless. Even though "invited" to come forward by the new immigration law, many don't because of negative past experiences with the authorities.

The problems of the homeless in this area are varied as pointed out in the 1986 report. These problems range from unemployment, to the low income of a single-parent family, to alcohol abuse. A point stressed in the report is that housing availability and conditions along with demographics play important parts in the problem of homelessness. The tremendous population growth during the last decade has placed great pressure on housing. For example, approximately 12,500 housing units within Palm Beach County are in substandard condition. The greatest number of these houses are in areas such as Belle Glade. Moreover, the Palm Beach County Public Housing Authorities report that in March 1986, 4,594 households and 14,580 persons were on waiting lists. The report also questioned community leaders, social service providers, and others concerning social problems and found that affordable housing was the number one priority service seen as needed in the county out of over 60 possible services to choose from. Emergency shelter was the fifth most frequently selected need.

The response to homelessness has followed the traditional pattern. Most assistance comes from religious and community organizations, along with some help from Palm Beach County. West Palm Beach, the largest city in the MSA, has provided little or no help. Various agencies provide limited services for problems such as spouse and child abuse, chronic mental illness and substance abuse, crisis pregnancy, and childhood homelessness. A survey in the 1986 report found that organizations such as the Salvation Army, Lord's Place (a family shelter), Safe Harbor Runaway Center, and Faith Farm provide 310 beds throughout the county for the traditional homeless, new and temporary homeless, homeless children, and mentally ill/substance abusers (respectively). In light of the estimated size of the homeless population, this response falls far short of what is needed.

FORT LAUDERDALE–HOLLYWOOD–POMPANO BEACH

The cities of Fort Lauderdale, Hollywood, and Pompano Beach are all part of Broward County, which lies south of the West Palm Beach MSA and north of the Miami MSA. Estimates of the number of homeless vary. The Statewide Task Force Report on the Homeless estimates that 804 homeless persons were seeking some type of services in March 1985. Other sources provide very different demographics, suggesting that the state report is conservative in its calculations. According to the "Program Proposal for Assisting Homeless of Broward County" (1986) issued by the Social Services Division of Broward County, there are approximately 2,000 year-round homeless in Broward County. These numbers are based upon a report by the Broward County Homeless Task Force Consortium. It is also suggested that during January through April, the figure increases to approximately 5,000. Furthermore, Daniel J. Schevis, director for the Broward County Social Services Division, told us in an interview that there are estimates of 2,000 to 10,000 homeless in the county, with seasonal variation probably causing such a wide range. He believes that usually there are 5,000 to 7,000 homeless in this area. The Broward County Social Services Division has been one of the most active governmental agencies in this region in work with the homeless and is probably the most knowledgeable concerning how many there are. We believe that a reasonable estimate of homelessness in this area would be at least 5,000 persons.

The homeless in this region are composed of several categories of persons. According to the "District Ten Homeless Task Force Report" (that is, Broward County) conducted by HRS in 1985 as part of the statewide report, there are three major groups. It is estimated that 61 percent of the homeless are new or temporarily homeless, 24 percent are chronic/traditionally homeless, and 15 percent are deinstitutionalized.

These three broad categories encompass a number of subgroups. The new homeless include unemployed families, single parents, and single adults, many from outside the state of Florida. A significant but unknown number includes children–"runaways" and "throwaways." Broward County has a long history of attracting runaways from throughout the country, especially due to its "beach and fun" image as portrayed in the news media and movies. There is a substantial population of Cuban and Haitian entrants in the area with 90 percent being Haitian. Many are illiterate, generally unskilled, and suffering from health problems when entering the country. While extended family relationships prevent some from being truly homeless, many live under substandard living conditions. To some extent, domestic, seasonal, and hired farm workers also contribute to the homeless population. Finally, deinstitutionalization has resulted in a sharp drop in patients at South Florida Hospital in the last decade. A significant number of these individuals are also homeless.

The causes and therefore the needs of these different homeless groups are varied. The HRS District 10 report highlights several key needs. Additional low-cost housing is definitely needed in the community. In 1985, approximately 7,656 additional housing units were needed. Shelter is perhaps the major unmet problem. This includes the need for beds and additional long-term residences along with a comprehensive program to help the homeless achieve economic independence. Related to this is the need for programs to provide employment and job training services. Other issues noted in the HRS report are the need for improvements in health care services, mental health services, and support systems. Another salient need is the development of programs for adolescents who have no home to return to or who refuse to return home.

Historically, the private sector, religious organizations, and voluntary groups have made the most effort to serve the homeless. Funding has come from contributions, the United Way, and local government agencies. The services have included emergency shelter, limited low-income housing, counseling for drug and alcohol abuse, mental health care, and food programs. In the past, the state has provided little or no financial assistance. Cities like Fort Lauderdale have apparently sought to ignore or suppress homelessness. For example, a moratorium on developing new social service agencies including homeless shelters presently exists in the city, while several years ago a proposed law would have had garbage cans sprayed with kerosene to prevent the homeless from looking for food in them. Vagrancy arrests have also been conducted. Clearly, additional services are needed in the community.

Recently, several positive steps have been taken to improve assistance to the homeless primarily by Broward County and organizations such as the Community Service Council, which have obtained support from various sources, including the Federal Emergency Management Assistance Program, the State Emergency Shelter Program, and the United Way. In 1985, Covenant House, the first shelter for runaways in the area, was established with approximately 88 beds. In 1987, the county, with support from FEMA, implemented a voucher system and case management staff to provide shelter (for example, in adult congregate living facilities, motels, and elsewhere) and other services to the homeless. The staff is comprised of several full-time, permanent workers who deal exclusively with the homeless. Finally, in 1987, the Salvation Army and Community Service Council began the first long-term residential facility for families, which can serve 35 people. Such developments are welcome, although they certainly do not fully address the problem of homelessness in this area.

MIAMI–HIALEAH

The second largest MSA in Florida is Miami–Hialeah in Dade County. As usual, estimates of the homeless in this region vary and lack precision, although the extent of the problem seems to be much greater than what is indicated by the Statewide Task Force Report on the Homeless. "A Report on the Homeless" (1987) issued by the Miami Coalition for Care to the Homeless suggests that the number of homeless ranges from 4,000 to 10,000 people in all of Dade County. Kay Flynn, executive assistant to the director for the Department of Human Resources of Metropolitan Dade County, made a similar estimate of 3,500 to 10,000 in an interview. According to Sidney Shapiro, senior human services program manager for alcohol, drug abuse, and mental health at HRS and liaison between the Statewide Task Force and the Miami Coalition for Care to the Homeless, the conventional estimate is around 10,000 with a possible maximum projection of 20,000. Finally, in a report entitled "Malign Neglect: The Homeless Poor of Miami" by the National Coalition for the Homeless (1986), 8,000 people are estimated to live in the streets and shelters of Miami City. The study also suggests that Miami lags behind every other American city in providing assistance to the homeless. In light of these projections, we believe that at least 8,000 to 10,000 homeless exist in this MSA region.

The homeless in this highly populated area are composed of several groups.

According to Sidney Shapiro, seven distinct groups exist. They are the new homeless—which includes people who have lost their jobs (some from the North), spouses without husbands, and low-wage workers. The deinstitutionalized form another category. Another group includes those who suffer to varying degrees from mental illness. Not unexpectedly, traditional street people and drug abusers are part of the homeless. Migrants and seasonal workers form another group. A further category is composed of Cuban and Haitian refugees. As reported in other nearby areas, many of these individuals fear that if they report to the authorities, they will be deported. As a result, they remain hidden and uncounted. A final group is composed of runaways and abused children. In the city of Miami there have even been reports of such individuals forming gangs.

"A Report on the Homeless" (1987), a survey of programs directly providing shelter or contracting for shelter for Dade County gives several other descriptive characteristics of the homeless. In the last year, 42 percent were persons who have been laid off longer than 6 months, 66 percent were persons who have no marketable skills, 57 percent were black, 30 percent were non-Hispanic white, and 9 percent were Hispanic. Sixty-seven percent were 19 to 40 years of age, 25 percent were alcoholics, 26 percent were drug users, and 20 percent were mentally ill applicants. Finally, 28 percent represented an increase in females applying for services, and 36 percent represented an increase in families applying for services.

As in other areas, there are various causes of homelessness. "A Report of the Homeless" (1987) focuses on three causes in Dade County. The first is the lack of affordable housing. As the report suggests, federal assistance began to disappear in 1980. The combination of decreasing assistance and increasing numbers of low-income families has been devastating. While actual documentation of the shortage of housing for low-income families and individuals is not available, some indicators of the extent of the problem do exist. For example, Miami suffered a 7 percent loss in housing inventory between 1979 and 1983. According to the *U.S. Census Annual Housing Survey: 1983*, a total of 20,700 units were removed from the housing stock countywide, with almost half taken from the city of Miami. Furthermore, during that time the percentage of renters paying more than 35 percent of their income for rent increased from 39 percent to 49 percent. Finally, operators of public housing in early 1987 were surveyed as to the number on their waiting lists. The results were: Metro-Dade County, 12,000; Hialeah, 2,000; Miami Beach, 1,000; and Homestead, 100.

The second cause of homelessness is mental illness and deinstitutionalization. There has been some response to this need. In the last two years, HRS has improved case management and tracking of deinstitutionalized clients and has increased residential treatment. The third cause is unemployment. In November 1986, the local unemployment rate was 6.2 percent, representing 56,639 people. Assuming that 1 percent of the labor force includes discouraged workers, another 10,000 individuals raises the total to approximately 65,000 unemployed people.

An unknown proportion of those people are homeless. Of course, numerous other causes could be added to these three discussed by the report. For example, Kay Flynn noted the impact of the "boat people" on the area in the early 1980s.

While there is a growing awareness of the problem and increasing attempts to deal with homelessness, as Sidney Shapiro pointed out, this region lacks a community-based political plan and effort. Overall, there has been inadequate recognition and response to the problem. Private, nonprofit groups and the county provide most of the available assistance. Within the government sector, Metropolitan Dade County has the primary responsibility for operating social services to deal with problems such as homelessness. Dade County provides approximately $7.7 million per year for health services, residential programs, shelters, and so on for the homeless.

The responsibility for dealing with the homeless has often fallen to the criminal justice system. "A Report on the Homeless" (1987) states that, over the years, the east wing of the Dade County jail has been a twenty-four-hour facility for the homeless. And in 1986 the city of Miami made 6,893 arrests of the homeless at an estimated total cost of $2 million. According to the report, the officers themselves said the system is not working—they are just moving the problem around.

Most of the existing programs provide short-term shelter for individuals. Programs that directly provide shelter are the Miami Rescue Mission, Miami City Mission, Camillus House, Miami Bridge, Metro-Dade Department of Human Resource Office of Emergency Assistance and Emergency Housing, and the Salvation Army. These groups provide beds for approximately 408 people. Obviously, this does not meet the needs of the large number of homeless in the area. It is worth noting that Camillus House, run by Brother Paul Johnson, is a major provider of assistance in the area and has been the object of many stories in the news media. In 1986, Camillus House served 272,772 meals to the homeless while bedding 70 people a night. Presently, the city of Miami wishes to move the shelter because it lies in the downtown area where a multimillion-dollar redevelopment project centered around the construction of a new sports stadium is taking place. Amidst the threat of condemnation, on-and-off negotiations continue as the city and the shelter discuss where to relocate, how much the city will assist the move financially, and the possibility of the shelter remaining at the present location and expanding its operations.

In view of the existing situation, an adequate response would require a number of actions. "A Report on the Homeless" (1987) makes four specific recommendations. Preeviction assistance should be expanded, thereby reducing the number of people evicted and homeless. A short-term receiving evaluation and referral shelter, open 24 hours a day, is also needed. Furthermore, additional long-term shelters for single individuals are required. Lastly, long-term shelters for families are definitely needed. These proposals focus on the immediate need for shelter with social service support. Underlying such recommendations is the need to address the broader causes of homelessness such as lack of housing, poverty, and unemployment, as well as the needs of refugees and the mentally ill/deinstitutionalized.

CONCLUSION

Based upon our investigation of the six largest MSAs in Florida, we estimate the number of homeless to be at least 3,000 to 3,500 in Jacksonville, 1,440 in Orlando, 2,200 to 2,800 in Tampa–Saint Petersburg–Clearwater (1,700 to 2,200 in the former and 500 to 600 in the latter two), 3,000 in West Palm Beach–Boca Raton–Delray Beach, 5,000 in Fort Lauderdale—Hollywood–Pompano Beach, and 8,000 to 10,000 in Miami–Hialeah. Consequently, the total number of homeless for Florida is at least 22,640 to 25,740 (approximately twice that of the statewide report's estimate). Again, it should be noted that this estimate is for urban homelessness, and therefore, the inclusion of the rural homeless would increase the estimate.

The composition of the homeless is diverse and, of course, varies by region. Briefly, we find that the major groups include unemployed or underpaid individuals and families (some from the North), single women (some of whom have been abused), Cuban and Haitian refugees, migrants and seasonal workers, deinstitutionalized/mentally ill, drug and alcohol abusers, runaways and throwaways, and traditional chronic homeless. Further variations also exist, such as the homeless population being composed of: whites, blacks, and to a lesser degree Hispanics; different ages and educational backgrounds; and sometimes families. Apparently, the traditional homeless are a relatively small proportion of the total, while those suffering from economic exigencies are a significant part of the population.

The sources of homelessness reflect the varied nature of the problem. However, certain needs repeatedly surfaced in the study. The lack of affordable housing and residential shelters clearly stands out. Unemployment, low-paying jobs, and lack of job training were causes of homelessness throughout the state. There is also a lack of management, tracking, and treatment of the deinstitutionalized and mentally ill. Other causes include a lack of programs for adolescents, abused women, and substance abusers, along with inadequate health-care services, support systems, and mental health systems for the various groups comprising the homeless.

While some noteworthy efforts have been made to aid the homeless and while such actions appear to be increasing, the public and private response clearly falls far short of adequately dealing with the problem. The state's response has been very clearly inadequate, and most of the cities have not dealt with the homeless in a constructive and substantive manner. Usually, the primary governmental effort has come from the counties. Much of the assistance that is provided comes from private, nonprofit organizations, although this varies from one region to another. In view of the size of this large and apparently growing problem, far more needs to be done to remedy the causes of homelessness in Florida. Such endeavors should include more assessments and proposals for solving the problem and greater political effort at the local and state level.

REFERENCES

Broward County, Florida—Social Services Division. 1986. Program Proposal for Assisting Homeless of Broward County. Room 433A, 115 South Andrews Ave., Fort Lauderdale, FL 33301.

Department of Health and Rehabilitative Services. 1985. District Ten Homeless Task Force Report. 201 West Broward Boulevard, Fort Lauderdale, FL 33301.

Harrington, Michael. 1984. *The New American Poverty*. New York: Holt, Rinehart and Winston.

Miami Coalition for Care to the Homeless. 1987. A Report on the Homeless. Dade County, Fl.

Pinellas County Coalition for the Homeless. 1987. About the Homeless of Pinellas County: Fact Sheet. Homeless Coaliton Survey (January).

Report by the National Coalition of the Homeless. 1986. Malign Neglect: The Homeless Poor of Miami. 105 East 22nd St., New York, NY 10010.

Report of the Needs Assessment Subcommittee of the Homeless Coalition. 1986. The Homeless Population in Palm Beach County. Community Services, P.O. Box 4006, West Palm Beach, FL 33402.

Rossi, Peter H., et al. 1987. The Urban Homeless: Estimating Composition and Size. *Science* 235 (March): 1336–1431.

Snow, David A., et al. 1986. The Myth of Pervasive Mental Illness Among the Homeless. *Social Problems* 33 (5): 407–423.

Statewide Task Force on the Homeless. 1985. Florida's Homeless: A Plan for Action. State of Florida: Department of Health and Rehabilitative Services.

Tobin, Thomas C. 1987. Treatment Center Might Come to St. Petersburg. The Pinellas Tribune section of the *Tampa Tribune* (June 9): 1, 9.

Traveler's Aid Society of Jacksonville. 1986. Intake Reports (January to November).

———. 1985. Annual Intake Report.

———. n.d. Five Year Study (1979–1984).

University of Florida/Bureau of Economic and Business Research. 1984. Florida Estimates of Population, April 1, 1984: State, Counties and Municipalities.

4

Homelessness in the Frostbelt: The Case of Illinois

Peter Kivisto

During the 1980s, homelessness has become a social problem receiving a growing amount of attention from journalists and, more recently, academics (Lamb, 1984; Hope and Young, 1986; Redburn and Buss, 1986; Bingham, et al., 1987). While it is an extraordinarily difficult task to ascertain the precise scope of the problem as well as to identify the major causes at play, there is sufficient evidence to suggest that the United States has not witnessed such an explosion of homelessness since the 1930s depression (Hombs and Synder, 1982).

Though homelessness did not disappear in the years between the depression and the neoconservative political victory in 1980, it did not register in the public consciousness as a significant social problem during much of this time. However, the recession of the early 1980s created an economic climate with clear parallels to that of the 1930s, and, although the numbers are exceedingly controversial, there is no doubt that the ranks of the homeless rose dramatically.

Part of the reason for the recent focus on homelessness is that, as Peter Marcuse (1987: 426) writes, "[it] is shocking. It shocks most people not because they are in danger of becoming homeless but because of what homelessness says about the society in which we live." In particular, it speaks to the growing bifurcation in our society between the haves and the have-nots.

Using the state of Illinois as a case study, this paper is an effort to understand the nature of the problem more precisely. Illinois is a good test case insofar as it can help to elucidate two issues that have been raised by research to date. The first concerns the similarities and differences between homelessness in the past and in the present. Because there was a considerable amount of research done on the homeless in Chicago before and during the depression (Anderson, 1923;

Locke, 1935; Sutherland and Locke, 1936; Solenberger, 1911), it is possible to make such comparisons. The second issue deals with regional differences. Specifically, because Illinois is a Frostbelt state that has experienced severe economic dislocations during the past decade, it might be useful in terms of making comparisons and contrasts to Sunbelt states.

While this paper will examine homelessness as a statewide problem, it is important to note that much of the literature assumes that the problem remains to a large extent one that confronts major cities. The accuracy of this assumption will be examined.

It is clear that because of Chicago, Illinois, is one of the states in the country with a severe homeless problem. Chicago is the third largest city in the country, and, according to estimates provided by the National Coalition for the Homeless, is tied for fourth in terms of the number of homeless persons contained in its borders. The coalition estimates place New York City first, with 60,000 homeless; Los Angeles second, with 50,000; Detroit third with 27,000; and Chicago and Houston fourth, with 25,000 each (*New York Times*, July 20, 1986, 5E).

This chapter is divided into three main sections that are intended to complement one another. The first reviews existing quantitative data, relying in part on a richer base of information in the case of Chicago than exists elsewhere. This will be complemented by ethnographic data obtained from unobtrusive observations of the homeless and from a limited number of extended taped interviews which seek to examine the problem both in Chicago and in smaller cities in the state and which seek to look at both the shelter population and the nonsheltered homeless. Finally, government policy initiatives will be briefly reviewed.

METHODOLOGICAL PROBLEMS

In 1936, Sutherland and Locke published the results of their study of the homeless in Chicago, *Twenty Thousand Homeless Men*. Writing in the midst of the depression, they sought to document the impact of this economic crisis and provide a portrait of men forced onto the streets and into the city's shelters. In so doing, they captured in microcosm the problem of homelessness at the advent of the establishment of, in Katz's (1986) terminology, "the semiwelfare state." A half century later, a research team headed by Peter Rossi produced a volume entitled *The Conditions of The Homeless in Chicago* (1986). Undoubtedly the most analytically rigorous study on the homeless to date, this costly investigation served unintentionally to illustrate the interrelationship between political and social research issues. While its findings will be discussed below, it can be suggested at the outset that it depicts the situation at a point when we have moved from, again in Katz's (1986) words, "the war on poverty to the war on welfare."

In the five decades between these two studies, far-reaching social and economic changes have occurred that have direct implications for the issue of the homeless. The manufacturing sector of the economy has eroded while the service sector has expanded. A consequence of this process of deindustrialization (Bluestone and Harrison, 1982) is that higher-paying, stable, unionized jobs have declined in number, forcing workers into the more marginal sectors of the economy where they compete with workers whose employment careers have been confined to this sector. Second, the ecology of cities has changed from the period of urban renewal to the gentrification of cities in the late 1970s, resulting, in many instances, in "the demolition of skid row" (Bahr, 1973; Miller, 1982; Siegal and Inciardi, 1982). Of particular significance, there is growing evidence to suggest that the federal bulldozer as well as private developers have destroyed a considerable amount of housing stock that had heretofore served the needs of the working poor (Slayton, 1987). Third, the deinstitutionalizing trend in the field of mental health, beginning with the creation of community mental health centers in the 1960s, has placed many mentally ill people with attenuated ties to family and community onto the streets (Snow et al., 1986). Forth, the exacerbation of problems within families has produced two new categories of the homeless: women (with or without children, frequently the victims of domestic violence), and young people under the age of 21 (Hopper and Hamberg, 1986).

The task of ascertaining the number of homeless people in the United States is inherently fraught with difficulties and ambiguities. Transient people, often with a desire to avoid dealing with bureaucratic functionaries, the police, and other representatives of established social institutions, are frequently unwilling to be counted. Alcoholics, drug abusers, and the mentally ill are often incapable of providing useful information even if willing to do so. The problem of ascertaining not merely the number of the homeless in the country, but what the demographic portrait looks like is even more complicated because the issue has been intensely politicized. The controversy surrounding the U.S. Department of Housing and Urban Development's (1984) report on the homeless and emergency shelters graphically testifies to the polemical character of counting.

In the case of Illinois, no studies have been undertaken to determine the homeless population statewide. However, considerable attention has been devoted to the problem in the Chicago metropolitan area. Now the nation's third largest city, Chicago has historically been a magnet for Midwesterners fleeing small-town provincialism, periodic economic crises in the farm economy, or merely seeking adventure. When Nels Anderson wrote his famous study, *The Hobo* (1923), 50 million people lived within a one-night train ride of the city. However, a number of medium-sized cities dot the state, the most important being Bloomington–Normal, Champaign–Urbana, Decatur, East Saint Louis, Moline-Rock Island, Peoria, Rockford, and Springfield (Johnson and Veach, 1980). Each of these cities has witnessed an increase in the number of homeless persons during the 1980s, though constraints on research funding have meant that there has been no effort to determine homeless estimates in a manner analogous to that of Chicago. In addition, there is growing impressionistic evidence that rural and small-town homelessness has risen, though the scope of this problem remains quite unclear, and reliable data do not exist.

It remains the case, nonetheless, that Chicago constitutes a clear locus of the problem. While the Illinois Coalition for the Homeless has estimated that there may be as many as 25,000 homeless persons in the city, Rossi et al. (1986: ix) concluded that on an average night in 1985 and 1986 there were slightly more than 2,000 persons without a home, and that the annual prevalence estimates did not exceed 7,000. Both studies have their shortcomings. The methodological rigor of the Rossi project was perhaps undercut by a logistical decision (actually, a safety concern for the research team) to send off-duty police officers with researchers as they conducted their street surveys between 1 A.M. and 6 A.M. (Rossi et al. 1986: 14). A likely consequence of this decision was that, in an effort to avoid legal authorities, some of the street homeless "disappeared" when the team arrived in a particular location. This would serve to produce an undercount in the actual number of the homeless. The coalition study, by contrast, was less methodologically rigorous and had smaller and somewhat less reliable samples upon which to base its estimates. Despite the disparity regarding overall population estimates, marked similarities emerge in the demographic profiles created by Rossi and his colleagues and by the Chicago Coalition (1983) study.

A DEMOGRAPHIC PROFILE OF THE HOMELESS

In the first place, the homeless today differ markedly from the migratory workers of an earlier era (Caplow, 1940). The homeless in Chicago at the beginning of the century, studied by Solberger (1911), might bear a greater similarity in this regard to the current homeless in a Sunbelt city such as Los Angeles. Second, in contrast to one popular myth, they are not in any significant way made up of members of a downwardly mobile middle class. Third, while homeless families certainly constitute a problem of major concern, the bulk of the homeless remain unattached males.

The Chicago Coaliton study (1983: 17) was unable to make a clear determination of the gender ratio, but implicitly (because they had a difficult time finding women to include in their survey) recognized that homelessness remains a predominantly male phenomenon. Rossi, et al. (1986: 60) concluded that 75.5 percent of the Chicago homeless were male.

The average age of the homeless was 40.3 years, fairly closely corresponding to the average age of all Chicago residents, which, according to the 1980 census, was 39.4 (Rossi et al., 1986: 61). There is a relatively even distribution according to age category. The Chicago Coalition (1983: 19) suggested that today's homeless are somewhat younger than those treated in the traditional literature. While this is probably true if contrasted to the skid-row alcoholics portrayed in the social problems literature during the 1950s and 1960s, there are good reasons to doubt whether the age distribution differs greatly from that of the depression-era homeless. One special category that will be singled out for attention below is that of youth.

One finding that indicates a change from the past concerns the racial composition of this population. Blacks are overrepresented in the ranks of the homeless. The Chicago Coalition study (1983: 18) reported that 56 percent of their respondents were black, while Rossi, et al. (1986: 63) put the figure at 53 percent. The former study found 41 percent of the homeless to be white, 2 percent Native American, and 1 percent Hispanic, while the latter study reported the percentages respectively at 30.7 percent, 5.1 percent, and 6.9 percent. This finding is not entirely surprising, given the fact that racial minorities are overrepresented in the ranks of the underclass and the working poor. Their slide into homelessness can be seen as occurring over a protracted period of time, during which their tenuous place in the labor market progressively eroded. Adding credence to this assessment is the fact that a significant portion of the homeless have lived in Chicago for long periods of time and thus are not recent migrants seeking to get a foothold in the local economy. Of the Chicago Coalition's respondents 51 percent reported having lived in the city all their lives, while only 12 percent said they had lived there for a few months or less (1983: 20). Rossi et al. (1986: 64) support these findings, concluding that 72.3 percent of the homeless have lived in Chicago for at least 10 years, while only 11.1 percent have resided in the city for less than a year.

Related to this finding is the issue of the length of time that individuals have been homeless. Rossi et al. (1986: 30) divide the population into three categories: "short-termers," who have been homeless for up to three months; "medium-termers," who have been homeless from between four months and two years; and "long-termers," who have been homeless for more than two years. There are one in four persons in the first category, one in two in the second, and one in four in the third. About 6 percent are the permanent homeless, individuals reporting that they have been without a domicile for 10 or more years.

According to Rossi et al. (1986: 31), the median income of the homeless was $99.85, the mean income being $168.39. The regular provision of income was derived from a number of sources, including General Assistance payments, Supplemental Security Income, Veterans Administration Disability, Aid to Families with Dependent Children, and unemployment benefits. Rossi et al. (1986: 33) discovered that for 31.6 percent of the respondents, at least a part of their monthly base income came from employment. This corresponds to the Chicago Coaliton (1983: 30) study, which found 29 percent of its respondents obtaining at least occasional income from day labor. Other sources of income included begging, collecting cans, paper, and other materials for recycling, and various illegal activities, including prostitution. In addition, to varying degrees the homeless availed themselves of various types of in-kind goods and services such as free meals, free clothing and, at least for a minority, food stamps.

Homelessness and Mental Illness

One recurring issue in the literature is the extent to which the homeless are mentally ill. Snow et al. (1986: 1336) have recently called into question the "myth of pervasive mental illness" in their study of the homeless in Austin, Texas. If correct in reference to Chicago, this would suggest that the new homeless are far different from the portrait presented by Wiseman (1970), which emphasized the pathologies (particularly alcoholism) of the denizens of Chicago's skid row in the 1960s. Both studies reviewed here would dispute the conclusions of Snow et al. (1986), implicitly suggesting that the current situation evidences considerable continuity with the recent past. Ross (1986: 36) determined that approximately two thirds of the homeless had been institutionalized in mental hospitals, detoxification units, prisons, or jails, with 38.4 percent of the total reporting two or more institutionalizations. The Chicago Coalition (1983: 120) researchers perceived that 43 percent of the individuals they interviewed were not sober at the time. Rossi et al. (1986: 128–129) concludes that there "was a very high prevalence of mental illness" among the homeless, particularly of depression and psychosis. This, of course, lends support to the argument that the deinstitutionalization campaign initiated in the 1960s continues to play a profound role in the overall problem.

Homeless Youth

One significant subgroup demands further comment. Since the 1960s, the height of the youth counterculture, homeless youth have been a phenomenon of the urban landscape (Chicago Coalition, 1985). However, homeless youth today have, in most instances, not left home motivated by the utopian sensibilities of young people two decades ago. Instead, they have generally fled intolerable conditions. As the author of the Illinois governor's Task Force on Homeless Youth final report contends, "they are leaving home, or being forced out of the home because of serious physical, sexual, and emotional abuses. They are ending up homeless because of a breakdown in their families and inability to find or use resources that are available" (Johnson, 1985: 13). The estimates provided by this report are quite high, suggesting that there may be as many as 21,535 homeless youth in the state, approximately half of them in Chicago, with the remainder being distributed rather evenly throughout other major metropolitan areas. Statewide, 4,335 youth were determined to have had some contact with at least one community social service agency (Johnson, 1985: 5).

Battered Women and Homelessness

Another subgroup is battered women, individuals who, with or without children, have fled a situation where they were the victims of domestic violence. While economic factors are clearly at play in forcing women into homelessness, due to what has been referred to as the "feminization of ghetto poverty" (Pearce, 1983), women rendered homeless because of domestic violence cut across class lines, though working-class and poor women are overrepresented as victims of abuse. During the past decade, an increasing number of facilities have been established to address the particular needs of battered women and their children, with numerous facilities in operation in Chicago and with each medium-sized city in the state having at least one.

Statewide Estimate

Whatever the shortcomings of research on Chicago, at the very least, a critical interpolation of the findings of the two major surveys undertaken to date provides us with some confidence in the overall portrait of the homeless in the city as depicted above and some clues about the actual number of homeless individuals. In contrast, outside Chicago it is extremely difficult to arrive at reliable estimates. Since the resources for a survey of the other urban areas in the state were unavailable, an effort was made to obtain crude estimates by relying on well-informed individuals who have direct contact with the homeless in their locale. Calls were made to the directors of at least two social service agencies dealing with the homeless in the above-noted eight middle-sized urban areas in the state. These directors were asked for their impression regarding scope of homelessness in their community. While all respondents prefaced their estimates with a warning about the problematic nature of such an exercise, several suggested that a general rule of thumb is to assume that there are about twice as many homeless as there are individuals reportedly served by shelters.

Using this ratio (and the Chicago studies can be cited to reinforce this 2:1 ratio), a conservative homeless figure in these eight localities would be 11,376. This is based on the fact that 5,183 unduplicated clients were provided shelter in fiscal year 1986 in facilities receiving funds from the State of Illinois Emergency Shelter Program (Illinois Department of Public Aid, 1987). This should be seen as a conservative estimate, since not all shelters in these cities are recipients of state funds. Using the same data, there are approximately 6,196 homeless individuals in localities in the state other than Chicago or the eight other cities. Finally, there are an estimated 29,216 homeless individuals statewide. These data would suggest a homeless population in Chicago of 11,644. This falls between those of the two Chicago studies reviewed earlier. This figure slightly exceeds the combined homeless population of the eight medium-sized metropolitan areas. Based on these estimates, the statewide estimate of homeless individuals would be 29,216, and Chicago would have about 40 percent of them. Thus, while homelessness is certainly a significant problem for major urban areas, the results of this analysis, which is admittedly predicated on very rough estimates, would indicate that it is a serious problem for other parts of the state as well.

THE EVERYDAY WORLD OF THE HOMELESS

In order to put flesh on these numerical bones, an ethnographic study was undertaken. This involved three facets and took place in two urban settings,

Chicago and Rock Island–Moline. The first facet entailed unobtrusive observations of the homeless outside the shelter setting in both cities during the day and evening. These observations are thus limited insofar as they were not undertaken during the night, particularly those hours when the Rossi research teams were conducting their investigation. However, the observations did provide useful information about how homeless men "get by" from day to day. Second, an intensive investigation took place at two sites in Rock Island—at a soup kitchen run at a Catholic church by Catholic Workers and at a mission run by a consortium of fundamentalist churches (the latter also ran a facility for battered women but was intent on preserving the anonymity of its location). Finally, during a four-month period in the winter of 1986–1987, in-depth taped interviews were conducted with 11 homeless individuals in both Chicago and Rock Island–Moline. In combination, this three-pronged approach adds depth to the earlier discussion.

On the basis of this research, the following composite portrait can be constructed. Some of the homeless spend their days working, either as day laborers or at regular jobs. Their days are thus similar to those of people with homes and jobs. Others spend a considerable portion of their days searching for work, either exploring realistic possibilities or pursuing their fantasies. In differing degrees, these types are less demoralized than the third type, those who are simply "biding their time." These homeless are the most visible to the public. They spend their days in parks, libraries, bus terminals, and similar public facilities, or, if they have money, in diners or bars. Much of the day is spent simply passing the time away, or in the case of alcoholics, drinking or seeking to obtain alcohol. Various survival strategies are evident among this group. For instance, they have devised ways of using public restrooms to clean up without being hassled by security guards. They tend to have a rather thorough knowledge of where they can obtain free food and under what conditions (for example, do you have to be sober?) and similarly where clothing and other handouts can be obtained. They are keenly aware that fast-food restaurants throw out large quantities of food at closing time, and many have become adept "dumpster divers."

While drinking is commonly a group activity, in most other instances the nonworking homeless tended to spend rather solitary days. Except for a minority which is very aggressive, and this group is probably made up of mentally ill individuals, most of the homeless seek to avoid threatening situations. A chief objective is to get through the day without being hassled. They place great value on being left alone. In this sense, those who were observed or interviewed clearly serve to reinforce the aptness of Caplow et al.'s (1968: 494) definition of homelessness as being a state of "detachment from society characterized by the absence or attenuation of the affiliative bonds that link settled persons to a network of interconnected social structures."

While many shelters have eliminated the trappings of "moral reform" so characteristic of missions a half century ago, the mission in Rock Island—albeit in a restrained way—saw its task as addressing the physical and spiritual needs of the homeless. A rigid structure of rules was in place, which the management deemed to be necessary in order to preserve order and decorum. To prevent conflict over what was being viewed, residents were not permitted to touch the television dials. People would be asked to leave if they were not sober or if their conduct was considered bizarre. Fighting meant immediate dismissal. Chapel was a requirement for anyone who planned to eat dinner (meals were served to nonresidents as well, and the facility was frequently used by elderly residents at a nearby public housing high rise), and the sleeping quarters were not accessible to residents until after the evening meal. The mission was defined as temporary refuge, and to that end, an individual could not stay there for more than 15 consecutive days. Nonetheless, approximately one third of the residents were regulars, individuals who usually spent a portion of each month in the mission. They generally sought shelter during the latter part of the month, when their monthly assistance checks had run out.

The one unwritten rule coming from the resident themselves was that individuals were to avoid "getting into someone else's business." The presentation of self in everyday mission life was not to be dictated or proscribed by other mission residents. The individual was free to reveal as much or as little about his past or present circumstances as he chose. Uninvited probing of a person's background was seen as an unwarranted intrusion. Privacy was to be respected. On the other hand, those who chose to talk about themselves at length were given considerable latitude, though if they became too overbearing, they were ignored.

In conducting interviews with 11 individuals, an effort was made to obtain background information, a description of the individuals' daily routines, and their attitudes regarding the future. The individuals could be divided into two general categories, short-term versus long-term homeless (with three years of homelessness being the dividing line), with those designations largely coinciding with the individual's age. The short-termers were mainly under 40, while all of the long-termers were over 40. In a locale such as Rock Island–Moline that has witnessed the elimination of 19,000 manufacturing jobs since 1980, it was quite possible that former unionized workers with years of service, high hourly wages, and homes might well have drifted into the ranks of the homeless—a somewhat modified version of the view that the new homeless include many from the middle class. Our interviews, combined with information provided from social service providers, indicated that this was not the case to any significant extent. The employment histories provided by interviewees suggested that these are unskilled workers who have experienced sustained periods of unemployment or underemployment.

The interviews were open-ended and generally lasted from 45 minutes to an hour. They were designed to be opportunities for the interviewees to engage in the "verbal construction and avowal of personal identities" (Snow and Anderson, 1987). This was neither an interior monologue nor a dialogue with representatives of the peer culture. Rather, it was a verbal exchange with a member of the mainstream of society. Thus, we were alert to the ways in which interviewees sought to provide various accounts of their homelessness, since it was likely that they would treat the interview as a situation in which they believed that their homelessness was being "subjected to valuative inquiry" (Lyman and Scott, 1970: 112). In particular, we were looking for the use of varied accounts, including various excuses or justifications.

While the interviewees were not inclined to adjudicate blame to themselves (except for two alcoholics, who rather matter-of-factly depicted their drinking as a major contributing factor to their problems), neither did they blame specific others or society as a whole. One might have assumed that the state of the local economy would have been cited, but such was not the case. While the interviewees were quite talkative about their present circumstances and, to a lesser extent, their futures, they tended to be rather circumspect about their past and about the specific events that led to their present condition. Thus, a twenty-year-old from Texas who had been traveling with a carnival said simply, "I was going to do good, but I didn't do good." One older man, originally from New England, had been homeless for approximately 15 years. Asked why he had originally left home, he replied that it was because he "had itchy feet." After recounting numerous cities where he had lived during this time and the wide range of jobs that he had held, he was asked what precipitated his various moves. He moved, he said, "when he had stayed long enough."

We probed to discover something about their family backgrounds, and a portrait of disaffiliation emerged. Several grew up in very troubled homes, in broken homes, or in foster homes. In general, they have had little or no contact with relatives. While five claimed to have never been married, the rest described one or more failed marriages. In two cases, it was not clear whether the men were actually legally married at present, but in each instance, there is little more than sporadic contact with family members. None suggested they hoped for marital reconciliations or, for those who said they had children, that they hoped to reestablish contact with their offspring.

While a certain amount of camaraderie could be observed in the mission lounge, the interviewees in both Chicago and Rock Island–Moline did not claim to have friends among the homeless. Indeed, there was a decided tendency to distance themselves from others. One respondent who was interviewed near the Greyhound bus terminal in Chicago's Loop gave a rather typical response: "I don't make friends. I make acquaintances. That's the way I was brought up." In western Illinois another said, "I space off people and times." In addition to a desire to stay away from "kooks" and "hotheads," a recurring theme concerned the inability to trust people; avoiding associations was seen as a way of insuring against being used or taken advantage of.

Future orientations differed largely on the basis of age and length of time on the streets. The older, long-term homeless were present-oriented. They were not inclined to talk about future plans, being largely concerned with daily survival strategies. On the other hand, they did not seem interested in embracing their role, certainly not in the romantic fashion of the vagabonds of folklore. Even in the one case where a respondent said he sought to be a "first-class bum," he somewhat defensively went on to suggest that this was a temporary goal, with employment possibilities to be explored in the next few months. The young, short-termers were inclined to describe their present circumstances as an unfortunate setback that would be rectified in the near future. Thus, the former carnival worker claimed that he was waiting for his name to get to the top of the list for a job training program. Another person was an aspiring musician whose goal, probably unrealistic, was to break into the gospel recording industry.

Parenthetically, we were surprised to discover how many times religion emerged as a topic, especially since we did not ask about it. Four of our respondents viewed themselves as very religious, and two others as religious (though, as one said, not "fanatical"). Religious backgrounds tended to be fundamentalist, and there was a passive, even fatalistic, cast to many of their comments. Thus, one individual, when asked what he was doing about the future, said, "I'm trusting in the Lord that things will get better."

Whether short-term or long-term, these individuals described similar day-to-day survival strategies. To survive meant knowing where and how to obtain food, shelter, and similar necessities. It meant knowing how to comport oneself when dealing with representatives from mainstream society, be they police, social workers, shopkeepers, or whatever. It meant knowing how to "avoid hassles." Clearly, some manage to survive better than others. Though never made quite so explicit in the interviews, the homeless tend to see their immediate world as divided into two categories: the exploiters and the exploited.

These homeless individuals are outsiders. For whatever reason—economic, psychological, social, or combinations thereof—these homeless men have become disaffiliated from the larger society and from the intimate world of family and friends. Some are clearly capable of reconnecting, while others are not; for some, homelessness will ultimately be a temporary, unrepeated phenomenon, while for others it will become a permanent way of life.

POLICY INITIATIVES IN THE 1980S

The preceding two sections have provided a composite, albeit necessarily partial, portrait of the homeless in Illinois. The ethnographic section focused on single adult males, both in shelters and on the streets. The two subgroups, women and youth, were not included in this aspect of the investigation. As the quantitative data reviewed indicate, adult males continue to constitute a sizable majority of the homeless population. Within this group alone, there is a considerable amount of variation regarding the causes of homelessness and characteristics of the population. It is clear that the complexity of the situation suggests that no single solution to the problem is possible. When the unique problems that confront homeless women and youth are also considered, the complexity of the situation is further compounded. Because the root causes of contemporary homelessness reflect structural changes, particularly in the economy and in families, a viable solution to the problem demands addressing these underlying factors. Short-term emergency measures will prove to be inadequate if they are not complemented by medium-range and long-term programs.

However, the federal government and the state of Illinois to date have opted for policies that view homelessness as an essentially short-term crisis. Before 1983, the federal government was involved neither in the provision of shelter for the homeless nor in funding private-sector agencies that were. The Emergency Jobs and Humanitarian Aid bill (P.L. 98–8) of 1983 provided for $100 million to be used for food and shelter programs; funds were to be funneled through the Federal Emergency Management Agency. The states received half of this allotment through an allocation formula that gave Illinois $2.5 million. During that same year, the state legislature provided $300,000 in emergency funding to eight shelters in Chicago (Illinois Department of Public Aid, n.d.).

The following year, the state's General Assembly authorized, in P.A. 83–1382, that the Department of Public Aid administer emergency shelter and food distribution programs. The act stipulated that the department be responsible for the distribution of funds to either local government or nonprofit agencies involved in the provision of temporary shelter and food assistance. During Fiscal Year 1985, the first full year the act was in effect, the department received an appropriation of $800,000. That was increased to $1,666,200 in the 1986 fiscal year and to $2,307,000 the following year. To date, the department has entered into 38 contracts with service providers. All are nonprofit agencies; no local governments have been awarded contracts (Illinois Department of Public Aid, n.d.).

While the U.S. Senate has approved a bill providing $923 million in aid to the homeless (*Washington Post*, 1987: A19), at the state level there are at present no legislative initiatives underway that would indicate either a substantial expansion of state funding to assist the homeless or a willingness on the part of the state to become more actively involved in housing provision. Local governments, likewise, have not opted for direct involvement in aiding the homeless, though there is a possibility that Chicago might move in that direction in the future. At neither the state nor the local level have any coordinated programs been proposed that would address the multifaceted character of homelessness or the underlying structural conditions that cause homelessness.

In the private sector, some local United Ways have sought to target increased allotments for the homeless, but in some economically distressed locales, such as Rock Island–Moline, the effect has been largely offset by declining charitable contributions. The Salvation army has similarly sought to expand both its shelter operation and its therapeutic programs for alcoholics but has also been limited in this endeavor by funding problems. Existing service providers are either designed to treat homelessness as an emergency problem or, as with the case of the Salvation Army, they provided a therapeutic response to the problem. While some shelters have sought to work cooperatively with job training programs and either provide psychological counseling or refer clients to other agencies, efforts to establish an integrated and comprehensive way of dealing with homelessness have been relatively unsuccessful. As with the governmental response to date, the private-sector service providers have not initiated policies or programs that are designed to attack the structural causes of homelessness.

One sees in the response to homelessness a particular instance of what Salomon (1985: 1) characterized as the American welfare state's "peculiar form": non-profit agencies assume primary responsibility for the delivery of services to those in need of shelter while the government becomes the chief source of funding for those agencies. This general pattern, despite criticisms from some advocates for the homeless, has not been questioned by political elites, the media, or the general population. There is little to suggest that this government–nonprofit agency relationship is likely to be modified in the future.

SUMMARY AND CONCLUSION

Homelessness in this Frostbelt state has, as the evidence presented in this chapter indicates, become a significant problem during the past decade. In comparison to the homeless during the depression, the contemporary homeless are less transient, somewhat younger, and more likely to have experienced alcoholism, drug dependency, or various forms of mental illness. In addition, in contrast to the past, racial minorities are grossly overrepresented in the ranks of today's homeless population. Finally, significant new categories of the homeless have emerged with distinct problems, including women (often the victims of domestic violence) and youth.

In fundamental ways, the homeless in Illinois differ little from the homeless elsewhere in the country: They are victims of economic recession and deindustrialization; they confront a shortage of affordable housing; and a significant percentage of them have histories of institutionalization in mental hospitals or prisons. They are marginal members of society who do not have the benefit of support networks provided by primary groups. The longer they remain in the "other America," the more likely their existential definitions of self serve to reinforce this marginal status.

Addressing the problem of homelessness is a complicated task because of the multiplicity of variables contributing to it and the structural embeddedness of the problem. The exceedingly restrained responses of goverment agencies (at all levels) to date does not suggest any reason for optimism. As a consequence, the homeless will continue to remain vivid symbols of a society in which social justice does not entail the right of all citizens to a guarantee that their basic needs of food, shelter, and medical care will be met.

ACKNOWLEDGMENTS

I would like to thank Padmini Gulati, Elizabeth Huttman, and Jamshid Momeni for their comments on an earlier version of this paper, originally presented at the annual meeting of the Society for the Study of Social Problems, in Chicago, Illinois, on August 15, 1987. I am especially indebted to Elliott Liebow for his detailed criticisms, comments on the relationship between government and nonprofit social service agencies, and general encouragement.

REFERENCES

Anderson, Nels. 1923. *The Hobo: The Sociology of the Homeless*. Chicago: University of Chicago Press.

Bahr, Howard. 1973. *Skid Row: An Introduction to Disaffiliation*. New York: Oxford University Press.

Bingham, Richard, et al., eds. 1987. *The Homeless in Contemporary Society*. Newbury Park, Calif.: Sage.

Bluestone, Barry, and Bennett Harrison. 1982. *The Deindustrialization of America*. New York: Basic Books.

Caplow, Theordore. 1940. Transiency as a Cultural Pattern. *American Sociological Review* 5: 731–739.

————, et al. 1968. Homelessness. *International Encyclopedia of the Social Sciences* 6: 494–499.

Chicago Coalition for the Homeless. 1983. "When You Don't Have Anything": A Street Survey of Homeless People in Chicago. Mimeographed report.

————. 1985. Position Paper: Youth Homelessness in Chicago. Mimeographed report.

Hombs, Mary Ellen, and Mitch Snyder. 1982. *Homeless in America: A Forced March to Nowhere*. Washington, D.C.: The Community for Creative Non-violence.

Hope, Marjorie, and James Young. 1986. *The Faces of Homelessness*. Lexington, Mass.: Lexington Books.

Hopper, Kim, and Jill Hamberg. 1986. The Making of America's Homeless: From Skid Row to New Poor. In *Critical Perspectives on Housing*, edited by Rachel Bratt et al., 12–40. Philadelphia: Temple University Press.

Illinois Department of Public Aid. 1987. Memoranda provided to the author by Gregory Coler, Director IDPA.

————. n.d. Fact Sheet and History (xerox).

Johnson, Daniel, and Rebecca Veach, eds. 1980. *The Middle-Size Cities of Illinois*. Springfield, Ill.: Sangamon State University Press.

Johnson, Gregory. 1985. Final Report: Governor's Task Force on Homeless Youth. Springfield, Ill.: Department of Children and Family Services.

Katz, Michael. 1986. *In the Shadow of the Poorhouse: A Social History of Welfare in America*. New York: Basic Books.

Lamb, H. Richard, ed. 1984. *The Homeless Mentally Ill*. Washington, D.C.: American Psychiatric Association.

Locke, H. J. 1935. Unemployed Men in Chicago Shelters. *Sociology and Social Research* 19: 420–428.

Lyman, Stanford, and Marvin Scott. 1970. Accounts. In *A Sociology of the Absurd*, 100–143. New York: Appleton-Century-Crofts.

Marcuse, Peter. 1987. Why Are They Homeless? *The Nation* (April 4): 426–429.

Miller, Ronald. 1982. *The Demolition of Skid Row*. Lexington, Mass.: Lexington Books.

New York Times, July 20, 1986.

Pearce, Diana. 1983. The Feminization of Ghetto Poverty. *Society* (November-December): 70–74.

Redburn, Stevens, and Terry Buss. 1986. *Responding to America's Homeless*. New York: Praeger Books.

Rossi, Peter, et al. 1986. The Condition of the Homeless in Chicago. Report of the National Opinion Research Center, Chicago, and the Social and Demographic Research Institute, Amherst, Mass.

Salamon, Lester. 1985. Partners in Public Service: Toward a Theory of Government-Nonprofit Relations. Paper presented at the annual meeting of the Society for the Study of Social Probelms, in Washington, D.C., on August 24.

Siegal, Harvey, and James Inciardi. 1982. The Demise of Skid Row. *Society* (January-February): 39–45.

Slayton, Robert. 1987. SRO Hotels and the Homeless in Chicago. Paper presented at the Midwest Sociological Society Meeting in Chicago, Ill., on April 17.

Snow, David, et al. 1986. The Myth of Pervasive Mental Illness Among the Homeless. *Social Problems* 33: 407–423.

Snow, David, and Leon Anderson. 1987. Identity Work among the Homeless: The Verbal Construction and Avowal of Personal Identities. *American Journal of Sociology* 92: 1336–1371.

Solenberger, Alice. 1911. *One Thousand Homeless Men*. New York: Russell Sage Foundation.

Sutherland, E. H., and H. J. Locke. 1936. *Twenty Thousand Homeless Men*. Chicago: J. B. Lippincott.

U.S. Department of Housing and Urban Development. 1984. A Report to the Secretary on the Homeless and Emergency Shelters. Washington, D.C.: Government Printing Office.

Washington Post, June 28, 1987, A19.

Wiseman, Jacqueline. 1970. *Stations of the Lost: The Treatment of Skid-Row Alcoholics*. Englewood Cliffs, N.J.: Prentice-Hall.

5

Homelessness in Massachusetts: Description and Analysis

Gerald R. Garrett and Russell K. Schutt

Individuals and families recently unable to afford any housing, mentally ill adults, and chronic alcoholics each appear in substantial numbers among the homeless of the 1980s. Although a growing body of research highlights the health problems of the homeless, detailed information on their social and financial resources and residential histories is often lacking (Bachrach, 1984b: 912–913; Brickner et al., 1985; Lamb, 1984b). This broader information is necessary to guide social service policy for the homeless and to help shelters plan for and respond to the needs of their clients.

In Massachusetts, as in other urban, industrialized states, the urgent needs of the growing numbers of homeless persons have strained the creativity of policymakers and the capacity of service providers. Studies by state and private organizations and by academic researchers are just now revealing an in-depth picture of Massachusetts's homeless to help shape relevant policies and services.

This chapter offers a brief overview of Massachusetts's response to the homelessness crisis, drawing largely on state and local reports that have described the scope of the problem and the policies and programs that have evolved in response to it. In addition, the chapter provides a comprehensive profile of Boston's single-adult homeless population. Data for this profile were obtained through representative sampling of intake records at one of Boston's largest shelters; evidence from other studies indicates that these clients closely resemble homeless single adults elsewhere in the state. The extensive intake data available at this shelter permit a detailed analysis of the health problems and service needs of the homeless.

THE HOMELESS IN MASSACHUSETTS

Approximately 8,000 of the commonwealth's 5.8 million residents are homeless, according to one recent estimate (Massachusetts Association for Mental Health, 1985: 9). Estimates of the number of unduplicated homeless people in a given year range from a low of 6,000 to as high as 15,000 (Emergency Shelter Commission and the United Community Planning Corporation, 1986: 5). Boston, Massachusetts's capital city, has the state's largest homeless population. A 1984 census of shelter clients and homeless persons on the streets estimated that from 2,000 to 2,700 individuals are homeless in Boston on any given day (Massachusetts Association for Mental Health, 1985). It should be noted that none of these figures include those who are doubled up in living quarters, the ''incipient homeless.''

Data obtained in several studies of Massachusetts's shelter users indicate that the commonwealth's homeless resemble the nationwide profile. About 83 percent are male; 17 percent are female. Racial composition resembles that for metropolitan Boston: 77 percent white; 22 percent black; 1 percent Hispanic. Median age is about 34; only about one in 10 is currently married, and the rest are almost evenly split between those always single and those divorced or separated. Nearly 4 of every 10 have completed high school, and about one in three had attended college (Emergency Shelter Commission and the United Community Planning Corporation, 1986; Massachusetts Association for Mental Health, 1985; United Community Planning Corporation, 1983).

In Massachusetts families who are homeless or at risk of becoming homeless have received special attention. In 1987, for example, the Massachusetts Executive Office of Human Services (EOHS) reported that approximately 500 families used the commonwealth's 26 family shelters; another 450 to 500 families were placed in hotels and motels in lieu of regular shelters. As many as 2,800 families passed through shelters and motels over a one-year period (September 1985–September 1986) and another 8,000 families were prevented from becoming homeless through special intervention by state agencies. About 80 percent of these families were single, female-headed households (EOHS, 1987).

Factors Promoting Homelessness

While Massachusetts has earned a place in the national spotlight for its economic prosperity, its ability to retain and attract industry, urban renewal, and an unprecedented urban building boom, it is in part these very factors that have contributed to the growth of Massachusetts's homeless population:

1. Urban renewal has brought a major decline in the number of affordable housing units, especially in Boston–Cambridge and the surrounding industrial suburbs, but also in the cities of Worcester, Springfield, New Bedford–Fall River, and Lowell. In Boston alone, the number of lodging houses declined from 1,650 in 1960 to about 300 by

1980; single-room occupancy (SRO) units fell from 24,000 to 6,000 during this same period. In the 1980s, the general cost of living as well as the price of housing has soared to one of the highest levels in the nation (Massachusetts Association for Mental Health, 1985).

2. Although Massachusetts has enjoyed one of the lowest unemployment rates among the 10 major industrialized states during the 1980s, labor market analyses show a marked shift toward technologically oriented positions requiring some degree of education and training. The impact of the job shortage for the poorly trained is compounded by reductions in public benefit programs, particularly federally sponsored social security entitlements. It is thus not surprising that more than 8 of every 10 homeless persons in Massachusetts have had only manual jobs and 6 of every 10 have had only unskilled manual jobs (Massachusetts Association for Mental Health, 1985).

3. As in other states, Massachusetts's policy to deinstitutionalize alcoholics and especially the mentally ill is also a major factor promoting the growth of its homeless population. While new policies and shifts in techniques for treating clients with psychiatric impairment led to large-scale reductions in the institutional population, noninstitutional supports to the poor, alcoholic, and physically or mentally disabled were inadequate to meet their needs. Even among those who were able to make satisfactory transitions from institutional to community life, "their poverty conspired to prevent their retention of affordable housing as their rooming houses and subsidized apartments were lost to gentrification and discrimination" (Massachusetts Association for Mental Health, 1985: 30).

The Response by Massachusetts

Efforts in the 1980s to respond to the crisis of homelessness in Massachusetts have been a joint venture of state agencies and the private sector. The first major step was taken in 1981 with the formation of the Massachusetts Coalition for the Homeless. Formed by service providers to address the short-term and long-term needs of homeless people, the coalition conducted the first statewide survey of homelessness in 1983. A complete inventory of facilities serving Massachusetts's homeless and a rough count of the number of homeless persons were the results.

Governor Michael Dukakis gave special attention to the plight of the homeless in his 1983 inaugural address, declaring homelessness to be a priority for social welfare efforts. Subsequent actions included formation of an Advisory Committee on Homelessness, with 53 members drawn from provider groups, business, advocacy and religious organizations, and the legislature and local government agencies. A statewide group of representatives from nonprofit agencies serving the homeless was then formed to advise state officials on how to target appropriate resources to areas with the greatest need. Thus, efforts in Massachusetts to formulate policy and strategies for service delivery have been tied closely to local circumstances.

The Dukakis administration also formed the Executive Office of Human Resources ("Resources" was changed later to "Services") to coordinate the efforts of individual agencies in responding to the needs of homeless individuals and families. An EOHR study profiled the homeless population in Massachusetts, identifying the need for services in suburban communities and the significant number of homeless families (EOHS, 1985). Subsequently, the Departments of Public Welfare, Public Health, and Mental Health initiated new shelter programs for the homeless in cooperation with other agencies.

The new interagency approach took into account the special needs of homeless families, alcoholics, and the physically and mentally disabled. Four goals were the focus of action: (1) prevention of homelessness, (2) provision of emergency services, (3) development and operation of support services, and (4) development of permanent housing (EOHS, 1985; Massachusetts Association for Mental Health, 1986).

One of the most significant milestones in Massachusetts's response to homelessness was a bill (Chapter 450 of the Acts of 1983) that broadened the role of state agencies in providing assistance to needy persons, including the homeless. Specifically, state welfare programs were mandated to assist eligible families to prevent destitution or to provide living arrangements in the home. In effect, the bill liberalized requirements for emergency assistance and enabled direct financial aid to both the homeless and potentially homeless families (Massachusetts Association for Mental Health, 1986).

The Massachusetts response to the crisis of homelessness thus represents a reciprocal relationship between public and private agencies. Executive action in the form of legislation, policy-making, and state-agency action has complemented efforts by communities, local agencies, and representatives from the public and private sectors statewide. Simultaneously, advocacy groups have played a key role in maintaining the visibility of homelessness as a community welfare issue and in promoting legislative and executive actions that serve the housing, medical, and financial needs of both the homeless and the potentially homeless.

THE HOMELESS IN BOSTON

The most comprehensive profile of the homeless in Massachusetts comes from the Long Island Shelter. One of the largest in Massachusetts, the Long Island Shelter opened in March 1983 on one of the off-shore islands near Boston Harbor. The shelter is operated by Boston's Department of Health and Hospitals and maintains 460 beds for homeless men, women, and a small but growing number of families. The shelter also provides food, nursing assistance, and referrals to other agencies for help with medical, psychiatric, and social needs.

Homeless clients (called by shelter staff "guests") are bused to the shelter from Boston City Hospital each night. Drugs and alcohol are not permitted at the shelter, but there are no restrictions on the types of individuals who may use it. Upon their arrival, the names of all guests are recorded; those who are new to the shelter are interviewed by a case manager. The intake form completed in this initial interview contains questions on demographic characteristics, work experience, medical problems, service needs, and related issues. A systematic random sample of these intake interviews are computerized regularly at the University of Massachusetts at Boston. Subsequent counseling and referrals to other agencies are noted in the file established after the initial interview. Many clients are also seen by a nurse, and a medical form is completed.

Methodology

Intake forms completed from March 1983 to July 1984 provide the primary source of data for this chapter. During this period, the shelter expanded in size from 100 to 200 beds. Until March 1984, an open-ended intake form was used to record guests' responses to general questions concerning their situation and problems. A systematic random sample of one quarter of these intake forms was drawn. The form was revised and expanded in March 1984; all these revised intake forms were coded. Sampled cases were then weighted to reflect the disproportionate sampling strategy used, resulting in an adjusted total of 501 cases. Two additional data sources were used. All cases in the first sample of 500 intake forms were checked against medical records at the shelter. Detailed medical information on the 82 cases for which medical records had been completed is presented. From May to July 1984, a complete list of shelter users was compiled from daily census sheets. An analysis of frequency of use is conducted with these data.

Overview of Shelter Guests

Most of the homeless clients at the shelter had been homeless for substantially less than one year. For example, 49 percent had been homeless one month or less; another 18 percent reported being homeless for at least one month but not longer than six months. Only 4 percent had been homeless for a year or longer. The median length of homelessness for new clients was 2.3 months. These figures are comparable to those reported in a study of the entire guest population at another Boston Shelter (Bassuk et al., 1984). New shelter clients frequently did not return to the shelter; of those in the initial sample 73 percent did not reappear at the shelter during May, June, or July 1984, even though the shelter's daily census indicated no decrease in shelter use during this period. Of those who did reappear, one in three clients came only for one or two nights; one third spent at least 10 nights per month. Shelter clients were a diverse group in terms of age, race, sex, and residential history. Median age for the period of March 1983 to July 1984 was 34. Twenty-four percent of the clients were under 26; 24 percent were 46 or older. Eight of every 10 clients were male. Although data on race were recorded only from March to July 1984, 62 percent of the clients during this period were white. Finally, 46 percent of the shelter population was born in Massachusetts, and nearly 8 of every 10 had had their last residence in Massachusetts.

These characteristics of the homeless at Boston's Long Island Shelter are similar to those reported in other studies in Boston. Bassuk et al.'s (1984) sample of the homeless at another Boston shelter found that 75 percent were men, compared to 80 percent at the Long Island Shelter. Mulkern and Spence's (1985) study of a street sample of Boston's homeless, however, found that 89 percent were male. In all three studies, the median age was 34. The percentage currently married was 11 percent in Bassuk et al.'s (1984) sample, 10 percent in the Long Island Shelter sample, and just 5 percent in the street sample. The percentage of white homeless was somewhat lower (62 percent) at the Long Island Shelter than in the other two samples (with about three quarters white). Bassuk et al. (1984) reported that 43 percent had finished high school, compared to 53 percent at the Long Island Shelter. This sociodemographic profile of Boston's homeless confirms indications of a shift in the composition of the homeless. While research in the 1950s and 1960s found homeless persons to be primarily older, white, male alcoholics (e.g., Blumberg et al., 1960; Bogue, 1963; Bahr, 1965; Bahr and Garrett, 1971, 1976), the homeless are now younger, more racially diverse, include a significant number of women, and have a wider range of problems (U.S. Department of Housing and Urban Development, 1984; Roper and Robertson, 1984).

The demographic characteristics of homeless clients at the shelter differed markedly from the Massachusetts population as a whole. Thus, shelter users tended to be younger and were more often male and members of minority racial or ethnic groups. According to the 1980 census, 44 percent of the state's population over 17 years old was 45 or older (U.S. Bureau of the Census, 1983: Table 62). Only 25 percent of the shelter's clients (not including children) were 45 or older. Men were particularly overrepresented in the shelter's population. Forty-eight percent of the Massachusetts population in 1980 was male (U.S. Bureau of the Census, 1983: Table 58); the corresponding figure for the shelter was 80 percent. Blacks and members of other minority groups comprised a disproportionate share of shelter users. While just 6 percent of the Massachusetts population were members of minority groups in 1980 (8 percent of the Boston Standard Metropolitan Statistical Area), 38 percent of the shelter's users were minorities (U.S. Bureau of the Census, 1983: Table 58). The percentage of the state's population who were black in 1980 was 4 percent, compared to 30 percent of the new shelter users.

Social and Financial Support. Lack of social support impairs the ability of the homeless to remedy their own condition and limits efforts of care providers to a short-term impact on that condition (Lipton et al., 1983). These problems were reflected in the minimal family ties of shelter guests. At least 49 percent had children, but only 10 percent were married at the time of the intake interview. In the Massachusetts population of 15- to 54-year-olds, just 6 percent of those who have ever been married have ever been divorced and 0.8 percent have ever been widowed (U.S. Bureau of the Census, 1983: Table 64). The corresponding figures for shelter users *in this age range* were 21 percent (currently divorced) and 2 percent (currently widowed). In addition, 24 percent of the new guests did not provide the case manager who interviewed them with the name of anyone else who could be contacted for them in an emergency.

Homeless guests also had little outside financial support. Seventy-two percent received no financial benefits at all (the comparable percentage in Bassuk et al.'s (1984) study of another Boston shelter was 78). The mean level of support for those receiving any benefits was $392 per month. Eleven percent received some type of welfare, and 15 percent obtained social security benefits. Thirty-one percent of the shelter guests (37 percent of the male guests) were veterans, but just 19 percent of these reported receiving veterans' benefits. This percentage of veterans among the homeless is similar to that for the male population in the state, 35 percent of whom were veterans in 1980 (U.S. Bureau of the Census, 1983: Table 70).

These figures suggest that the response to the problems of the homeless cannot rely primarily on the resources of the homeless themselves. A few—less than 5 percent—received enough benefits to support a more stable life-style. Identification and counseling of these guests might help to resolve their immediate problem of lack of shelter more quickly. On the other hand, one fourth of the guests were particularly socially isolated—lacking even a person who could be contacted in an emergency. More intensive social work would probably be required to help these guests establish supportive connections to the larger society.

Experience with Education and Work. The educational backgrounds of the new guests at the shelter were diverse. Nineteen percent had attended grade school, and an additional 29 percent had completed less than four years of high school. The remaining 53 percent were high school graduates (4 percent through a GED). Fifteen percent had education beyond high school, and 3 percent had graduated from college.

These figures indicate that many of the homeless had made significant educational progress, but a comparison with the educational level of the Massachusetts population in 1980 reveals that shelter users were less well educated. Seventy-two percent of the Massachusetts population at least 25 years old were high school graduates and 20 percent had finished four or more years of college (U.S. Bureau of the Census, 1983: Table 66). The corresponding figures in the shelter sample were 56 and 4. The same pattern appeared among those between 18 and 24 years of age. Eighty-three percent of Massachusetts residents in this age range were high school graduates, compared to 43 percent of shelter guests. While 10 percent of Massachusetts's 18- to 24-year-olds had completed at least four years of college, none of the shelter's clients had done so.

Most homeless clients had some work experience. Forty-six percent had worked at some time in jobs that involved a skill, while 54 percent had not worked in jobs likely to involve any skill prior to the interview. Twenty-nine percent had performed such skilled work in their most recent job. Half of the guests had worked at some time within the year preceding their first appearance at the shelter, although 15 percent had not had any job.

Recent research in New York City (*New York Times*, September 30, 1984), as well as earlier studies in Chicago (Bogue, 1963) confirm that the homeless are not uniformly low in educational level but do include smaller percentages of more educated persons. The number of homeless with at least a high school education and the frequency of job experience among them still suggest that many are potentially employable.

Health Problems. Physical illness and other health problems are more prevalent among the homeless than in the general population (Bogue, 1963; Wiseman, 1970). Recent studies have found about one third to be chronic alcoholics. The deinstitutionalization of mental patients has expanded the ranks of the homeless with many who are mentally ill (Arce et al., 1983; Bassuk et al., 1984; Carmody, 1984; Jones, 1983; Lamb, 1984a). These health problems each appeared among the clients at the Long Island Shelter.

Eighty-five percent of the Long Island Shelter sample had been in some type of hospital in the past—almost half of them within the previous year. The distribution of years since last hospitalization for those ever hospitalized (N = 262) was as follows:

Years since Last Hospitalization	Shelter Guests (%)
0–1	45
2–5	29
6–9	10
10 or more	16

A total of 18 percent noted a physical illness in the intake interview, and 7 percent reported injuries. Another 10 percent reported having been hospitalized for psychiatric problems, and an equal percentage reported current psychiatric problems. When these two indicators were combined, 29 percent appeared to have had some psychiatric problems—a figure somewhat low compared to the 40 percent of users of another Boston shelter reported to be psychotic by clinician interviewers (Bassuk et al., 1984).

Alcohol abuse or alcoholism was common among the shelter's guests. One third reported a problem with alcohol use, while 8 percent indicated that they had a problem with drugs. When all indicators of alcohol abuse in the intake interview were combined, the percentage of guests appearing to have a problem with alcohol rose to 43. A total of 41 percent who were asked in interviews from March to July 1984 whether they had been treated for alcohol or drug use responded affirmatively. Of those who reported a problem with alcohol use, 83 percent said they had been treated for alcoholism in the past.

The proportion of Boston's homeless with a history of alcoholism or alcohol abuse is consistent with similar studies in Los Angeles (Ropers and Robertson, 1984), San Diego (Wynne, 1984), and New York (Crystal, 1983), although Bassuk et al.'s (1984) clinicians diagnosed just 29 percent of shelter users as alcoholic. Comparative evidence reported elsewhere (Schutt and Garrett, 1987) indicates that the proportion of alcoholics among the homeless population has remained roughly stable over the past 25 years.

The combined incidence of health problems among individuals provides another useful description of their health status. One third of the new guests gave no indication of health problems. Twenty-three percent mentioned a problem with alcohol only or in combination with a physical illness; another 20 percent mentioned alcoholism in combination with a mental health problem. Fifteen percent gave some indication of mental illness, in some cases in conjunction with a physical health problem, while 8 percent only mentioned a physical illness.

Health forms were completed by nurses for 16 percent of the 1983–1984 intake sample. Some of these guests were seen by nurses because of specific health problems, while others were evaluated in periods when it was possible to send all new guests to a nurse for evaluation.

The information on the health forms provides a more detailed description of health problems than does the intake information. Since it was obtained through clinical evaluations, it is more reliable. However, several critical health problems were not assessed adequately on these forms (intestinal problems, kidney disease, and recent trauma). In addition, the cases having health forms were not a representative sample of the homeless using the shelter. Women, members of minority ethnic groups, and the elderly were overrepresented in the nursing sample. However, those likely to have any health problems did not seem to be substantially overrepresented. While 17 percent of those reporting any health problem (psychiatric, physical, alcohol-related, or injury) in the intake interview appeared in the nursing files, 12 percent of those who reported no such problem also appeared in the nursing files (see Schutt, 1985 for more details).

Nurses identified current psychiatric problems for 55 percent of the guests for whom they indicated any psychiatric evaluation. Forty-two percent were noted as being drinkers, although only 32 percent reported they were moderate or heavy drinkers. Fifty-eight percent were classified as having a physical health problem and 20 percent were classified as being injured.

The most common health problems found by nurses were dental, followed by blackouts, respiratory disorders (lung disease), and previously broken bones (Table 5.1). At least one third of the shelter guests for whom an evaluation was recorded by the interviewing nurse had had at least one of these problems. Physical health manifestations of alcoholism were common. In addition to the 45 percent who reported having had blackouts, 31 percent reported having had delirium tremens (DTs), and about 26 percent had had seizures. The percent

Table 5.1
Specific Health Problems Cited by Shelter Guests in Nursing Interview

Health Problem	Current Health Problem (%)	Past Health Problem (%)	Total %	(N)*
Hallucinations	18	7	25	(38)
Seizures	13	13	26	(42)
Delirium tremens	17	14	31	(42)
Blackouts	26	19	45	(43)
Rashes	4	5	9	(60)
Ulsers	0	5	5	(59)
Frostbite	1	8	8	(57)
Lice	1	4	5	(57)
Blood pressure (exam)	13	1	14	(62)
Arterial pressure (exam)	10	na	na	(na)
Circulatory system	12	4	16	(52)
Lungs (exam)	7	na	7	(60)
Lung disease	5	26	32	(56)
Eye problem	11	na	11	(52)
Diabetes	10	na	10	(56)
Liver	5	2	7	(56)
Eye/Ear/Nose/Throat	26	2	28	(51)
Back pain	4	8	12	(55)
Broken bones	2	36	38	(56)
Dental	31	37	69	(22)

na: Not available and/or not applicable.
* Percentages may not add to 100 due to rounding.

reporting that they had experienced hallucinations (which could indicate schizophrenia or alcoholism) was 25.

Skin disorders were less frequent. Approximately 9 percent had had a rash, 8 percent had experienced frostbite, and about 5 percent had had lice or ulcers. Thirty-two percent reported chronic obstructive pulmonary disease, TB, or pneumonia, and 7 percent had a lung problem. Seven to 10 percent had had a liver disorder or diabetes. Some 12 percent had experienced back pain, and 28 percent had had eye, ear, nose, or throat problems. Dental problems were reported by 69 percent.

The nursing records indicate that information obtained in intake interviews understates the health problems of the homeless. Nursing records tend to agree with self-reports of physical illness, injury, and alcoholism, but suggest substantial underreporting of psychiatric problems in the intake interview.

Services for the Homeless

Even when they first entered the Long Island Shelter, as the data below (N = 401) indicate, most guests had already had contact with one or more other service agencies.

Agencies Contacted	Shelter Guests (%)
Hospital	14
Mental health service	21
Shelter	41
Alcohol-related service	10
Social service agencies	25
None	18

These data show that the homeless in Boston interact frequently with service agencies, although shelters themselves were more common points of contact with the service system. When asked about their needs at the time of the intake interview, these clients focused on four concerns: 82 percent expressed a need for housing; slightly more than one third wanted a job; and about one third indicated a need for food and/or health care. Only 3 percent failed to express any service-related needs.

Patterns of Homelessness

Understanding the problems of the homeless requires determining the sources and consequences of these problems. Identification of those groups most susceptible to particular types of health and other problems can result in more effective targeting of resources and planning of intervention strategies.

By itself, life on the street can exact a heavy toll on physical and mental well-being. Of those mentioning psychiatric problems 38 percent had been homeless for at least seven months, as had a comparable percentage of those mentioning only alcoholism (Table 5.2). Nearly half (47 percent) of those mentioning a problem with alcohol in conjunction with another health problem had been homeless at least seven months. About the same percent of those only mentioning a physical health problem had been homeless at least seven months. Only 17 percent of those not mentioning any health problems had been homeless seven or more months.

Those with psychiatric problems seemed to use the shelter more frequently than did others, if they used it at all from May to July (Table 5.2). However, clients indicating a problem with alcohol use were only slightly more likely to use the shelter than those with no health problems.

The prevalence of illness in general as well as of specific health problems varied across particular groups among the homeless (Table 5.3). In general, as the data in Table 5.3 show, the frequency of health problems increased with age, was greater among men than among women, and was lower among those from outside of Massachusetts, among those who were married, and among those not giving the name of an emergency contact person (cf. Stoller, 1984: 265).

Table 5.2
Health Problems by Length of Homelessness and Frequency of Shelter Use

Health Problem	Homeless 7 Plus Months		Using Shelter 10 Plus Days	
	%	N	%	N
No Health Problem	17	113	20	15
Alcoholism only[a]	38	119	25	24
Psychiatric only[b]	38	47	41	10
Physical only	45	22	6	2
Alcoholism[c]	47	49	19	7

a: Includes alcoholism and physical problems.

b: Includes psychiatric and physical problems.

c: Includes alcoholism and psychiatric problems.

The likelihood of having any health problems did not vary with years of education. Veterans were somewhat more likely to have physical health problems than nonveterans, but otherwise their health problems were similar to those of men who were not veterans.

Self-reported psychiatric problems were much more prevalent among minorities than among whites, usually in conjunction with alcoholism. Those under 30 were more likely to have psychiatric problems not linked to alcoholism than were older guests. Psychiatric problems were more prevalent among men than among women but only because of the greater likelihood of men having both a psychiatric problem and a problem with alcohol. Psychiatric problems were less common among those married at the time of the intake interview. There was no systematic relation between education and health problems. Self-reported psychiatric problems were not associated with age, having children, job experience, or receipt of benefits.

Several groups were particularly prone to alcoholism. Alcohol abuse was reported much more often among men, those over 30 years of age, and those divorced, widowed, or separated. White guests were much more likely to report alcoholism as their only problem than were blacks and members of other minority groups, but minority group members reported a higher level of alcoholism in conjunction with psychiatric problems. New clients who had been homeless for a longer period, those who had previously resided in Massachusetts, and those with a person to contact in an emergency were also more likely to report alcohol problems.

Services needed also varied across different groups of shelter users (Table

Table 5.3
Health Problems by Social Characteristics of Guests

Characteristics	None %	Alcoholism %	Psychological[b] %	Physical Only %	Alcoholism & Psychological %
			Health Problems[a]		
AGE:					
17-29 (N=187)	41	22	20	7	10
30-49 (N=210)	31	34	14	6	16
50-80 (N=90)	22	43	13	11	12
SEX:					
Male (N=400)	31	34	16	6	14
Female (N=101)	45	20	17	12	6
RACE:					
White (N=27)	27	47	11	2	13
Minority (N=17)	24	17	15	13	30
LAST RESIDENT:					
Mass. (N=267)	29	38	13	5	16
Other NE (N=30)	36	22	14	10	18
Other (N=41)	55	20	13	7	4
MARITAL STATUS:					
Married (N=38)	49	25	2	9	14
Single (N=211)	34	28	17	8	12
Divorced (N=84)	16	49	13	3	20
Widowed (N=16)	28	40	10	4	18
Separated (N=22)	28	55	2	0	15
CHILDREN:					
Yes (N=134)	26	38	13	5	17
No (N=142)	32	35	13	8	12
CONTACT PERSON:					
Yes (N=378)	30	33	18	7	12
No (N=123)	45	23	11	8	13
VETERAN[c]:					
Yes (N=143)	27	34	14	10	15
No (N=240)	31	34	18	3	14
EDUCATION:					
1-8 yrs. (N=64)	33	32	13	9	13
9-11 yrs. (N=98)	25	37	16	6	16
12 yrs. (N=128)	34	31	14	4	17
13 yrs up (N=9)	29	37	13	12	9

a: Percentages may not add up to 100 due to rounding.

b: Includes combined psychiatric and physical health problems.

c: Percent of males only.

Table 5.4
Services Needed by Guest Characteristics

Characteristics	Services Needed[a]				
	Housing %	Job %	Food %	Health Care %	None %
SEX:					
Male (N=368)	80	38	42	31	3
Female (N=87)	86	29	43	24	4
RACE:					
White (N=24)	35	25	5	47	21
Minority(N=16)	56	26	12	40	7
AGE:					
17-29 (N=174)	84	37	47	24	4
30-49 (N=187)	78	42	41	30	2
50-80 (N=84)	84	26	36	34	3
VETERAN STATUS:					
Yes (N=128)[b]	84	39	44	32	3
No (N=228)	78	38	42	31	3
MARITAL STATUS:					
Married (N=36)	86	29	53	24	1
Single (N=195)	84	32	54	28	4
Divorced (N=79)	79	26	49	41	3
Widowed (N=15)	94	20	44	22	9
Separated (N=19)	76	34	31	33	2
CHILDREN:					
Yes (N=120)	85	21	49	32	1
No (N=131)	80	30	46	37	4
CONTACT PERSON INDICATED:					
Yes (N=352)	83	36	46	30	3
No (N=103)	78	37	29	25	3

a: Multiple responses permitted.

b: Males only.

5.4). Self-reported needs for housing were greatest among members of minority ethnic groups and those without alcohol- or drug-related problems. Needs for a job were reported most frequently by men, by those under 50, by those not receiving any financial benefits, and by those without an alcohol- or drug-related problem. A need for health care was reported most often by men, whites, those divorced, and those *with* alcohol- or drug-related problems. The new clients who reported a need for food were more likely to be members of minority groups, younger, more educated, and from out of state.

CONCLUSIONS

Although collected at one large shelter in Boston, the data reported here yielded a profile of Massachusetts's homeless that is similar to that obtained in other studies in Boston and elsewhere in Massachusetts. Due to the broad coverage of the Long Island Shelter's intake data, the profile has been more comprehensive than most; identification of factors associated with health problems of the homeless has also been possible.

Those individuals who remain homeless for an extended period are more prone to health problems and thus less likely to be able to reestablish a settled existence in the future. Few receive any financial benefits, and many have problems with mental and/or physical health, including alcoholism, The likelihood of continued homelessness, or at least of major and continuing dysfunction, is substantial. Given the young age of many homeless persons, prolonged homelessness connotes a major loss of human resources—the resources required for the interagency efforts to prevent homelessness in Massachusetts are likely to be well spent.

A mix of services is needed for the homeless. Between one quarter and one half have psychiatric problems at the time of their becoming homeless. Psychiatric problems tend to increase with length of homelessness, and those with psychiatric problems were more frequent shelter users. The systematic provision of mental health services in the shelter itself may thus be a viable interim solution to the problems posed by the lack of adequate community and institutional care facilities. Such services might have an important impact on the numbers of shelter users (American Psychiatric Association, 1984; Lamb, 1984b). A similar conclusion seems warranted in the case of physical health care. The homeless in Boston manifested a high level of physical health problems, and the physically ill tended to use the shelter more frequently.

The clinic arrangement that seems appropriate for the mentally or physically ill is not as likely to be effective with alcoholics. Drinking was associated with many health problems. However, alcoholics were more mobile, less likely to rely on the shelter, had been homeless longer, and were less interested in a job and housing. For this group, referrals to traditional alcohol treatment programs may still be the most appropriate strategy—although the high level of prior experience with alcohol treatment programs among the homeless indicates that such treatment must be supplemented with other forms of intervention.

Years of urban renewal, a high-tech economy, declining federal supports for welfare, and deinstitutionalization are each reflected in the composition of the homeless population in Massachusetts. These diverse influences complicate the contemporary problem of homelessness; the Massachusetts approach of developing support services and more permanent housing in addition to emergency services represents the type of multipronged response that is needed.

ACKNOWLEDGMENTS

We are grateful to Kevin P. Mulvey, Richard Lunden, and Alicia Johnston for research assistance, and to Richard Weintraub, William Dillon, Debbie Chausse, and Tom Scott for their support of this project. This research was funded in part by a grant from the National Institutes of Health through the BioMedical Research Support Grant Program, University of Massachusetts at Boston.

REFERENCES

American Psychiatric Association. 1984. Recommendations of APA's Task Force on the Homeless Mentally Ill. *Hospital and Community Psychiatry* 35 (September): 908–909.

Arce, A. A., M. Tadlock, M. J. Vergare, and S. H. Shapiro. 1983. A Psychiatric Profile of Street People Admitted to an Emergency Shelter. *Hospital and Community Psychiatry* 34 (September): 812–817.

Bachrach, Leona L. 1984a. Interpreting Research on the Homeless Mentally Ill: Some Caveats. *Hospital and Community Psychiatry* 35 (September): 914–916.

———. 1984b. Research on Services for the Homeless Mentally Ill. *Hospital and Community Psychiatry* 35 (September): 910–913.

Bahr, Howard M., and Gerald R. Garrett. 1976. *Women Alone*. Lexington, Mass.: Lexington Books.

———. 1971. *Disaffiliation among Urban Women*. New York: Columbia University, Bureau of Applied Social Research.

Bassuk, Ellen L., Lenore Rubin, and Alison Lauriat. 1984. Is Homelessness a Mental Health Problem? *American Journal of Psychiatry* 141 (December): 1546–1550.

Blumberg, Leonard, et al. 1960. *The Men on Skid Row*. Philadelphia: Department of Psychiatry, Temple University School of Medicine.

Bogue, Donald J. 1963. *Skid Row in American Cities*. Chicago: Community and Family Studies Center.

Brickner, Philip W., Linda K. Scharer, Barbara Conanan, Alexander Elvy, Marianne Savarese, eds. 1985. *Health Care of Homeless People*. New York: Springer.

Carmody, Deirdre. 1984. City to Spend $100 Million on Homeless. *New York Times*, October 10.

City of Boston. 1986. *Making Room: Comprehensive Policy for the Homeless*. Boston: Office of the Mayor.

Crystal, Stephen. 1982. *Chronic and Situational Dependency: Long-term Residents in a Shelter for Men*. New York: Human Resources Administration.

Emergency Shelter Commission and the United Community Planning Corporation. 1986. *Boston's Homeless: Taking the Next Step*. Boston: Emergency Shelter Commission, City of Boston, and United Community Planning Corporation.

EOHS (Executive Office of Human Services). 1985. *Massachusetts Report on Homelessness*. Boston: EOHS, Commonwealth of Massachusetts.

———. 1987. *Homeless Families in Massachusetts: Progress and Action*. Boston: EOHS, Commonwealth of Massachusetts.

Jones, R. E. 1983. Street People and Psychiatry: An Introduction. *Hospital and Community Psychiatry* 34 (September): 807–811.

Lamb, H. Richard. 1984a. Deinstitutionalization and the Homeless Mentally Ill. *Hospital and Community Psychiatry* 35 (September): 899–924.

———. 1984b. *The Homeless Mentally Ill*. Washington, D.C.: American Psychiatric Association.

Lipton, F. R., A. Sabatini, and S. E. Katz. 1983. Down and Out in the City: The Homeless Mentally Ill. *Hospital and Community Psychiatry* 34 (September): 817–821.

Massachusetts Association for Mental Health. 1985. *Homelessness: An Integrated Approach*. Boston: MAMH.

Mulkern, Virginia, and Rebecca Spence. 1984. Preliminary Data from the Department of Mental Health's Study on Homelessness. Memo, October 12.

Ropers, R., and Marjorie Robertson. 1984. *The Inner-City Homeless of Los Angeles: An Empirical Assessment*. Los Angeles: Los Angeles Basic Shelter Project.

Schutt, Russell K. 1985. Boston's Homeless: Their Backgrounds, Problems and Needs. Unpublished manuscript.

Schutt, Russell K., and Gerald R. Garrett. 1987. The Homeless Alcoholic: Past and Present. In *Homelessness: The National Perspective*, edited by M. Robertson and M. Greenblatt. New York: Plenum.

Stoller, Eleanor Palo. 1984. Self-Assessments of Health by the Elderly: The Impact of Informal Assistance. *Journal of Health and Social Behavior* 25 (September): 260–270.

United Community Planning Corporation. 1986. *Boston's Homeless: Taking the Next Step*. Boston: Emergency Shelter Commission and The United Community Planning Corporation.

U.S. Bureau of the Census. 1983. *1980 Census of Population*. Vol. 1, Ch. C, Part 25: General Social and Economic Characteristics, Massachusetts. Washington, D.C.: Government Printing Office.

U.S. Department of Housing and Urban Development. 1984. *A Report to the Secretary on Homelessness and Emergency Shelters*. Washington, D.C.: U.S. Department of Housing and Urban Development.

Wiseman, Jacqueline. 1970. *Stations of the Lost*. Englewood Cliffs, N.J.: Prentice-Hall.

Wynne, J. 1984. *Homeless Women in San Diego*. San Diego: County of San Diego, Department of Health Services, Alcohol Program.

6

Homelessness in Missouri: Populations, Problems, and Policy

Julia S. Kunz

Drawing on existing studies, this chapter attempts to describe the current state of knowledge of homelessness in Missouri, including numbers and types of homeless populations, factors contributing to underlying problems, and policy initiatives emanating from studies and advocacy groups. Missouri's experience probably parallels that of other areas with two possible exceptions. Data, especially from the St. Louis area, show much higher averages of family members among the homeless than do national statistics. Not yet systematically studied, Missouri may have more homeless in rural areas related to the farm crisis and loss of small businesses than the more urbanized states.

The chapter maintains that homelessness in Missouri is a growing condition and will continue to be so unless major federal and state policy interventions are undertaken. The declining supply of low-cost housing and a changing economy with more unemployment and lower-paying jobs coupled with inadequate public initiatives for the poor are the basic factors underlying homelessness in the studies reviewed. This structural interpretation provides a theoretical backdrop for the chapter. The author suggests that a third factor, less tangible and measureable, also contributes to homelessness—a declining sense of public/personal well-being.

The approach taken is a review and synthesis of existing studies, which are primarily descriptive, quantitative, and policy-oriented in nature. The chapter is divided into three sections, which cover populations, problems, and policy, and begins with a discussion of homelessness as a social process.

CONTRASTING HOMELESS POPULATIONS: VISIBLE–HIDDEN, RURAL–URBAN, AND FAMILIES–INDIVIDUALS

Homelessness as a Process

The theoretical formulation that underlies this chapter is that homelessness is a social process imbedded in the housing market, the changing economy, and public welfare policy. While there is much variety in the separate populations that make up the composite group called homeless, they are all enmeshed in the process of homelessness. That process includes a decreasing supply of low-cost housing resulting from a variety of factors, including a retreating federal commitment to low-income housing and unprofitable market factors. Because housing is treated as a commodity in the United States, units can be offered at low cost only with substantial subsidies in financing and rents. With fewer federal subsidies and rising housing costs, existing low-cost units have been lost through redevelopment to higher uses and disinvestment (the inability or failure to maintain units in good condition) often leading to condemnation and abandonment.

The dynamics of the housing market are linked with larger changes in the economy that have resulted in increased poverty, higher rates and longer periods of unemployment, declining average wages, and a small but significant shift in wealth from lower- to upper-income groups. Higher-paying industrial jobs have been traded for lower-paying service positions with an overall loss in jobs for the unskilled. Add to this the insufficiency of public assistance benefits and training and educational opportunities for the poor, and a picture of growing numbers of lower-income people competing for a decreasing supply of low-cost housing emerges (Figure 6.1). The result is a steady stream of homelessness when the failure to pay rent or utilities ends in eviction or utility cutoffs, or when overcrowding and unsafe living conditions lead to interpersonal friction or condemnation.

Visible-Hidden Populations

Concepts of visible and hidden homelessness help illustrate the process of homelessness. The visible homeless on the streets and in shelters represent only a small portion of the potentially homeless. Recent Missouri studies suggest that the visible homeless (those requesting shelter or staying in shelters, or living on the street in urban areas, and those living in parks and along roads in parked cars in rural areas) approach 40,000 persons statewide.[1] The hidden homeless, defined as those doubled up with family or friends or living in unsafe housing, may number up to seven times that number based on several indicators. According to the 1980 census, there were 109,694 rental units in Missouri showing indications of substandard housing (such as overcrowding and/or incomplete plumbing and/or lacking a central heating system)—about 20 percent of the total rental housing supply. While units indicating signs of poor housing are not all low-

Figure 6.1
Homelessness in the Making

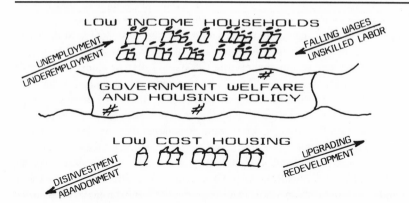

Converging factors in the U.S. economy create and maintain a large pool of low-income households while market factors siphon off the supply of low-cost housing. Government welfare and housing policy in the 1980s has not attenuated the former and has exacerbated the latter.

rent units, many, if not most, are likely to be. These approximately 110,000 units would house about 285,000 people based on the average Missouri household size of 2.6 persons (Missouri Association for Social Welfare, 1987a: 2).

Other indirect indicators of hidden homelessness include numbers on waiting lists for public and Section 8 housing, and the shared living arrangements of those requesting shelter. Requests for emergency shelter received by the St. Louis Relocation Clearinghouse showed that most requests came from households doubled up with family or friends—60 percent in 1983 and 68 percent in 1984 (Missouri Association for Social Welfare, 1985: 33).

The hidden homeless are apparently not being counted in census studies, including the Annual Housing Survey conducted in Kansas City and St. Louis, which shows patterns of decreasing overcrowding and substandard conditions over the past decade. New approaches are needed to describe and measure this phenomenon.

There is every indication that homelessness will continue to increase in the foreseeable future as the supply of low-cost housing is further eroded without replacement, and wages and income do not keep pace with rising housing costs. The visible homeless in shelters and on the street may be helped through social services and transitional housing programs, and some will find permanent housing. But the larger process of homelessness in the making means that a steady stream of newly homeless households will continue to converge on limited emergency services unless there is major intervention in the housing market, the economy, and public welfare and housing policy.

Rural and Urban Populations

Homelessness is typically regarded as an urban phenomenon, and indeed, Missouri's two major cities, Kansas City and St. Louis, situated on the state's east and west borders, have the largest number of homeless people in the state.

Annual shelter users in the St. Louis area were reported as at least 10,000 unduplicated persons within shelters for 1983 and 1984 (Missouri Association for Social Welfare, 1985: 32). This figure encompassed shelters for domestic violence, but not transitional living arrangements. It did not address across-shelter duplication or the sizable but undetermined number of people turned away for lack of space. The total St. Louis homeless population has been estimated at 15,000 persons by one observer (*St. Louis Post-Dispatch*, October 6, 1986).

Requests for shelter in the St. Louis area seem to have increased since the early 1980s. The St. Louis Relocation Clearinghouse reported 1,485 requests in 1983 and 1,877 requests in 1984. Data from the St. Louis Homeless Reception Center for a 12-month period in 1986–1987 show 2,574 requests for assistance. The data sets are not strictly comparable, as the clearinghouse gathered separate information on 1,561 additional households requesting permanent housing in 1983 and 1,891 in 1984. While the Homeless Reception Center does not distinguish between requests for emergency shelter and requests for permanent housing in its data collection, the name and organizational affiliation would suggest that most callers would be interested in emergency shelter. These 2,574 households contained 6,541 persons, 59 percent of them children.

The research committee of the St. Louis Homeless Services Network hopes to conduct a census of area emergency shelters several times over the next year to determine the size of the shelter population based on a reverse sampling methodology used to estimate hidden populations (Darcy and Jones, 1975).

The homeless population in Kansas City is estimated to be between 7,000 and 12,000 persons in official counts. The Hotline for the Homeless, representing Kansas City's ten major shelters, registered requests from 7,634 unduplicated persons in 1986 (Liebling, 1987). The figure stands in contrast to a Kansas City Health Department study that reported that a total of 5,548 unduplicated persons were provided shelter during 1985, reflecting an 11 percent decline from the number served in 1984 (Gist and Welch, 1986: i). Of course, many of the 1986 requests for shelter went unmet, mostly among families where the average demand for space was 38 per week with an average availability of 15 spaces (Liebling, 1987).

These St. Louis and Kansas City figures suggest a significant increase in the homeless population since the 1982 report of the Missouri governor's office to the National Governors' Conference Task Force on the Homeless. At that time, Missouri's homeless population was estimated at 15,830 based on data provided from St. Louis and five smaller cities on the number of people served in shelters. Data from Kansas City were notably missing. The 1982 figures represented a doubling since 1980 according to service providers (Missouri Association for

Social Welfare, 1985: 8). As indicated above, estimates of the visible statewide homeless population today approach 40,000 persons, indicating some slowing of growth in the past few years.

There has been no systematic effort to count the homeless in Missouri's rural areas aside from studies from smaller cities, such as Columbia and Springfield, which report the size of their homeless populations as about 6,000 and under 1,000 respectively (Lincoln, 1986: 1; Lovell, 1987: 9), and a few county figures. About 1,500 people were reported homeless on any given day in St. Charles County, and 200 homeless persons were reported in Dunklin County in Missouri's boot heel (*St. Louis Post-Dispatch*, April 27, 1987; *Daily Dunklin Democrat*, May 5, 1987). Evidence of visible homelessness in rural areas comes from reports of people living in cars along county roads or staying in public campgrounds beyond the normal season (Missouri Association for Social Welfare, 1987a: 19).

Two statewide reports have called attention to the problem of rural homelessness (Missouri Association for Social Welfare, 1985; Goward, 1986). In farming areas, the foreclosure of banks, farming-related businesses, and family farms has left households jobless, homeless, and in some cases, suicidal. Debts owed by Missouri farmers increased from $4.8 billion in 1979 to $7.1 billion in 1983 (Goward, 1986: 19). There were about 2,000 liquidations and bankruptcies statewide in the first quarter of 1985, a 79 percent increase over the previous year. Nine banks were closed across the state in 1985 (Goward 1986: 20).

Five categories of the rural homeless were described in the first report: (1) the traditional homeless, (2) the new poor, (3) the mentally ill, (4) the displaced farmers and farm-related workers, and (5) the new hermits (Streeter and Frank, 1985: 49). Shelters in Jefferson City and Columbia estimate that between 20 percent and 30 percent of their guests can be classified as traditional homeless or street people who survive by panhandling, collecting aluminum cans, and scouring through garbage containers for food (Streeter and Frank, 1985: 49).

The new poor, victims of the changing economy and hard times, are seen in the "travelers" in search of jobs and a new start. One shelter in Columbia, located on Interstate 70 midway between St. Louis and Kansas City, estimates that 20 percent of its guests are travelers. Some come from rural areas, and some are enroute to distant places to build new lives (De Simone, 1985: 22).

There are no estimates of the number of mentally ill homeless in rural areas, but one Columbia shelter, located only 30 miles from Fulton State Hospital, estimates that 35 percent of its guests have been discharged from mental hospitals and about half of those appear to need treatment (De Simone, 1985: 20).

Few displaced farmers appear to end up in shelters, although Springfield and Kansas City shelters reported serving farm families (Goward, 1986: 20). Perhaps they find help from family or friends or secure permanent housing in town. One observer noted the movement of adult children and their families back to the original homestead with their parents when they lost their own real estate on failing farms. One Missouri farm family made the rounds of shelters from

St.Louis through Iowa to Minneapolis–St. Paul before receiving assistance to start anew (Missouri Association for Social Welfare, 1987a: 18–19).

Little is known about the new hermits, often thought to be Vietnam veterans and back-to-the-landers, but they can be found in the southern Ozarks of Missouri.

The interactions between rural and urban homelessness are increasingly appreciated by service providers. With few services in rural areas, the homeless tend to gravitate to urban areas. However, most of the homeless in Kansas City and St. Louis are residents of the respective areas, with transients comprising from 10 percent to 35 percent of the shelter populations (Morse et al., 1985: 48; Gist and Welch, 1986: i). About 10 percent of the requests for emergency assistance through the Homeless Reception Center in St. Louis came from outside the city-county area in 1986–1987. Only 2 percent (52 cases) of these were from ZIP Codes in outlying Missouri (St. Louis Homeless Reception Center, 1986–1987). Urban service providers are overwhelmed by the homeless already present in their areas and have little to offer to the rural migrants. On the positive side, the farm crisis has evoked a number of rural helping organizations that provide help to people in their own communities.

Family Members versus Individuals

The U.S. Department of Housing and Urban Development (1984: 22–30) study of homeless people in emergency shelters and on the street, like other national studies, reported that most of the homeless (65 percent to 66 percent) were single men. Only 13 percent to 14 percent were single women, and family members were reported to comprise 21 percent. The U.S. Conference of Mayors more recently reported that the homeless population is composed of 56 percent single men, 15 percent single women, and 28 percent families with children (*Safety Network*, June 1987).

Striking differences were reported in a 1984 study of homeless people in St. Louis (Kunz and Murray, 1984) and confirmed by recent data from the St. Louis Homeless Reception Center (1987). In 1983 about 60 percent of the households and about 83 percent of the total persons were family members. In 1986–1987, about 68 percent of the households and about 87 percent of the total persons requesting emergency assistance were family members. Most of these family members—well over half of the requests in 1983 and approaching two-thirds in 1986–1987—are single women with children. The following figures show the family composition of households requesting emergency shelter assistance in St. Louis in 1983 and 1986–1987. The 1983 data are annual percentages from the St. Louis Relocation Clearinghouse, while the 1986–1987 data are percentages from the St. Louis Homeless Reception Center, May 1986 through April 1987.

Family Composition	1983	1986–1987
Women with children	54	63
Single women	22	21
Single men	13	9
Couples with children	6	3
Couples without children	4	1
Men with children	1	1
Extended family	NA	1
Other/unknown	NA	1

As the above figures indicate, both in 1983 and 1986–1987, women with children constituted the majority of households requesting emergency shelter assistance.

It is important to qualify the percentages of types of households requesting shelter with experience-based estimates of actual shelter use. While single males represent only 9 percent to 13 percent of the requests, they probably account for at least one third of the unduplicated shelter population. Many single men go directly to the relevant shelters without calling for assistance; some others live on the street. The remaining two thirds of the sheltered homeless would be comprised of women and children, two-parent families, and single women. This would reduce the percentage of family members to about one half of the sheltered homeless—but still more than twice the proportion accounted for in the U.S. Department of Housing and Urban Development (HUD) (1984) national sample.

There is no readily apparent explanation as to why the predominance of family members in St. Louis differs so greatly from national studies (St. Louis was not included in HUD's 1984 study). One methodological reason is that the HUD (1984) study did not include homeless people sheltered temporarily in motels and apartments, most of whom consist of families. A few observers noted the large number of welfare clients in St. Louis and the inadequacy of benefit levels as well as strict guidelines. The city has very high poverty rates—63 percent among black children (Missouri: Association for Social Welfare, 1986: 111). Other substantive reasons could be related to both housing redevelopment and disinvestment causing displacement, and discrimination in rentals against families with children. Workers trying to place homeless families in permanent housing have documented widespread discrimination against families, which exacerbates the shortfall of affordable units. It is also possible that St. Louis has a better data-collection system in place and is reporting a more accurate picture of the homeless than some other areas.

Data gathered from the Kansas City area also suggest a larger proportion of the homeless made up of family members than the HUD (1984) national sample. In 1986, 50 percent of the calls on the Hotline for the Homeless were from families or couples. Children comprised 35 percent of the total persons (Liebling, 1987). An earlier report stated that about 35 percent of the homeless actually sheltered in Kansas City emergency shelters were women and children (Whitney, 1986: 1).

Homelessness and Poverty, Race, Sex, and Housing

Studies from the St. Louis area, which have included more demographic data on homeless households than studies elsewhere in the state, show that poverty, race, sex, and a history of shared housing are important correlates of visible homelessness (Kunz and Murray, 1984; Morse et al., 1985; St. Louis Homeless Reception Center, 1986–1987). Between two thirds and three fourths or more of the homeless people in St. Louis are racial minorities, virtually all black; the smaller percentage (two thirds) reflects a 1984 in-shelter survey and the larger, current requests for shelter assistance. About 85 percent of household heads requesting shelter at present are female, a 9 percent increase over the 76 percent in 1983. Most of the homeless are very poor; about 88 percent reported no employment in both 1983 and 1986–1987. Average annual income of those requesting shelter in 1983 was $2,400. Two fifths reported no income in 1983; 29 percent reported no income in 1986–1987. In 1983, 37 percent of the households were receiving Aid to Families with Dependent Children (AFDC) benefits; in 1986–1987, 42 percent were receiving AFDC.

A history of shared housing is another correlate of homelessness. Of the households requesting shelter in St. Louis in 1984, two thirds (68 percent) were living with friends or relatives. This was an increase from 60 percent of such households in 1983. Data analyzed in that year showed that the average length of residence for the 43 percent of households living temporarily with others was less than six months. For the 17 percent of households living permanently with others, the average length of residence was five years. Much of this doubling up can probably be attributed to the lack of low-cost housing. Of households requesting shelter in 1983 and living on their own, 37 percent were living in market-rate rental units; less than 1 percent were in Section 8 or public housing; only 3 percent were in owner-occupied units. The 1984 increase in households doubled up resulted from a comparable loss of households in market-rate rental housing, which dropped from 37 percent to 29 percent (Kunz and Murray, 1984: 7; Missouri Association for Social Welfare, 1985: 33).

Precipitating Crises Suggest Underlying Problems

Of the precipitating events that moved households into homelessness in 1983 and 1984, interpersonal crises, primarily friction with family or friends, were reported most often—by about one half of households requesting emergency shelter in St. Louis (Kunz and Murray, 1984: 9). From stories shared by the homeless, many such crises seem a predictable result of economic or other setbacks that necessitate doubling up with others in overcrowded conditions. When tensions reach a breaking point, the guests are forced to leave.

Recent data from the St. Louis Homeless Reception Center, while not directly comparable because of changes in coding categories, show that 48 percent of the housing emergency reasons reveal interpersonal problems as the precipitating factor. The majority are related to an inability to continue living in a family situation.

The second largest area of crisis events in both 1984 and 1986–1987 was environmental, including such things as poor housing, utility problems, eviction, condemnation, and fire. Of households requesting assistance, about 24 percent in 1984 and about 23 percent in 1986–1987 reported such crises. Most of these crises are directly related to the shortfall of low-cost housing.

Relocation crises were reported by about 13 percent of households in 1983 and about 12 percent in 1986–1987. Other reported crises were far less pervasive, including overcrowding, loss of income, and problems related to mental health or health treatment. Others reached the time limit for staying in their present shelter.

In comparing the crises reported by households in 1983 with their family composition and type of housing, the findings showed that certain kinds of households in certain living situations had certain crises. Single women and men or women with children in a living situation with others were most likely to report interpersonal crises. Women with children living in market-rate rental units were most likely to report environmental crises. Couples living temporarily with others were most likely to report relocation crises. Couples with or without children and single men in market-rate rental units were most likely to report economic crises. Women with children or couples with children living temporarily with others were most likely to report overcrowding (Kunz and Murray, 1984: 12–13). These relationships suggest that social factors rather than the personal attributes of homeless people are at the base of crises precipitating homelessness.

These linkages help define the shape of homelessness: doubling up leading to interpersonal friction, poor single mothers struggling to survive in unsafe housing, couples moving from place to place for a fresh start, breadwinners losing jobs and then apartments, and children growing up without a sense of permanence. In these findings, homelessness is *not* primarily defined by mental illness, substance abuse, or even personal inadequacy. There are larger economic and public issues at work.

UNDERLYING PROBLEMS: LOSS OF HOUSING, POVERTY, AND A DECLINING SENSE OF WELL-BEING

As the correlates of homelessness from St. Louis's studies of homeless households were low income, minority race, female sex, and a history of shared housing, the *structural* correlates of homelessness seem to be inadequate low-cost housing; poverty due to unemployment, low wages, and insufficient welfare benefits; and a declining sense of public and personal well-being. Based on this hypothesis, one would expect to find a relationship between the number of homeless and such measures as the vacancy rate for low-rent units, level of poverty, welfare payment levels, wage levels, unemployment rate, and percent of budget spent for social and mental health services.

Shortfall of Low-Cost Housing

Homelessness in Missouri results primarily from a diminishing supply of low-cost housing. According to one national study, about 500,000 low-rent units are lost annually through the combined effects of conversion, arson, abandonment, inflation, and demolition (Hopper and Hamberg, 1986: 22). A Kansas City response to a national homelessness questionnaire indicated the following priority ranking of causes of the affordable housing shortage: (1) rent increases, (2) lack of replacement of lost affordable housing, (3) curtailment of government housing subsidy programs, (4) gentrification, (5) landlord abandonment, (6) deterioration, (7) massive urban business redevelopment, (8) conversions, and (9) fire (Pape, n.d.).

Based on the 1980 census, the shortfall of affordable housing for low-income (0 to 50 percent of the median) renter households in Missouri was nearly 75,000 units, assuming that households paid no more than one fourth of their income for gross rent. Gross rent includes utilities (electricity, gas, and water) and fuels. If the rent level is raised to one third of income, the shortfall drops considerably to under 23,000 units.[2] Figure 6.2 shows the shortfall of affordable rental units for low-income Missouri households in 1980 (U.S. Bureau of the Census, 1983a: 39; 1983b: 200; 1983c: 313). The figures are based on a comparison of the number of available rental units with rents up to one fourth or one third of 50 percent of the median renter household income for the jurisdiction with the total number of renter households with incomes at that level (Missouri Association for Social Welfare, 1987a: 11).

About three fourths of the shortfall occurs in urban areas of the state (2,500 or more inhabitants) and about one fourth in rural areas. About one half of the shortfall occurs in the St. Louis Standard Metropolitan Statistical Area (SMSA) and about one fourth in the Kansas City SMSA (not adjusting for out-of-state boundaries and higher median incomes in those areas).

These figures suggest that many low-income Missourians are paying large percentages of their income for rent. According to the census, median gross monthly rent as a percentage of income was 24.2 percent for all Missouri households in 1980. Renter households with incomes under $5,000 paid 50 percent or more of their income for gross rent, however. Rental housing units comprise about 85 percent of available low-cost units in Missouri according to census figures (Missouri Association for Social Welfare, 1987a: 14).

The current shortfall of affordable housing for low-income households may be 50 to 100 percent greater than the 1980 figures based on the loss and deterioration of existing units, rising housing costs in relation to income, and increasing poverty and homelessness in Missouri since 1980 (Missouri Association for Social Welfare, 1987a: 1).

Figure 6.2
Shortfall of Affordable Rental Units for Low-Income[a] Missouri Households in 1980

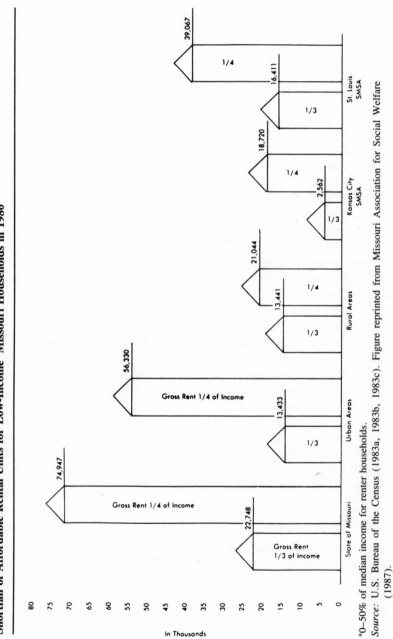

[a]0–50% of median income for renter households.

Source: U.S. Bureau of the Census (1983a, 1983b, 1983c). Figure reprinted from Missouri Association for Social Welfare (1987).

There are no reliable figures on the loss of units, but knowledgeable observers report that there have been significant losses because of redevelopment, disinvestment, and abandonment. As reported above, an estimated 20 percent of existing rental units in 1980 evidenced one or more measures of poor housing.

Data from the Annual Housing Survey for the city of St. Louis for 1980 and 1983 suggest a worsening of housing quality during this period. There was a 30 percent increase in the incidence of selected structural deficiencies, from 56,600 to 73,500.[3] It is not possible to determine from the 1983 presentation how much of the increase is due to worsening conditions in the same units or an increased number of units with deficiencies (Missouri Association for Social Welfare, 1987a: 14).

The loss of units from displacement, especially gentrification, is a continuing problem in Kansas City and St. Louis. St. Louis, having lost a significant share of middle-income households during the 1970s, has undergone revitalization programs in some neighborhoods, which have displaced low-income households. The loss of boarding homes (single-room occupancy units) is also an increasing problem in recent years.

The increase in median rents in recent years has been about twice the increase in median incomes, according to the Annual Housing Survey conducted in Kansas City and St. Louis. Between 1980 and 1983, median income for renter households in the St. Louis metropolitan area rose by 15.6 percent while gross median rent rose by 30.6 percent. Between 1978 and 1982, median income for renter households in the Kansas City metropolitan area rose by 22.9 percent while gross median rent rose by 46.0 percent (Missouri Association for Social Welfare, 1987a: 15).

Another indirect measure of the shortfall of low-income housing is the number of households on waiting lists for public housing. There were 17,000 households in the city of St. Louis on waiting lists when the lists were closed in mid–1986. Households waiting since 1980 are just now getting in. The vacancy rate for public housing in Kansas City has shrunk to less than 1 percent from 26 percent in 1977. An administrator of an existing Section 8 program in central Missouri reported a drop in turnover rate from 30 percent to 5 percent in the past year (Missouri Association for Social Welfare, 1987a: 2).

Insufficient Income

Growing numbers of Missourians in poverty during the early 1980s increased the competition for scarce low-cost units. Missouri suffered more than the nation as a whole in the 1982 recession, resulting in a poverty rate of 16.8 percent in 1983 and 1984.[4] The comparable national rates were 15.3 percent and 14.4 percent. The 1983 Missouri rate reflects an increase of 38 percent over the 12.2 percent rate in the 1980 census (Missouri Association for Social Welfare, 1987b: 41).

Along with the nation, Missouri experienced structural changes in its economy, losing 21,000 manufacturing jobs between 1980 and 1985, with the increase of most new jobs since 1982 in the service sector (Missouri Association for Social Welfare, 1986: 16). According to national figures, about one half of the new jobs generated between 1978 and 1984 paid near poverty level wages (Ehrenreich, 1986: 19). A recent congressional study reported that high unemployment and falling wages—and not the rise of single-parent households—were most responsible for increased poverty during the 1980s (*St. Louis Post-Dispatch*, December 22, 1986).

Missouri's unemployment rates account for some of the increase in poverty, rising from a low 4.5 percent in 1979 to a high 9.9 percent in 1983 and leveling off to 6.1 percent in 1986. From 1982 to 1983, poverty rose much faster than unemployment and stayed at a high level while unemployment dropped (Missouri Association for Social Welfare, 1986: 15). Falling wages probably explain much of the difference. The minimum wage, which pays only 63 percent of the poverty line for a family of four, would need to be raised to $4.35 an hour just to regain its 1981 purchasing power. It is also important to note that unemployment figures are based on a sample of households and fail to count the homeless. They do not include discouraged workers, and part-time workers are counted as employed, even if underemployed.

The inadequacy of Missouri's welfare system perpetuates the poverty of the unemployed. About 4 percent of Missouri's population receives AFDC—an average of 66,000 cases per month in 1986. Missouri's AFDC benefits are among the lowest in the nation. The average three-person household receives $282 monthly, thirty-seventh in grant levels of the 50 states and only 37 percent of the federal poverty level. The addition of food stamps would bring total purchasing power to only 57 percent of the poverty line, and about one third of Missouri AFDC households are not receiving this extra benefit. A primary reason has to do with the large number of families doubled up with relatives whose assets and income become part of the qualifying criteria (Missouri Association for Social Welfare, 1987b: 14, 22).

The decreasing value of benefits also contributes to poverty. AFDC benefits increased by nearly 12 percent in the past six years while the cost of living has increased by more than 30 percent, resulting in an 18 percent loss in purchasing power (Missouri Association for Social Welfare, 1987b: 14). Declining value plus an outdated standard of need that has not been adjusted since 1975 produces a sub-survival existence for recipients. Homelessness is the natural consequence of paying for food, clothing, or other necessities in lieu of rent or utilities.

The AFDC-UP (Unemployed Parents) program for two-parent families operates in Missouri, but comprises only about 6 percent of the total AFDC caseload. Almost 9 out of 10 families in the program live in outstate Missouri (not Kansas City or St. Louis). While it has helped those in rural areas who have been affected by the farm crisis and the unemployed in the lead mining belt, the program has a work history requirement that thwarts its applicability to the long-term unemployed and never-employed new families in urban areas (Missouri Association for Social Welfare, 1987b: 4, 73).

There is no cash assistance available to healthy single persons in Missouri, no matter how destitute, although they may qualify for food stamps. For those medically certified as unable to work for at least 90 days, a general relief payment of $80 monthly is available, which could lead to substantially higher Supplementary Security Income (SSI) payments. General relief provides pocket money for some of the homeless mentally ill (Missouri Association for Social Welfare, 1987b: 24–25).

Declining Sense of Public and Personal Well-being

The third problem area can at best be suggestive. The common culture does not have a way to talk about or measure the domain of public well-being. When there are problems, we speak of the need for expanded mental health programs in the public arena, and in the religious sphere, we focus on spirituality. Both are individual-oriented approaches to personal well-being, which is defined here as the ability to cope with life (and death) in a sustaining, creative manner in the context of family and community.

Public well-being is more difficult to define and measure. Recent sociological works describe the loss of community traditions shaped by religion and early political history, such as *The Cultural Contradictions of Capitalism* by Daniel Bell, *The Culture of Narcissism* by Christopher Lasch, and *Habits of the Heart* by Robert Bellah et al. These works suggest that the dynamics of the larger society are unhealthy. The rising suicide rates among American teens and among farmers harken back to Emile Durkheim's classic study of suicide and may be indicators of a weakening social fabric.

Early estimates of the homeless population indicated that a sizable proportion were mentally ill. More current investigations in Missouri show relatively small numbers of the homeless with chronic mental illness. According to the Missouri Department of Mental Health study of a sample of residents in St. Louis emergency shelters in 1984, about one fifth of the homeless had chronic mental health needs and slightly more than one third had crisis or acute needs (Morse et al., 1985: ES3). In Kansas City, Swope Parkway's Homeless Health Program also reported that 20 percent of the homeless mentally ill have chronic forms of mental illness (Van Sant, 1987).

Using cluster analysis, the St. Louis study identified four distinctive subgroups among the homeless, based on problems and service needs. While a majority of the homeless (53 percent) fell into an "average needs" group, two other distinct groups with mental health needs and drinking problems emerged. These two groups comprised over one third (36 percent) of the total sample. A fourth, but small group, was labeled "socially advantaged" (Morse et al., 1985: 65–66).

Not surprisingly the St. Louis study found that many of the homeless apart from the designated subgroup showed mental health needs. Mental illness seems a likely result of the loss of self-esteem and dignity that comes from unemployment, being on welfare, or being totally dependent on others to meet one's needs in a society that places high value on riches and autonomy.

National demographic factors suggest a strong potential for growing numbers of mentally ill persons in the future. As the baby boom generation reaches maturity, the absolute number of adults at risk of developing schizophrenia and later other chronic disorders is high. The onset of schizophrenia normally occurs in young adulthood when pressures to take on work, family, and social responsibilities are greatest.

As described in the first part of this chapter, the most common precipitating crisis resulting in homelessness was interpersonal friction. While this seems closely related to overcrowded conditions of families doubled up or the tensions unleashed by having inadequate income for basic needs, the homeless seem to have more than their share of personal crises. The Missouri Department of Mental Health study reported that homeless people had experienced extremely high levels of life crises in the year before they first became homeless—3.3 times greater than the normal population and 1.9 times greater than the mean number of depressed psychiatric patients. Life crises such as the loss of loved ones or social and financial difficulties were measured on an accepted scale (Morse et al., 1985: 49). While the author holds to an explanation of homelessness in largely structural terms, this finding suggests the tentative hypothesis that from the large population of households living in poverty and competing for scarce housing, the presence of life crises is an important determinant in pushing households at risk into homelessness.

Studies of the homeless per se often show a loss or absence of family or social ties. According to a recent Chicago study, while almost 9 in 10 homeless people had surviving relatives and family members, only about three in five maintained even minimal contact with them. One in three homeless people reported no contact with any relatives or friends (Rossi et al., 1987: 1339). The St. Louis study reported that over one half of the homeless had never been married, and about one fifth were currently separated, with another 14 percent divorced (Morse et al., 1985: 47). Over two thirds of the callers requesting shelter assistance through the St. Louis Homeless Reception Center during the past year were unmarried; 14 percent were separated and 7 percent divorced. The loss of social networks is surely a factor in homelessness, but whether it is causative in the sense of changing social values or a derivative of the state of homelessness or both is unclear.

It is possible that the loss of family and community traditions in our fast-paced society provides a seedbed for mental illness. Robert Bellah's *Habits of the Heart* describes the rise of a therapeutic mentality, which defines individual values as the ultimate measure. While this has been a force for freedom from a restrictive past, it offers no corporate future. Some view the incidence of domestic violence, a cause of homelessness, as an indicator of changing family values. It is uncertain how much of this violence reflects formerly hidden behaviors and how much is triggered by the changing roles of men and women in our society. Perhaps it is evidence of a crisis in social values in the same sense that rising suicide rates among teens and farmers are. While such crises cut across income lines, the poor often have fewer resources for dealing with them and combatting their contribution to homelessness.

This is especially true in a low-tax state such as Missouri, which ranks forty-ninth in state and local tax revenues and forty-seventh in state and local expenditures. While the Reagan administration was making deep cuts in social programs in the early 1980s, Missouri was also cutting back on state expenditures—$293 million between Fiscal Years 1981 and 1984 (Missouri Association for Social Welfare, 1987b: 44). Social programs were being cut at a time of rising need, casting grave criticism on public policy, the third section of this chapter.

PUBLIC POLICY: FOCUSING ON PREVENTION AND PRESERVATION

All indications point to increasing homelessness in the future unless strong measures address the underlying problems. Many of the studies reviewed for this chapter have recommendations for public policy, indicating some direction, if not consensus, for state and federal governments. Policies that focus on prevention of homelessness and preservation of existing housing resources should have a strong hearing. Two statewide studies by the Missouri Association for Social Welfare, *Homelessness in Missouri* (1985) and *Low Income Housing in Missouri* (1987a), offer recommendations in these areas. A recent report by the Missouri Lieutenant Governor's Task Force on Homelessness also offers statewide recommendations (1987).

Housing Policy

A focus on retaining and upgrading existing housing stock makes sense from a number of perspectives: declining federal commitment to public housing in the 1980s, a public climate of tight dollars, and a large number of low-cost units at risk of both redevelopment to higher uses and disinvestment leading to condemnation and abandonment. In the wake of retreating federal dollars, a number of state and smaller jurisdictions have enacted housing trust funds as a means of rehabilitating and building low-cost units. A statewide housing trust fund bill introduced in the Missouri Senate during the past legislative session encountered opposition from real estate companies that proved fatal. The trust fund would have been financed by interest earned on escrow accounts from various real estate transactions (Missouri Association for Social Welfare, 1987a: 37).

A linkage proposal, based on the Missouri 353 redevelopment statute, which would require residential and commercial developers to provide or pay for a proportionate share of low-income housing through a housing trust fund, was under discussion in Kansas City last year, but failed to gain City Council approval. Some work has been done on a similar proposal in St. Louis (Missouri Association for Social Welfare, 1987a: 41–42).

In addition to funding major rehabilitation and new construction, housing trust funds can provide loans or grants for the repair and upgrading of existing units that are presently unavailable or unprofitable for landlords. Efforts to maintain existing inhabited units are an important part of a conservation strategy.

Emergency assistance programs that help low-income households meet overdue rent or utility bills that would otherwise cause them to become homeless are also a good investment in the maintenance of existing housing. Efforts to fund the AFDC Emergency Assistance Program in Missouri for one-time grants to families at risk of homelessness or in need of funds to procure housing have failed in the past several years. Twenty-six states do participate in the program.

Anti-displacement measures in redevelopment areas have come under discussion in St. Louis and Kansas City; the latter has an ordinance. The loss of boarding hotels has been of particular concern in St. Louis.

There seems to be a growing consensus that the federal role in housing must be restored and expanded (Missouri Association for Social Welfare, 1987a: 7). Even with substantial initiatives at state and local levels, housing needs of low-income people will not be met without federal funds for the maintenance of existing public housing and the creation of new units through rehabilitation and construction. The movement toward total reliance on a voucher system dependent on the existing housing supply will not satisfy most housing needs. Some households toward the upper end of the eligible income scale will be able to find attractive housing by paying a larger portion of their income for rent, supplementing the vouchers. For many, if not most, low-income households, however, already strapped budgets for other necessities will not permit such freedom, and their inability to find low-cost housing because of the tight supply will result in homelessness.

One of the significant and still available sources of federal funds for low-income housing is Community Development Block Grants (CDBG), with current House Bill H.R. 4 stipulating that at least 75 percent of the funds be directed toward low- and moderate-income households. The present law requires that only 51 percent of the funds be so directed. Diminished federal regulation of CDBG funds necessitates oversight by citizens concerned about low-cost housing.

The Missouri Housing Development Commission, a state agency that finances the development of housing for low- and moderate-income families through the sale of tax exempt bonds, began a demonstration moderate rehab program this year. It is available to developers, especially nonprofit agencies, who have units that can be rehabilitated for up to $10,000 each, using no-frills materials. Funds committed thus far would rehab only about 300 units of low-cost housing (Missouri Association for Social Welfare, 1987a: 22).

The commission is also administering the tax credits for low-income housing from the Tax Reform Act of 1986. Over $6 million in low-income housing tax credits was allocated for Missouri for 1987, but much of that will probably go unused because of the necessary start-up time and the inability to complete projects by year's end. The credit is 9 percent a year of the value of units in a project occupied by low-income tenants and not otherwise benefiting from federal subsidies (Missouri Association for Social Welfare, 1987a: 35).

Creative alternatives to traditional housing programs are beginning to thrive in Missouri, making a small, but worthy contribution to the problem. Home-sharing programs are functioning in St. Louis, Springfield, Joplin, and Kansas City. Sweat equity programs, such as Habitat for Humanity, are active mostly in Kansas City and St. Louis (Missouri Association for Social Welfare, 1987a: 46–48).

Another nontraditional approach called shadow housing offers potential aside from federal funds. The shadow market refers to the many ways of enlarging and improving the existing supply through restoration, transformation, and conversion. Nationally, the shadow market accounted for one third of the increase in low-cost units occupied by owners and one half of the increase in units occupied by renters between 1973 and 1980. About 85 percent of the low-cost rental housing supplied by the shadow market was unsubsidized (Missouri Association for Social Welfare, 1987a: 31). Dependent on changes in local building codes, zoning, and land use regulations, the shadow market could transform older, single-family housing into two-family homes or apartments and encourage the use of older and currently vacant or underused commercial and industrial space. An early proposal to transform old City Hospital in St. Louis into low-cost apartments is a good example of shadow housing.

Anti-poverty Measures

Housing policy must be coupled with efforts to increase incomes of poor households to permit them to afford housing and avoid homelessness. Current discussions on welfare reform are likely to yield new measures aimed at helping welfare clients move into the work world with the help of child care and health insurance. Expanded educational and training programs are needed for unskilled clients. The availability of viable employment is a key issue. A recent study by the Missouri Association for Social Welfare included many recommendations for reforming the system in Missouri (1987b: 7–11).

Discussions in the one hundredth Congress concerning welfare reform are focusing on a limited appropriation of $1 billion. There is little talk of job creation in this forum. But in other, smaller circles, the issues of full employment and public works employment are given serious consideration. Without better paying job opportunities that can pay for basic needs, poor households will continue to be at risk of becoming homeless.

There seems to be consensus among welfare advocates in Missouri that a federal standard, indexed for inflation, is necessary for establishing an equitable floor for those dependent on welfare (Missouri Association for Social Welfare, 1987b: 9). Only token increases in Missouri benefit levels have been sustained in recent years.

Discussions at the national level focus on the concept of a family living standard that would provide additional federal monies to states which increase benefit levels. Households employed at low-wage jobs would have their incomes supplemented to the family living standard. Basing benefit levels on a percentage of state median income would provide for differing area costs. It should be noted, however, that legislation of this kind would offer no new opportunities to the two thirds of households in poverty who do not receive AFDC.

The Missouri welfare study estimates that 16,000 to 22,000 clients are ready, willing, and able to work, and by implication, that either the jobs or support services are not there to permit them to work (Missouri Association for Social Welfare, 1987b: 28). Various welfare reform proposals were under discussion in the 1987 Missouri legislature, ranging from mandatory learnfare and workfare to a voluntary program with a guaranteed job paying $1 above minimum wage upon completion. No proposals passed, not even the governor-backed learnfare program. None of these proposals addressed the needs of single destitute people or families not on welfare who are out of work. To the credit of the legislature, however, Medicaid benefits were extended to poor pregnant women and children up to age five and are to be phased in over several years.

Efforts to raise the minimum wage are alive at the federal level, although a recent Missouri proposal did not advance. An increase to $4.35 an hour would regain its 1981 purchasing power, but provide only 82 percent of the poverty level for a family of four.

Community-Oriented Human Services

The high level of life crises and interpersonal problems among the homeless population suggest that the prevention of homelessness must include such services as community-based mental health programs and crisis-intervention services for low-income people. As an example of the former, the Missouri Department of Mental Health promoted an expansion of community-based services to the chronically mentally ill in the recent legislative session.

A Task Force on the Homeless Mentally Ill of the Missouri Association for Social Welfare has developed service recommendations. These recommendations call for outreach to shelters by mental health agencies to identify the mentally ill and assess their needs, along with emergency and training support for shelter staff. Other recommendations—for drop-in centers offering basic support, referrals, and counseling; intensive case management services; special transitional housing programs; and long-term housing with support services—cover the spectrum of crisis/acute and chronic mental health needs.

The fact that some households move into and out of homelessness indicates that transitional programs with social services to help households move from dependency to independent living are also an important prevention measure. Providers of service to the homeless stress the importance of case management services to help clients regain, or perhaps develop for the first time, necessary skills for productive life-styles.

The Missouri Department of Mental Health study of the homeless in emergency shelters found that one fifth of the St. Louis area homeless had a prison record from the past, prior to homelessness, which may indicate the need for additional post-prison support services (Morse et al., 1985: 48).

The author's bias toward structural solutions to the problem is in part a response to official definitions of the homelessness problem as essentially one of personal disabilities. This can and has become a shorthand way of dismissing the social justice issues involved. The high prevalence of poverty backgrounds among the homeless and the relationships and factors described and discussed throughout this chapter indicate that far more than personal illness or disability is involved. Along with housing and economic reforms, it would be instructive to study the poor who have not become homeless in order to understand what prevention measures might work. The presence of significant family and community ties is probably an important factor. For the homeless who have lost them, the reconstruction of these ties in new ways may be vital.

NOTES

Direct all correspondence to Julia S. Kunz, Research Consultant, 4497 Pershing Ave., St. Louis, MO 63108

A special thank you to Sara Barwinski, Dorothy Dailey, Peter De Simone, and Calvin Streeter for reviewing earlier drafts of the chapter, and to Beth Liebling for providing access to Kansas City materials.

1. This 40,000 figure is an estimate based on reports from St. Louis, Kansas City, Columbia, and Springfield, and assuming increases in 1982 reports for several other cities, plus a guestimate of the rural population. It has been reported in several studies and received media attention in Missouri. It reflects the visible homeless and does not include the potentially homeless in halfway houses, prisons, and transitional facilities, or the hidden homeless doubled up with friends or relatives or living in substandard housing.

2. The shortfall is based on the following census data for Missouri: 50 percent of 1979 median income of renter-occupied units was $5,199. The number of renter households with 1979 income under $5,000 was 128,041. The number of units with gross rents about 1/4 of income ($110) was 53,094. The number of units with gross rents about 1/3 of income ($145) was 105,293.

3. The structural deficiencies included a basement with signs of water leakage, roof

water leakage, open cracks or holes in the interior walls or ceiling, holes in the floor, and broken plaster or peeling paint on the ceiling or inside walls.

4. The 1984 rate is assumed to remain at the 1983 level based on the Census Bureau's estimation from the Current Population Survey that poverty in the Midwest remained unchanged.

REFERENCES

Bell, Daniel. 1976. *The Cultural Contradictions of Capitalism*. New York: Basic Books.

Bellah, Robert, et al. 1985. *Habits of the Heart: Individualism and Commitment in American Life*. Berkeley, Calif.: University of California Press.

Daily Dunklin Democrat. 1987. March Study Found 200 Homeless People in Area. May 5.

Darcy, L., and D. L. Jones. 1975. The Size of the Homeless Men Population of Sydney. *Australian Journal of Social Issues* 10: 208–215.

De Simone, Peter. 1985. Homeless in Mid-Missouri. In *Homelessness in Missouri*, 19–26. Jefferson City: Missouri Association for Social Welfare.

Ehrenreich, Barbara. 1986. Is the Middle Class Doomed? *Seeds* 12: 16–21.

Gist, Richard M., and Quintin B. Welch. 1986. *Estimates of Period Prevalence of Homelessness in Kansas City, Missouri—1985*. Report No. 27. Kansas City, Mo.: Missouri Health Department, Office of Health Research and Analysis.

Goward, Russell, Chair, Social Services and Medicaid Interim Committee on the Homeless. 1986. *A Report to the Speaker, Missouri House of Representatives: Homelessness in Missouri*. Jefferson City, Mo.

Hopper, Kim, and Jill Hamberg. 1986. The Making of America's Homeless: From Skid Row to New Poor, 1945–1984. In *Critical Perspectives on Housing*, edited by Rachel G. Bratt, Chester Hartman, and Ann Meyerson, 12–40. Philadelphia: Temple University Press.

Kunz, Julia, and Susan Murray. 1984. *Sheltering the Homeless*. St. Louis, Mo.: St. Louis Relocation Clearinghouse.

Lasch, Christopher. 1978. *The Culture of Narcissism*. New York: Norton.

Liebling, Beth. 1985. *Causes of Homelessness and Pilgrim House Report*. Kansas City, Mo.: City Union Mission.

———. 1987. Hotline for the Homeless Statistics. Kansas City, Mo.: City Union Mission.

Lieutenant Governor's Task Force on Homelessness. 1987. *Homelessness in Missouri*. Jefferson City, Mo.: Office of Lieutenant Governor Harriet Woods.

Lincoln, Scott, Compiler for Task Force on the Homeless. 1986. *Homelessness in Columbia*. Columbia, Mo.: Office of Community Services, City of Columbia.

Lovell, Dorsey, Chair, Committee to Study the Problems of the Homeless and Hungry. 1987. *Report of the Committee to Study the Problems of the Homeless and Hungry in Springfield, Missouri*. Springfield, Mo.: Community Development Department, City of Springfield.

Missouri Association for Social Welfare. 1985. *Homelessness in Missouri*. Task Force on Survival, Betty Marver, Chair. Jefferson City, Mo.: MASW.

———. 1986. *Hunger in Missouri*. Sara Barwinski, Peter De Simone, Sharon Kliethermes, and Julia Kunz for Task Force on Hunger. Jefferson City, Mo.: MASW.

———. 1987a. *Low Income Housing in Missouri*. Julia Kunz for Low Income Housing Task Force. Jefferson City, Mo.: MASW.

————. 1987b. *Welfare Reform in Missouri*. Welfare Reform Committee, Betty Marver, Chair. Jefferson City, Mo.: MASW.

Morse, Gary, et al. 1985. *Homeless People in St. Louis: A Mental Health Program Evaluation, Field Study and Follow-up Investigation*. Jefferson City, Mo.: Department of Mental Health.

Pape, William R. No date. Response to Questionnaire from The Partnership for the Homeless. Kansas City, Mo.: Metropolitan Lutheran Ministry.

Rossi, Peter H., et al. 1987. The Urban Homeless: Estimating Composition and Size. *Science* 235: 1336–1341.

Safety Network. 1987. National Coalition Factsheet Info: Who, Why, How Many and How Much? May.

St. Louis Homeless Reception Center. 1986–1987. Form A: Profile of Families Seeking Shelter Information. St. Louis, Mo.: Department of Human Services, City of St. Louis.

St. Louis Post-Dispatch. 1986. Area Homeless, Friends Walk to Capital. October 6.

————. 1986. Increase in "New Poor" Laid to Unemployment. December 22.

————. 1987. St. Charles County's Homeless. April 27.

Streeter, Calvin L., and Robert Frank. 1985. Bitter Harvest: The Question of Homelessness in Rural America. In *Homelessness in Missouri*, 45–55. Jefferson City, Mo.: Missouri Association for Social Welfare.

U.S. Bureau of the Census. 1983a. *Detailed Housing Characteristics: Missouri*. 1980 Census of Housing, Vol. 1, Part 27, Table 62:39. Washington, D.C.: Government Printing Office.

————. 1983b. *Metropolitan Housing Characteristics: Kansas City, Mo.–Kan. Standard Metropolitan Statistical Area*. 1980 Census of Housing, Vol. 2, Table A–4:200. Washington, D.C.: Government Printing Office.

————. 1983c. *Metropolitan Housing Characteristics: St. Louis, Mo.–Ill. Standard Metropolitan Statistical Area*. 1980 Census of Housing, Vol. 2, Table A–4:313. Washington, D.C.: Government Printing Office.

U.S. Department of Housing and Urban Development. 1984. *A Report to the Secretary on the Homeless and Emergency Shelters*. Washington, D.C.: HUD, Office of Policy Development and Research.

Van Sant, Jane, Chair, Task Force on Homeless Mentally Ill of the Missouri Association for Social Welfare. 1987. Minutes of the Task Force. Kansas City, Mo.: Transitional Living Consortium.

Whitney, Stuart E., Chair, Ad Hoc Committee on Shelter for the Homeless. 1985. *Preliminary Report*. Kansas City, Mo.: City of Kansas City.

————. 1986. *Expansion of Affordable Housing*. Third Preliminary Report. Kansas City, Mo.: City of Kansas City.

7

Homelessness in New Jersey: The Social Service Network and the People Served

Gerald R. Gioglio

On January 22, 1986, more than 200 of New Jersey's public and private social service agencies were asked to participate in a study of homelessness in the state. The research was authorized by the commissioner of the New Jersey Department of Human Services in response to recommendations made by Governor Thomas H. Kean's 1983 Task Force on Homelessness. The task force suggested a study to help identify the causes of homelessness and to provide information on the characteristics, problems, and needs of homeless persons. The need to collect information on emergency services available through the shelters was also recommended, along with the call for a census of New Jersey's homeless population (Governor's Task Force, 1983).

METHODOLOGY

The research plan was designed and carried out by staff of the department's Division of Youth and Family Services' Bureau of Research, Evaluation, and Quality Assurance. First, a mailed survey of shelter operators was conducted in October 1985. Information from that study was used to prepare for a one-day study of homelessness and social service use, held in January 1986. A summary of findings from these efforts are presented here. For more details, the reader may refer to the final report of the research project entitled, *Homelessness in New Jersey: A Study of Shelters, Agencies and the Clients They Serve* (Gioglio and Jacobsen, 1986).

Given the controversy surrounding street counts and the methodological difficulties inherent in counting the homeless (Hombs and Snyder, 1982; House of of Representatives, 1984; U.S. Department of Housing and Urban Development, 1984), a decision was made not to count or include street dwellers in the research effort. Rather, emphasis was placed on acquiring a demographic profile of those homeless and imminently homeless persons and families who used the state's various social service programs and emergency shelters. The goal was to obtain critically needed baseline information on services provided to homeless persons and to gain insight into the complexities, causes, and nature of homelessness in the state.

The research, then, focused on a "captive audience" of shelter residents and those persons or families aided by the state's public and private social service agencies. It also generated a "snapshot" of service provision to homeless and imminently homeless persons who sought assistance on the day of the study.

For the purpose of this study, "homeless" was defined as being temporarily or permanently without shelter, or receiving cash or services to prevent a loss of existing shelter. Imminently homeless was defined as being in *immediate need* of cash or services to prevent a loss of existing shelter. Unless indicated otherwise, both of these terms will be subsumed through the use of the single word "homeless."

The primary governmental agencies involved in the research included all the existing units of the Division of Youth and Family Services (DYFS) at the time (37 district offices and three adoption resource centers). DYFS provides social services to children and families, particularly to the abused and neglected, including protective services, foster care, day care, and adoption services. Also included were all 21 county boards of social services/county welfare boards (CBSS/CWA). These county-based agencies provide a wide range of social service programs to adults, families, and the poor, such as counseling, family planning, housing assistance, and homemaker services as well as cash assistance programs, including Aid to Families with Dependent Children (AFDC) and Medicaid.

In addition, a random sample of 70 of the state's municipal welfare boards was chosen from a list of 460 local offices made available by the Division of Public Welfare, a component of the New Jersey Department of Human Services. Municipal welfare boards provide financial assistance for adults under age 65 who are without dependent children and are not eligible for other programs. Also included were: (1) all 34 emergency homeless shelters and the 21 specialized shelters (for battered women and runaways) that existed at that time; and, (2) 42 (two per county) private, nonprofit social service providers known to assist homeless persons. Participation rates ranged from 82 percent for the shelters to 100 percent for the DYFS and CBSS/CWA units. The overall completion rate was 84 percent.

Shelters, agencies, and providers were given supplies of intake forms and caseworker logs designed for use in this study. These instruments were used to collect information on persons or families who approached them with problems related to homelessness between 12:01 A.M. and 12 midnight on the day of the study. The intake forms were used to gather information on individuals or families who were *not* on active agency or provider caseloads on that day. The caseworker logs requested aggregate information on clients from *currently active* provider and agency caseloads where homelessness was a factor in the case. Logs were not distributed to the shelters or to those agencies or providers that provided services on a temporary or episodic basis.

Intake forms collected information on the type of client seeking assistance (unaccompanied persons and one- or two-parent families), various demographic data, primary and secondary reasons for homelessness, and information on prior homelessness or institutionalization. Caseworker logs sought baseline data on the total number of adults and children who were homeless and the number of children placed in foster care due to inadequate housing options.

A series of training sessions was held during the month preceding the study. All participants were asked to send a staff member to be briefed on the project and to act as a liaison between the research team and their respective offices. The liaisons were trained in the use of the research instruments and advised of the logistical procedures including the receipt, dissemination, and collection of the completed intake forms and logs. Liaisons were instructed to identify all staff at their offices selected for the study (intake workers, social workers, and so on), to train them, and to assist their staff during the actual conduct of the study. The liaisons were also responsible for collecting and forwarding the completed instruments to the main research staff.

POPULATIONS SERVED

A summary of the number of homeless persons served by agencies and shelters is shown below.

Caseload	Total Homeless	Number of Children	Percent Children
DYFS	5,175	3,584	69
CBSS	5,962	3,716	62
MWB	1,108	22	2
Providers	2,202	1,076	49
Total	14,447	8,398	58

It may be pointed out that the MWB (municipal welfare board) totals are generalized across the state, based on data from a random sample. On January 22, 1986, when the research was conducted, there were 14,447 homeless or imminently homeless persons on agency caseloads. These were persons and families already known to agencies and receiving social services or financial assistance from state, county, or municipal welfare or private social service agencies. The critical and most disturbing finding, as the above figures show, is that almost three fifths (58 percent) of these clients were children.

Relatedly, as demonstrated below, 2,046 homeless persons also approached a shelter or one or more agencies that day. Here, among those who approached the agencies seeking cash or services for problems related to homelessness, 53 percent were children. At the shelters, fully one quarter of the residents were children.

Intake	Total Homeless	Number of Children	Percent Children
All agencies/providers	764	406	53
All shelters	1,282	315	25
Total intakes	2,046	707	35

Because an unknown number of persons may have been served by more than one service organization, combining the totals presented above has been avoided. Totaling the two may indicate a minimum number of service incidents involving the homeless for that date, but it should not be construed as representing an unduplicated count of homeless clients receiving services that day.

Individuals and Families

Shelters and agencies were asked to identify the client family units that approached them for shelter or assistance on the day of the study. Table 7.1 compares these various client family units by selected characteristics. The shelters reported 966 family units housed, as compared with 306 family units served by the agencies. Shelters, for the most part, served unaccompanied persons, while the agencies served families. Approximately 84 percent of the shelter population was made up of unaccompanied adults, especially males, but 60 percent of the family units served by agencies were families with children.

In the shelters, families with children averaged 3.0 persons per unit; there were 3.5 persons per family unit in those families visiting the agencies. A disturbingly large number of female-headed families (49 percent of all family units) was reported by the agencies. Also disheartening was the 13 percent figure for single-parent, female-headed families living in shelters. On January 22, 1986, these families made up a major subgroup of New Jersey's homeless.

Locale

There was some thought among social service providers that homeless people were "migrating" to cities where social services were available. There was also some speculation that the homeless were being "shipped" (as a "social service action") to the larger cities from neighboring states or from less populous counties in New Jersey. Conversations with shelter operators indicated that they believed such practices did occur. Therefore, shelter residents and agency clients were asked to identify the last geographic location they came from prior to seeking help from these organizations. Their responses indicate that, in New Jersey,

Table 7.1

Intake Data: Frequency Distribution, Client Family Units Served by Shelters and Agencies

Family Type	Shelters Number	(N=966) Percent	Agencies Number	(N=306) Percent
Unaccompanied males	677	70.0	58	19.0
Unaccompanied females	138	14.0	40	13.0
Single parent females	125	13.0	150	49.0
Single parent males	5	<1.0	6	2.0
Single parent males	10	1.0	28	9.0
Couple	8	<1.0	24	8.0
Unknown	3	<1.0	na	na
Last Geographical Location				
Same town/city	483	50.	116	38.0
Same county/other city	213	22.0	135	44.0
Another county	116	12.0	28	9.0
Another state	125	13.0	24	8.0
Another country	29	3.0	3	1.0
Received Gov't Assistance				
No assistance	454	47.0	156	51.0
Municipal welfare	319	33.0	25	8.0
County welfare	116	12.0	104	34.0
SSI	77	8.0	21	7.0

na: Not available and/or not applicable.

seeking shelter and services for conditions of homelessness is a decidedly local circumstance.

Indeed, as it may be noted from data in Table 7.1, one half of the shelter residents and 38 percent of the agency clients report coming from the same town or city where they seek shelter or services. Adding those not from the same municipality but from the same county results in 72 percent of the shelter population and 82 percent of the agency clients reported as coming from either their own county or their immediate locale.

These findings on locale are comparable to those reported for the state of New York in 1984. The New York shelter operators reported that 77 percent of their shelter residents come from the same municipality where they were being sheltered, with an additional 10 percent coming from outside the municipality, but from the same county (New York Department of Social Services, 1984).

Government Assistance

Garrett and Schutt (1986), sampling intake records from a homeless shelter in Boston, reported that few of the shelter residents received any financial benefits. In New Jersey, agency clients and shelter residents were also asked if they received any municipal or county welfare and/or Supplemental Security Income (SSI). Roughly one half of these agency clients (51 percent) and shelter residents (47 percent) reported that they did not receive assistance from any of these sources. A greater percentage of shelter residents, again mostly adults, reported receiving municipal welfare (known in New Jersey as general assistance). County welfare, basically AFDC, was reported as available to about one third of the agency clientele. Unfortunately, given the nature of the research, it was not possible to secure in-depth information on why so many people did *not* receive financial help from these sources. There are several possible reasons, including ineligibility, not having been referred to these sources of aid, unwillingness to apply, incapacitation, or other difficulties in negotiating the social service system.

Questions related to incapacitation and willingness to seek help were part of the mailed survey of operators discussed in Gioglio and Jacobsen (1986)l. Here, shelter operators were questioned on the ability and willingness of shelter residents to follow up on referrals. Operators of emergency shelters reported that an average of 7.5 percent (range: 0–60 percent) of these residents were not capable of following up on referrals. Twenty percent were unwilling to do so because of personal choice or life-style (range: 2–90 percent), and 15 percent (range: 0–50 percent) were seen as being unable to follow up due to organizational barriers in the state's social service system (range: 0–50 percent). In the specialized shelters, 1.5 percent were deemed incapable, 10 percent were unwilling, and 10 percent were unable to follow up on referrals.

Table 7.2 provides greater detail on the demographic characteristics of persons in the 966 sheltered and 306 agency-served family units discussed above. Regarding racial characteristics, 50 percent of all shelter residents were black and 14 percent were Hispanic. Similarly, of those seeking help from the agencies, 41 and 11 percent were black and Hispanic, respectively. Given that New Jersey's black population stands at about 13 percent and Hispanics at 7 percent (New Jersey Department of Labor, 1981), both groups were disproportionately overrepresented in the homeless population. Minorities, then, also constitute a major subgroup of New Jersey's homeless population.

The homeless at shelters were predominantly adults between the ages of 18 and 39. The average age for male adults was 35 years, for adult families, 33.3 years. Sheltered children averaged 5.4 years old. Agencies predominantly served children of families. The average child served was 7.2 years old. Adult females at agencies were 33.3 years old; agency-served males were, on average, 38 years old.

Finally, shelter residents were asked only if they were U.S. military veterans; 186 (19 percent) indicated prior military service. Given that approximately 12.5 percent of the total state population are veterans, the veteran population was somewhat overrepresented in New Jersey's homeless shelters. As such, veterans constitute a major subgroup within the state's sheltered homeless population. Veterans in the shelters were predominantly male (97 percent), as would be

Table 7.2
Intake Data: Frequency Distribution, Clients Served by Agencies and Shelters

Characteristics	Shelters		Agencies	
	Number	Percent	Number	Percent
Sex:				
Male	846	66.0	302	40.0
Female	396	31.0	451	59.0
Unknown	40	3.0	6	1.0
Race:				
White	462	36.0	367	48.0
Black	641	50.0	313	41.0
Hispanic	179	14.0	84	11.0
Age:				
0-17	315	25.0	393	52.0
18-29	336	26.0	166	22.0
30-39	300	23.0	122	16.0
40-49	151	12.0	35	5.0
50-59	90	7.0	11	1.0
60 and over	59	4.0	11	1.0
Unknown	32	3.0	26	3.0
Veteran Status (N=966):				
Veteran	186	19.0	na	na
Nonveteran	780	81.0	na	na
Black veteran	87	47.0	na	na
Hispanic veteran	12	6.0	na	na

na: Not available and/or not applicable.

expected; were mostly blacks and Hispanics (53 percent); and were somewhat older (average age 44) than the total sheltered male population. Compared to the general shelter population they also showed slightly higher rates of homelessness due to substance abuse. Across other variables the veterans' experiences parallel those of other shelter residents.

REASONS FOR HOMELESSNESS

In 1985, the U.S. General Accounting Office (GAO), in a report entitled *Homelessness: A Complex Problem and the Federal Response*, identified "multiple and interrelated" factors that contributed to the condition of homelessness. These factors included increased unemployment in the 1970s and early 1980s, deinstitutionalization of mentally ill persons and the lack of available community-based services for them, increases in personal crises such as divorce, release from jail or hospital, traveling, domestic violence, fires and health-related prob-

Table 7.3
Intake Data: Frequency Distribution, Family Units' Primary Reasons for
Homelessness

Reason	Shelters Number	(N=966) Percent	Agencies Number	(N=306) Percent
Eviction by landlord	216	22.0	99	32.0
Eviction by primary tenant	152	18.0	55	18.0
No money for shelter	56	6.0	29	9.5
Loss of job	124	13.0	20	6.5
Housing destroyed	48	5.0	17	6.0
Domestic violence	111	11.0	14	5.0
Personal choice/traveling	57	6.0	12	4.0
New to area	17	2.0	9	3.0
Left jail	33	3.0	6	2.0
Left/to admission to Mental Hospital	34	3.0	5	2.0
Substance abuse	43	4.0	3	<1.0
Other	31	3.0	24	8.0
Unknown	44	4.0	13	4.0

lems, cuts in public assistance programs, and the decline in the low-income housing supply (U.S. General Accounting Office, 1985).

While it was assumed that the homeless in New Jersey confronted similar problems, attempts were made during the study to focus on the most important reasons that persons approached the shelters and agencies for help. Therefore, during the intake process, homeless persons were asked to pinpoint the *one* most important reason for being without shelter. They were also asked to report other secondary reasons for arriving at a condition of homelessness.

The primary reasons for homelessness, by family unit, are detailed in Table 7.3. As the data in Table 7.3 indicate, eviction by a landlord or by a primary tenant (a person or family with whom one shares housing) are reported as the two most important reasons for homelessness. Forty percent of the shelter residents and 50 percent of the agency clients reported eviction by landlord or primary tenant as the primary cause. By way of comparison, a study conducted in New York found that the "immediate reason" for homelessness among those in emergency shelters was also eviction (60 percent). Thirty-seven percent of the total shelter population had reportedly been doubled up and were not able to remain in that living situation (New York Department of Social Services, 1984).

Because of the exploratory nature of this research, information regarding the personal, social, or economic factors that result in actual eviction was not collected. Many factors can be involved. For example, Seitz and Ziegler (1985), reporting on New Jersey's Homelessness Prevention Program, pointed out that "households receiving public assistance require most, if not all, of their income for housing costs. The inevitable result for many households is eviction for nonpayment of rent.'' At the time of their study, a typical family of three in New Jersey received $385 per month from Aid to Families with Dependent Children; however, the authors noted that ''the average fair market rent for a two-bedroom apartment . . . was $450 per month.'' Hartman (1986) pointed out other factors that could result in housing displacement, including:

undermaintenance and abandonment practices of landlords and building managers that render the housing uninhabitable . . . accidental or intentional fires (the latter sometimes known as ''selling out to the insurance company''); conversion of rental units to condominiums . . . conversion of residential property to non-residential uses; and demolition of residential property in order to . . . redevelop it as higher-priced residential quarters.

Added to this are tensions and pressures of overcrowding (often as a result of sharing housing with relatives or friends) that can lead to eviction by a landlord or primary tenant.

Eviction, of course, like any other primary reason for homelessness, is a precipitating event that leads to homelessness. But, for Hopper and Hamberg (1984), such events themselves need explanation. That is, the social and economic factors leading to a condition of eviction and homelessness are both complex and interconnected. In New Jersey, the interconnections among eviction, economic difficulties, and levels of government financial assistance become more apparent when considering eviction in relation to secondary reasons for homelessness.

From the following data, we may note that more than a majority of New Jersey's evicted homeless were nonwhite and that children were involved in 15 percent of the evicted family units living at shelters and in 71 percent of the evicted families seeking help from the agencies. The following percentages are based on 368 shelters' and 154 agencies' family units evicted by landlords and/ or primary tenants.

Characteristics	Shelters (%)	Agencies (%)
Age: 40	66	83
Race: nonwhite	67	56
A family, children present	15	71
Secondary reason: Homelessness: loss of job	21	17
Secondary reason: no money for rent	27	43
Do not receive municipal or county welfare or SSI	60	48
In emergency shelter within the last year	35	17

Based on these data, approximately one fifth of the evicted agency clients and shelter residents point to a loss of a job as a secondary reason for their condition; 27 percent point to having no money for rent. Forty-three percent of the evicted homeless approaching agencies also report this as a secondary reason for homelessness. Note that 60 percent of the evicted who reside in shelters and 48 percent of the evicted at the agencies reportedly *do* receive SSI or some form of municipal or county welfare.

Equally disturbing is the finding that about one fifth of the evicted shelter residents and one third of the evicted agency clients reported being in an emergency shelter within the year preceeding the study. These findings point to a cyclic and chronic condition that has not been alleviated by available government and community-based assistance. Other top-ranking reasons for homelessness included a loss of job (13 percent) and domestic violence (11 percent) for shelter residents, and the lack of money left for shelter (9.5 percent) and job loss (6.5 percent) for agency clients.

Among the shelter residents who reported the loss of a job as the primary reason for homelessness, 97 percent were unaccompanied adults; 87 percent were men. When questioned about former employment, adult males can suddenly find themselves among the ranks of the dependent poor. One must realize that unemployment insurance is one of the few social welfare programs available to men. Unfortunately, all too often these benefits run out before new jobs can be found, a problem exacerbated by the fact that, in the 1980s, supplemental and extended unemployment benefits (as many as 26 weeks beyond the basic 26-week program) were eliminated. Hopper and Hamberg (1984) describe this as "calamitous" for those who confront joblessness by making the experience of unemployment more precarious than it has been in the recent past. They report, for example, that while "unemployment peaked at 10.8 percent in late 1982, it had also climbed above 9 percent during the 1974–75 recession." Of course, during the latter recession, extended benefits for the unemployed were available; but, during the 1980s, this particular safety net was not available to the long-term unemployed. By way of example, Hopper and Hamberg point out that in September 1983 only 32.8 percent of the 9.8 million officially unemployed were collecting unemployment benefits. For many formerly employed males who have exhausted these benefits, only general assistance, SSI (if disabled), or AFDC (if dependent children were involved) remained as possible buffers between poverty and total dependency.

Finally, domestic violence ranked high among the primary reasons for homelessness reported by shelter residents. Approximately 28 percent of those homeless for reasons of domestic violence were found at the emergency shelters; of course, the overwhelming majority lived at the specialized shelters established for this purpose.

MENTAL HEALTH AND HOMELESSNESS

Deinstitutionalization and the impact this policy has had on homelessness have been topics of considerable ongoing debate and controversy (Appleby and Desai, 1985; Okin, 1985; Bassuk, Rubin, and Lauriat, 1984; Lamb,

1984; Lipton, Sabatini, and Katz, 1983). Key issues include shortcomings in discharge procedures, funding for (and the efficacy of) the community care system, and the prevalence of mental disorder among the homeless population.

Advocates for the homeless, for example, report that between one fifth and one half of all homeless people in America are ex-mental patients (Hombs and Snyder, 1982; Baxter and Hopper, 1984). Robertson (1986) discusses the strengths and weaknesses of several studies that estimate the number of homeless who were previously institutionalized. She found that the rates ranged from 9 percent to 42 percent.

Of course, the deinstitutionalized are only one subgroup within the mentally ill homeless population. Also included are those in need of mental health services who have not been institutionalized but are not receiving or finding adequate care, and those unfortunate people who have developed forms of mental disorder as a consequence of their homelessness. That is, mental illness is both the cause and effect of homelessness.

Only 10 percent of New Jersey's shelter residents reported that they, or an accompanying family member, had been institutionalized during the preceding year, and 5 percent of those visiting the agencies gave this self-report. These self-reports of mental health–related problems seemed to be at odds with the October 1985 survey of New Jersey's shelter operators and various other studies. One possible explanation can be found in the work of Garrett and Schutt (1986), who compared intake interviews with shelter residents to matched nursing records for the same persons. The authors found a significant amount of underreporting of psychiatric problems on the intake forms compared to information on nursing records. This and the results of the New Jersey study suggest that perhaps a mental health professional should participate in future research that uses intake forms as a data-collection technique.

To get a more complete overview of mental health–related factors among New Jersey shelter residents, data about all mental health variables were entered into a multiple response matrix to generate a new variable called *mental health factor*—a broader measure of mental health need beyond simple institutionalization. The new variable included information on deinstitutionalization or the denial of admission to a mental health facility as a primary or secondary reason for homelessness, the history of institutionalization, the use of medication for nervous, emotional, or mental problems, and the use of a community mental health center during the preceding 12 months.

The combination of these variables demonstrated that 279, or 29 percent, of those living at shelters reported one or more mental health–related factors. Within this population, approximately 36 percent (10 percent of all shelter residents studied) were institutionalized for mental health reasons during the preceding year, more than half were using medication for mental health–related reasons, and almost three quarters had used the services of a community mental health center within the last year.

The following data compare the population of shelter residents who did not report any mental health–related factors to those who did.

Respondents' Characteristics	Without Mental Factor (%)	With Mental Factor (%)
Unaccompanied adults	83	91**
Females	28	32
Whites	33	42**
In emergency shelter on 1/22/86	80	88*
In emergency shelter last year	31	48**
Gets welfare or SSI	47	67**
Evicted	38	37
From own city/county	72	74
Veteran	20	19

It must be pointed out that the percentages without a mental health factor are based on 681 shelter residents who did not report any mental health factor, while the percentages with a mental health factor are based on 279 shelter residents who reported having one or more of these health factors. The single and double asterisks indicate significant differences at $p < .05$ and $p < .01$, respectively.

Using the chi-square test, we determined that a significantly larger amount of unaccompanied adults and whites were found among those with a mental health–related factor. Persons in this category were also more likely to have been in an emergency shelter at some point during the preceding year and to be found in an emergency shelter (as opposed to a specialized shelter) on the date of the study. It was encouraging to discover that significantly more of the mental health population, compared to those reporting no mental health factor, were receiving county or municipal welfare monies or SSI. However, once again it seems clear that cash assistance alone is not sufficient to address the varied needs of this vulnerable population.

The detail on eviction is notable among the nonsignificant findings that appear in the above data. Note that those with a mental health–related factor were as likely as those not reporting such factors to cite eviction as their primary reason for homelessness. In fact, comparisons between the mental health population and those not reporting such problems revealed no significant differences in *any* of the primary reasons given for becoming homeless. Finally, those expressing mental health factors were also just as likely as those without such problems to come to the shelters from their immediate locale. Thus, the socioeconomic and personal factors involved in arriving at homelessness frequently converge; that is, the demographics and experiences of those with mental disorders often parallel those of their homeless peers who do not report mental disorders.

However, the combination of homelessness and mental illness is a cruel double burden for these unfortunate people. Although many appear to be connected to funding sources and relatively large numbers use mental health services, these citizens need special assistance if they are to thrive in their communities. In 1983 a report on federal efforts regarding the shelter needs of the mentally ill found that homeless people, particularly those with mental health–related problems, needed help in finding and qualifying for services and benefits. The report stated that:

among the problems are lack of knowledge of available resources, difficulty in sorting out services offered by different agencies, difficulties in dealing with "complex bureaucracies," lack of program coordination, stigma against mental illness in some programs, lengthy periods to determine eligibility and lack of knowledge about application procedures and eligibility. (U.S. Department of Health and Human Services, 1983)

Barring this type of ongoing help, the need for emergency shelter for the mentally frail seems almost certain to continue.

HOMELESSNESS AND FOSTER CARE

Tomaszewicz (1985), in a study of 690 children placed in foster care in New Jersey between January and September 1983, reported that homelessness was the single most frequent problem experienced by these families. He found that forty percent of the families studied were homeless at the time of placement or had experienced homelessness in the twelve to eighteen months preceding the placement studied.

There was great concern that foster care was being used as a social service response in cases involving homelessness. Therefore, all units of the New Jersey Division of Youth and Family Services were asked to report the number of children on active caseloads who were placed in foster care either totally or partially due to inadequate housing options.

As previously shown, 3,584 children on the DYFS caseload were reported as homeless on the day of this study. Thirty-three percent (1,187) of these children were also reported as being in foster placement on that date. Further, when viewed as a percentage of the entire DYFS foster care caseload ($n = 6,790$), the 1,187 homeless children in placement constituted 18 percent of all children in foster care. It should be pointed out that in an unknown number of cases, other factors such as abuse or neglect may have been involved in the decision to place homeless children in foster care. Such factors were beyond the scope of this research. In the Tomaszewicz (1985) study, 134 of the 690 families studied (19 percent) placed a child in a foster home as an immediate result of some form of homelessness or housing difficulty. Within this group of 134 families, nearly three quarters (73 percent) placed children in foster care solely due to homelessness. In the remaining cases, homelessness joined child abuse and other pathologies as a reason for foster placement. Thus, in both these studies from New Jersey, homelessness is clearly identified as an important variable in the decision to place children apart from their families.

The impact that such an influx of children has on an already overburdened foster care system is apparent when one considers the costs involved. According to the DYFS Budget Office, the average monthly cost for a child in foster care placement at the time of the study was $262. This money is used to purchase board, clothing, and various nonmedical items and services. It does not include administrative costs related to case management and supervision. Multiplying this conservative figure by the 1,187 children placed into foster care partially or totally due to homelessness came to $311,000 for the month of January 1986 alone—or, if these figures remained constant, some $3.7 million annually.

CONCLUSIONS

The renowned sociologist C. Wright Mills (1959) suggested making a distinction between "personal troubles" and "public issues of the social structure." Personal troubles are individual occurrences having to do with one's personal biography, character, relations with significant others and with those areas of social life that are within the scope of one's immediate environment. A personal trouble, simply, is a private matter.

Public issues are those concerns that go beyond immediate environment and personal makeup. They are structural issues that have to do with the nature and character of society as a whole. These are macrolevel public concerns that affect, intersect, and, one might argue, cause the personal troubles of individual men and women; problems and troubles that the ordinary individual will not be able to solve. By their very nature, these public issues require a public response.

Homelessness, when identified with alcoholism and skid-row life-styles, was often viewed as a personal trouble of individuals responsible for their own plight. More, the abundant, albeit substandard, supply of single-room occupancy housing kept them out of the public sight and mind.

The "safety net" for these unfortunates was all too often cast out only by urban missionaries. The program involved detoxification, soul-saving, and pulling oneself up by one's own secondhand bootstraps.

It is no longer possible to view homelessness in this way. Homelessness today is no longer just an individual problem if it ever was. It is truly a problem of the social structure. It is a public issue that individuals cannot be expected to resolve on their own. Indeed, as the growing number of emergency shelters indicates, it is increasing and becoming a defining characteristic of this era.

But the accouterments of homelessness still include poverty, alcoholism, and disease—add now mental disorder, drugs and the absence of affordable housing. Include former workers left without jobs or resources in a changing national economy, mothers without partners in shifting family structures, children torn from neighborhood and school, and the trappings are complete. The faces of the homeless have changed, and so have the forms. The enclaves of homelessness transcend metropolitan skid rows to include small towns and suburbs. Urban missions, jails, and detox centers are joined by municipal shelters, "welfare hotels," and foster homes. Here the "more fortunate" find shelter while untold numbers sleep in cars, abandoned buildings, and cardboard boxes. Meanwhile, the state and nation prosper. National wealth increases, housing values rise, the number of those who work increases in tandem with those who live without permanent shelter.

There's the rub, and perhaps the key to understanding the structural nature of homelessness in America. Prosperity and homelessness do not exist in isolation or as contradictions. In our country today they seem inexorably linked; some might theorize that they are directly and linearly connected. All too often, people are dislocated as a by-product of economic activity. Consider the variables: urban renaissance and skyrocketing rents, bullish markets and abandoned factories, agribusiness and farm foreclosures. It could be argued that prosperity itself now qualifies for the list of "primary reasons for homelessness."

Viewing homelessness as truly a problem of the social structure is a straightforward, simple, and clear conclusion. It is truly a problem, national in scope, that requires creative intervention from both public and private sectors. As a defining characteristic of this era, homelessness is a macrolevel socioeconomic problem likely to be with us for years to come. State governments and private agencies have made advances in meeting the immediate needs of the homeless for food and emergency shelter. However, it becomes clear that long-term, national solutions are essential if this structural problem is to be ameliorated.

NOTE

The opinions expressed in this article are the author's and do not necessarily represent those of the New Jersey Department of Human Services or the Division of Youth and Family Services. Further, any interpretation of this article made by contributors to this book are their own, and are not those of these state agencies.

REFERENCES

Appleby, Lawrence, and Prakash Desai. 1985. Documenting the Relationship Between Homelessness and Psychiatric Hospitalization. *Hospital and Community Psychiatry* 36 (7): 732–737.

Bassuk, Ellen, Lenore Rubin, and Alison Lauriat. 1984. Is Homelessness a Mental Health Problem? *American Journal of Psychiatry* 141 (12): 1546–1550.

Baxter, Ellen, and Kim Hopper. 1984. Shelter and Housing for the Homeless Mentally Ill. In *The Homeless Mentally Ill*, edited by H. Richard Lamb. Washington, D.C.: American Psychiatric Association.

Garrett, Gerald R., and Russell K. Schutt. 1986. Homelessness in the 1980s: Social Services for a Changing Population. Presented at the 1986 Annual Meeting of the

Eastern Sociological Society, New York City. University of Massachusetts at Boston, Boston, MA 02125.

Gioglio, Gerald R., and Ronald Jacobsen. 1986. *Homelessness in New Jersey: A Study of Shelters, Agencies and the Clients They Serve*. Trenton, N.J.: New Jersey Division of Youth and Family Services, Bureau of Research, Evaluation, and Quality Assurance.

Governor's Task Force on the Homeless. 1983. *Report of the Governor's Task Force on the Homeless*. Trenton, N.J.: New Jersey Department of Human Services.

Hartman, Chester. 1986. *The Housing Part of the Homeless Problem*. Washington, D.C.: Institute for Policy Studies.

Hombs, Mary Ellen, and Mitch Snyder. 1982. *Homelessness in America: A Forced March to Nowhere*. Washington, D.C.: Community for Creative Non-Violence.

Hopper, Kim, and Jill Hamberg. 1984. *The Making of America's Homeless: From Skid Row to New Poor, 1945–1984*. New York: Community Service Society of New York.

Lamb, H. Richard. 1984. *The Homeless Mentally Ill*. Washington, D.C.: American Psychiatric Association.

Lipton, Frank, Albert Sabatini, and Steven Katz. 1983. Down and Out in the City: The Homeless Mentally Ill. *Hospital and Community Psychiatry* 34 (9): 817–821.

Mills, C. Wright. 1959. *The Sociological Imagination*. New York: Oxford University Press.

New Jersey Department of Labor. 1981. *1980 Census Counts of Population by Race and Spanish Origin*. Trenton, N.J.: Office of Demographic and Economic Analysis.

New York Department of Social Services. 1984. *Homelessness in New York State: A Report of the Governor and the Legislature*. Albany, N.Y.: Author.

Okin, Robert. 1985. Expand the Community Care System: Deinstitutionalization Can Work. *Hospital and Community Psychiatry* 36 (7): 742–745.

Robertson, Marjorie J. 1986. Mental Disorder among Homeless Persons in the United States: A Review of Recent Empirical Literature. *Administration in Mental Health* 14 (1): 14–27.

Seitz, Helen, and Roy Ziegler. 1985. *Preventing Homelessness in New Jersey: A Report on the First Year of Operation of the New Jersey Department of Community Affairs' Homelessness Prevention Program*. Trenton, N.J.: New Jersey Department of Community Affairs.

Tomaszewicz, Michael. 1985. *Children Entering Foster Care: Factors Leading to Placement*. Trenton, N.J.: New Jersey Division of Youth and Family Services, Bureau of Research, Evaluation, and Quality Assurance.

U.S. Congress, House of Representatives. 1984. Joint Hearing before the Subcommittee on Housing and Community Development of the Committee on Banking, Finance, and Urban Affairs and the Subcommittee on Manpower and Housing of the Committee on Governmental Operations. Washington, D.C.: Government Printing Office.

U.S. Departments of Health and Human Services, and Housing and Urban Development. 1983. *Report on Federal Efforts to Respond to the Shelter and Basic Living Needs of Chronically Mentally Ill Persons*. Washington, D.C.: Government Printing Office.

U.S. Department of Housing and Urban Development. 1984. *A Report to the Secretary on the Homeless and Emergency Shelters*. Office of Policy Development and Research. Washington, D.C.: Government Printing Office.

U.S. General Accounting Office. 1985. *Homelessness: A Complex Problem and the Federal Response*. Washington, D.C.: Government Printing Office.

8

Homelessness in New York: A Demographic and Socioeconomic Analysis

Thomas Hirschl and Jamshid A. Momeni

With compassionate government—with government wise enough to know its limitations, courageous enough to reconcile order with justice, intelligent enough to bring opportunity and hope to those who have neither—we can shelter the homeless.

—MARIO M. CUOMO
Governor of New York State, February 1987

Homelessness is a creeping disease of our times, a disease that is spreading across our state and across the nation, leaving disruption and misery in its wake. Each new project, each new bed that we add, restores warmth and continuity to lives that have been drastically altered by the loss of a home.[1]

—CESAR A. PERALES
New York State Social Services Commissioner, February 1987

As reported by the New York State Department of Social Services (1987: i) New York State passed the first legislation authorizing the public care of the homeless in 1886, more than a century ago. In 1896, the first Municipal Lodging House was opened in New York City (NYC). In the 1930s, a former women's prison (now Camp LaGuardia) and several other commercial lodging houses were rehabilitated and converted into shelters for the increasing numbers of homeless. In the 1950s and earlier New York State provided for the homeless in New York City only. In recent years the problem has by no means been limited to NYC. The homeless population in New York State in general, and in the major metropolitan areas in particular, has increased dramatically (Council of Community

Services of Northeastern New York, 1983; Morrissey et al., 1985; City of New York, 1985, 1986a, 1986b, 1986c, 1986d; Struening, 1986). A 1983 statewide hearing indicated the inability of the small shelters to meet the ever-increasing demand for shelter throughout the state.

In January 1983, New York City was sheltering an average of 4,676 homeless men and 636 homeless women in 18 facilities. In January 1987, that number had grown to almost 9,000 homeless men, and 1,100 homeless women housed in 28 facilities. On February 15, 1987 a record number of 10,595 homeless single persons were housed in the City of New York. Throughout the state, the rise in demand for shelter by single individuals has resulted in the proliferation of newly opened local shelters as well as requests from three counties for the use of state armories in their localities to house the homeless. (New York State Department of Social Services, 1987: i)

The purpose of this paper is to conceptualize the problem of homelessness in New York State through a comprehensive review of empirical studies on home- lessness. Particular attention is paid to the regional distribution, family, and racial/ethnic composition of the homeless population. Because New York State encompasses a large and diverse population, one would expect the homeless population to reflect this diversity.

DATA AND METHOD

A major data source for this chapter is a 1983 statewide study of homelessness commissioned by the governor's office (New York State Department of Social Services, 1984). It represents the only attempt to measure homelessness at the state level and provides the best source of comparable data across New York's varied localities and regions. Other data sources include city-wide studies of New York City, Albany, and Schenectady, as well as the 1980 Census of Population and Housing.

Methodological obstacles to enumerating the homeless are well known (Rossi et al., 1986; U.S. Department of Housing and Urban Development, 1984). Although the number of homeless persons using public shelter facilities is typ- ically known, the number of homeless living outside the framework of the shelter system ("on the streets") is difficult to determine. One common estimation method is to infer the total number of homeless from the number of homeless sleeping in shelters (cf. Freeman and Hall, 1986).

This method was used in the New York State Department of Social Services (1984) study. The total number of homeless was estimated from a count of homeless sleeping in shelters by applying a multiplier to this count. The multiplier was constructed by the U.S. Department of Housing and Urban Development (1984) in studies of Boston and Baltimore where both the homeless using shelters and those not using public shelters were enumerated. The multiplier was com- puted as a ratio between these two counts.

Another method for computing a multiplier was developed by Freeman and Hall (1987) in a study of 500 randomly selected homeless persons in New York City. Some of the sampled homeless were currently sleeping in shelters and some were not. Using questionnaires, Freeman and Hall (1984) determined the percentage of nights that respondents slept in shelters during the recent past; this information was used to compute conditional probabilities that homeless people currently in shelters and currently not in shelters would sleep in a shelter on any given night. The multiplier was computed from these conditional probabilities. Based on their calculations, Freeman and Hall (1986: 3) concluded that there were 3.23 homeless persons for every homeless person in a shelter.

Homeless persons sleeping in New York State shelters were estimated by the New York State Department of Social Services (1984) using a survey of shelter providers. Shelter providers were asked in May 1983 to state the maximum number of persons sheltered, the minimum number sheltered, and the average number of persons sheltered on any given night in the recent past. The Department of Social Services used the average number of persons from each shelter provider to derive an estimate of the total number.

A total of 250 shelter providers were included in the survey. They were self-selected from a larger list of over 1,000 public and private agencies that "had at some time made themselves known to the Department [of Social Services] as concerned with emergency food and shelter" (1984: 6). A letter was sent out to more than 1,000 agencies asking whether they were shelter providers. A total of 856 agencies responded to the letter, and 250 responses were affirmative.

Confidence for this method of deriving a sampling frame is based on the fact that the Department of Social Services is a statewide organization with offices in every New York county/borough. An agency in New York State that provides shelter to the homeless is probably known to the Department of Social Services. Moreover, all of the more than 1,000 agencies originally surveyed were asked whether they knew of other agencies that provided shelter to the homeless. Additional letters were sent to all other named agencies.

Recall error for the number sheltered may be a problem, however. Accurate recall depends on the record-keeping practices of the shelter providers, and this accuracy varies. The Department of Social Services staff conducting the study recognized this problem, and verification with each shelter provider was conducted over the telephone. Unfortunately, standard errors for the final estimates are unavailable.

Another data source is the New York City's (1987) estimate of the total number of homeless using the municipal shelter system. This estimate was derived from records of the Human Resources Administration, the city agency responsible for the shelter system. Other data sources include three surveys of New York City shelter users (Freeman and Hall, 1987; Hopper, Susser, and Conover, 1985; Struening, 1986), two surveys of Albany shelter users (Hagen, 1987a; 1987b), a study of homelessness in Schenectady County (Hoddy, 1987), and a study of homelessness in a rural New York county (Hirschl, 1987).

Table 8.1
Number and Regional Distribution of Homeless Persons in New York State

Region	1983 No. Homeless[a]	1980 Population	Homeless per 1,000 Population
Adirondacks	207	879,312	2.4
Albany (L)	713	795,019	9.0
Albany (H)	1,001	795,019	12.6
Buffalo (L)	902	1,242,826	7.3
Buffalo (H)	1,266	1,242,826	10.2
Catskills (L)	280	704,325	4.0
New York City (L)	38,408	7,071,639	54.3
New York City (H)	53,938	7,071,639	76.3
New York City suburbs (L)	2,344	4,068,738	5.8
New York City suburbs (H)	3,291	4,068,738	8.1
Rochester (L)	1,231	971,230	12.7
Rochester (H)	1,728	971,230	17.8
Southern Tier	326	1,182,013	2.8
Syracuse (L)	1,014	642,971	15.8
Syracuse (H)	1,424	642,971	22.1

a: The number of homeless is estimated from the number of sheltered homeless by applying multipliers of 2.3 (HUD, 1984) and 3.23 (Freeman and Hall, 1986). Both multipliers are derived from studies of large urban areas and may not be used in rural areas of NY (Hirschl, 1987). Only the sheltered homeless figures are given for rural areas— Adirondacks, Catskills, and Southern Tier.

L: Refers to an estimate obtained by applying the HUD's multiplier, generally a lower estimate.

H: Indicates an estimate obtained by applying the Freeman and Hall's multipier, generally a higher estimate.

Source: New York State Department of Social Services (1984), and City of New York (1987).

REGIONAL DISTRIBUTION

An outstanding feature of New York State's 1980 population of 17.6 million is its uneven regional distribution. Over 40 percent of the state's population lives within the five boroughs that constitute New York City (population 7.1 million). There are five other metropolitan statistical areas within the state with populations greater than 500,000; two of these, Buffalo and Nassau-Suffolk, have metropolitan populations greater than 1 million. At the other extreme, there is a great deal of sparsely settled rural territory such as Hamilton County in the Adirondacks region, which contains no urbanized areas or incorporated places.

Table 8.1 indicates that homeless persons are also unevenly distributed across the state. Data for the table are taken from shelter counts (New York State Department of Social Services, 1984), and two multipliers are applied to give a low (L) and high (H) estimate of total homeless.[2] The total of homeless persons in New York State in 1983 is estimated to range between 45,000 and 63,000. It may be noted from Table 8.1 that NYC proper, containing about 40 percent of the state's total population, contains about 85 percent of the state's total homeless persons. The NYC suburbs consisting of five counties—Suffolk, Nassau, Putnam, Westchester, Orange, and Rockland—contained over 23 percent of the state's total population and only 5.2 percent of the homeless persons. Further, as noted from Table 8.1, the density of homelessness in Albany, Buffalo, Rochester, and Syracuse appears to be much more than the density in the NYC suburbs. As a whole, there were between 2.6 and 3.6 homeless persons per 1,000 in New York State. This is significantly less than the 1 percent of the total population estimate advanced by homeless activists.

Homelessness does not appear to be a major problem in rural areas of the state. The three largely rural regions (Adirondacks, Catskills, and Southern Tier) had 200 to 300 homeless persons in 1983. This finding is corroborated by a recent study of homelessness in rural Cortland County (Hirschl, 1987). Although there are indications of a low-income housing shortage in Cortland, the Cortland County Department of Social Services reports that only two homeless families per month were seeking assistance as of Spring 1987.

There is evidence, as the figures in Table 8.1 point out, that homelessness is growing rapidly in New York City, however. Applying the multiplier of 2.3 developed by HUD, the number of New York City homeless increased from 38,408 in 1983 to 59,800 in 1986—an increase of about 56 percent between 1983 and 1986. Applying the Freeman and Hall multiplier of 3.23, it increased from 53,938 homeless persons to 83,980—more than 51 percent—during the same period. This increase has led to a rapid expansion of the shelter system for homeless individuals and especially for homeless families (City of New York, 1987). Homelessness has reached crisis proportions in New York City.

Homeless Families in New York

An important aspect of the homeless problem is whether homeless persons are single individuals or are parts of large family units. Because families have different shelter needs from individuals, shelters designed for individuals may not be appropriate for families.

In 1983, over half (55.4 percent) of all homeless persons using shelters were in family units. The NYC suburban region had the highest percentage of persons in families (72.5 percent). The percentage of homeless persons in families in rural regions (Adirondacks, Catskills, and Southern Tier) was 57.6 percent, slightly higher than the state's average.

There has been an increase in homeless families in New York City. The percentage of New York City homeless in families increased from 55.4 percent in 1983 to 63.7 percent in 1986 (City of New York, 1987). This increase in homeless families has increased the demand for family facilities. Nearly $125 million of the $238.9 million allocated by New York City for homeless programs in Fiscal Year 1987 is specifically targeted for homeless families (City of New York, 1987: 27). Much of this money is used to fund accommodations in hotels designated by the city for this purpose. Based on a 1983 study, the average size for families in shelters was found to be 3.6 for NYC and 3.2 for Upstate New York (New York State Department of Social Services, 1984: 8).

RACIAL/ETHNIC COMPOSITION OF THE HOMELESS

A salient aspect of homelessness in New York State is its racial and ethnic composition. Even though only 13.7 percent of the state's total population is black, over half (55.2 percent) of the state's homeless are black. In part, this composition is due to the preponderance of New York City homeless. According to the 1980 census data, 25.2 percent of the NYC population were black, and nearly 20 percent were Hispanics. However, in 1983, 60.3 percent of New York City homeless were black, compared to 39.4 percent for the rest of the state. Outside New York City, the majority of homeless were white. The only other city in New York State where the majority of homeless were black is Rochester (50.3 percent). In the New York City suburbs, 36.7 percent of all homeless were black.

Two other surveys also found that a majority of shelter users in New York City were black. In a 1985 survey of 832 New York City shelter residents, Struening (1986) found that 72 percent were black. Blacks comprised 53 percent of a 1985 New York City survey of 223 first-time shelter users (Hopper, Susser, and Conover, 1986). Blacks are disproportionately represented among the homeless in a city that is 25.3 percent black.

In Albany, 59.7 percent of all homeless were white and 15.8 percent were black in 1983 (New York State Department of Social Services, 1984). A subsequent study by Hagen (1987b) indicates that the black component of homeless in Albany may be greater. In a random sample of homeless persons served by the Capital District Travelers Aid Society, Hagen (1987a, 1987b) found that 53 percent were white, and 40 percent were black. In Schenectady County, where blacks and Hispanics comprise 3 and about 1 percent of the general population respectively, 17 percent of the homeless were found to be black and 4 percent were Hispanics (Hoddy, 1987: 13).

In 1983, Hispanics comprised 24.7 percent of the homeless for the state as a whole. New York City had the highest percentage of Hispanic homeless (35.4 percent). Asian and Pacific Islanders constituted 1.8 percent of the New York State general population, and only 0.3 percent of the homeless statewide in 1983. American Indians, Eskimos, and Aleuts comprised 0.22 percent of the state's population in 1980, 0.2 percent of the homeless persons in families, and 0.6 percent of the homeless single individuals in 1983 (New York State Department of Social Services, 1984). However, in a sample of 832 New York City shelter users Struening (1986) found that 2 percent were Native American.

CAUSES OF HOMELESSNESS

A cursory review of literature indicates that the cause of homelessness is a complex problem and that the homeless are a diverse group. Individuals and families become homeless for a variety of reasons. Attempts to attribute homelessness in New York State to any single factor, such as institutional discharge (otherwise known as "deinstitutionalization"), are simply wrong. A sample of 189 homeless persons in Schenectady provided 23 specific reasons as the primary cause for homelessness. These 23 reasons fell into seven major categories: family disputes, 24 percent; transience-related reasons, 18 percent; eviction, 16 percent; drug and emotional problems, 10 percent; natural disaster, 8 percent; money problems, 8 percent; and "others," 16 percent (Hoddy, 1987: 13). This finding points to an important fact: that lack of affordable housing cannot be blamed for all the homelessness in America. As these data indicate, family disruption is the cause of one case of homeless out of every four in Schenectady County. Any measure that would prevent family violence and disruption, a pervasive phenomenon among all social classes in America, must have an impact on homelessness. Nonhousing factors such as drug problems and mental illness are also important factors. The very low rate of homelessness among Asian Americans also points to the fact that factors other than lack of affordable housing are at play.

Reasons for homelessness can be conceptualized at two levels. First, there are contextual factors such as economic conditions, which operate throughout the state and nation. Homeless people may be unconscious of these factors, or at least unaware that a large number of people become homeless as a result of their economic condition. Second, there are self-reported reasons that the homeless themselves give for being homeless.

Contextual Factors

An important contextual factor related to homelessness is a statewide housing shortage that is especially acute in the New York City area. A study by the New York State Division of Housing and Community Renewal (1984) estimated a "housing gap" (that is, the number of units needed but not available to house the existing population of the state adequately) equal to 1.02 million units. Sixty-two percent of these units were needed in New York City. This estimate indicates only the quantity of needed housing; if affordability is figured into the estimates the actual housing shortage may even be higher.

A second contextual factor is the decline in low-income housing assistance despite continuing high poverty levels. According to big-city mayors, the rising homelessness should be blamed on budget cuts. "Cuts in federal housing budgets over the last seven years are the major cause of homelessness among a growing number of working families with children, big city mayors and homeless families have told a House task force" (Mariano, 1987: D1). Poverty rates for persons

in New York and the Northeast have remained about 10 percent in the aftermath
of the 1982–1983 recession (U.S. Bureau of the Census, 1987: 5). At the same
time, low-income government housing assistance efforts have declined. Since
1981, federal funding for subsidized housing has been slashed by nearly 70
percent (City of New York, 1987: 15). Increases in the public-assistance shelter
allowance in New York State have not kept pace with rising rents, inducing a
growing number of the state's low-income families to pay rent with money
budgeted for food and other necessities (New York Department of Social Services, 1984: 37).

Currently, the state is trying to increase housing assistance to the poor through
the Housing and Homeless Assistance Program. But the level of effort is far
below prior efforts led by the federal government. The Homeless and Housing
Assistance Program is projected to create, preserve, or upgrade 1,076 units in
New York City and 642 units in the rest of the state between 1983 and 1987
(New York State Department of Social Services, 1986: 12). In comparison, over
26,200 units were funded by state and federal programs between 1970 and 1981
in New York City alone (City of New York, 1987: 15). Poverty levels in New
York are higher in the 1980s than in the 1970s; yet, housing assistance to the
poor has fallen off dramatically since 1981.

A third contextual factor is the community health movement, which began in
the late 1950s and entailed a policy of relocating chronically mentally ill patients
from institutions into community settings (Goldman and Morrissey, 1985). This
policy has had noticeable impacts within New York State. The number of in-
patients in state mental institutions dropped from 93,000 in 1955 to 23,000 in
1983 (New York State Department of Social Services, 1984: 39). One result is
a large number of former mental patients living in private housing on fixed
incomes. In 1981 the Community Service Society estimated that approximately
50,000 former mental patients were living in New York City (City of New York,
1987: 16). High city housing prices make it difficult for many of these former
patients to subsist on fixed incomes.

Self-Reported Causes

Respondents to the statewide survey were asked to select the "primary cause
for clients' becoming homeless" from the following list: eviction by landlord
or primary tenant, destruction of housing unit, family disruption, discharge from
institution, and other (New York State Department of Social Services, 1984:
Appendix B). The results indicate that eviction was the leading cause of homelessness. Eviction, either by a primary tenant or by a landlord, was the self-
reported cause of homelessness for 65.9 percent of all homeless in New York
State in 1983. This percentage was higher for families than for single individuals.
Regionally, eviction rates were higher for New York City homeless, probably
reflecting reduced affordability among households due to higher city housing
costs.

Institutional discharge was not a major self-reported reason for homelessness. In 1983, only 4.5 percent of all homeless persons in New York State were homeless due to institutional discharge. The percentage was considerably higher for homeless individuals (7.8 percent) than for persons in homeless families (1.4 percent). Eviction appears to be a more common cause of homelessness among families.

Institutional discharge was a more common self-reported cause of homelessness in "out-state" regions (9.3 percent). The percentages were highest in three medium-sized metropolitan areas: Albany (21.7 percent), the New York City suburbs (11.8 percent), and Rochester (12.8 percent). A 1987 study of homelessness in the Albany area (Hagen, 1987b) indicates that the Albany percentage of institutionally discharged may be less than the percentage found by the New York State Department of Social Services (1983). Hagen (1987b) found that only 13 percent of a random sample ($N = 180$) was homeless due to institutional discharge.

Other results from the statewide study indicate that family disruption (8.1 percent) and the physical destruction of one's home (4.2 percent) were also significant reasons for homelessness. In addition, a high percentage of respondents (27.1 percent) stated that "other" reasons were the primary causes for their homelessness. This indicates that there were significant primary causes of homelessness not spelled out in the survey questionnaire. Study results from Albany and New York City suggest that these other reasons include unemployment, mental illness, alcohol or other substance abuse, and interpersonal relations (cf. Hagen, 1987a; Hopper, Susser, and Conover, 1985).

ESTIMATING THE HOMELESS-VULNERABLE

Homelessness appears to be a much greater problem in New York City than in the rest of the state. A disproportionate number of the state's homeless previously lived in the city. New York City represents 40.3 percent of New York State's population and 73.6 percent of its homeless (New York State Department of Social Services, 1984). In addition, it is also apparent that homelessness is increasing rapidly in the city. The City of New York (1987: 8) estimates that the city's homeless population grew more than 300 percent between 1981 and 1986.

A key question that emerges from this scenario is where do the homeless come from? The 1983 statewide study (New York Department of Social Services, 1984) indicates that a majority of New York City's homeless are former residents who were evicted from dwellings. This suggests that housing affordability is a prime reason for homelessness; for example, a portion of the city's residents were unable to afford housing costs and became homeless after a spell of severe poverty (City of New York, 1987: 11–16).

To test this explanation, a measure of "homeless vulnerability" was constructed, and the New York State file of the *1980 Census of Population and*

Housing, Public Use Micro Data was used to estimate the number of homeless-vulnerable. If the affordability explanation is correct, there should be a large number of persons in New York City who are poor and whose housing rent is a large percentage of household income.

Households living below poverty with a high rent burden have less income to devote to nonhousing items. An interruption in income puts persons in these households in the position of withholding housing payments to compensate for the income loss. Depending on possibilities of acquiring help from government income maintenance programs and/or networks of family and friends, persons in such a household will be vulnerable to becoming homeless.

Homelessness vulnerability is defined as persons in households below the 75 percent poverty cutoff where rent is more than half of the household annual income. Households living below the poverty level are, by definition, unable to afford the basic necessities. These households must find some method of dis-saving (Samuelson, 1973: 213); that is, they need a strategy for consuming more than current income. Since legal credit may be unavailable to a poor household, withholding or delaying rent represents one such strategy. For a household with a rent burden greater than 50 percent of its income, this strategy is a probable and logical alternative.

Rent burden was computed by analyzing the 1980 contract rent and dividing this figure into 1979 household income (multiplied by a factor to adjust to 1980 dollars). All households below the 75 percent poverty cutoff were selected from the Public Use Micro Data file; from this group we selected households whose contract rent was equal to or greater than 50 percent of their annual income. This amounted to 348,900 households defined as homeless-vulnerable.

The results of this procedure are displayed in Table 8.2, which compares the demographic characteristics of the homeless using shelters in 1983 to the homeless-vulnerable in 1980. In 1980 there were 820,900 persons living in households vulnerable to homelessness. The majority of these persons (74.1 percent) were living in New York City. The percentages of homeless-vulnerable and homeless sheltered in New York City vis-à-vis the remainder of the state were virtually equal. To some extent, this statistical equality lends face validity to the homeless-vulnerable construct.

As the data in Table 8.2 show, a significantly higher proportion of homeless-vulnerable are family members than are the sheltered homeless. The high percentage of homeless-vulnerable families in 1980 may explain why post–1980 increases of homeless persons in New York City have been heavily composed of persons in family units (City of New York, 1987: 11–12). We expect that a high percentage of homeless persons would emerge from among the homeless-vulnerable.

It is possible that a person identified as a family member before becoming homeless would lose this membership subsequent to becoming homeless. No doubt the problems of maintaining a family unit under the conditions of homeless-

Table 8.2

Characteristics of the Sheltered Homeless and Homeless-Vulnerable Populations in New York State

Characteristics	Sheltered Homeless (%)[a]	Homeless Vulnerable (%)[b]
In Families	55.4	80.2
Not in Families	44.6	19.8
White	18.8	44.9
Black	55.2	35.0
Hispanic	24.7	31.2
In New York City[c]	73.6	74.1
Outside New York City	26.4	25.9
Male	53.6	41.7
Female	46.4	58.3
Children age 1-6 years	na	18.8

a: Based on sheltered homeless population of 20,210.

b: Based on a homeless-vulnerable population of 820,900.

c: New York City is defined as the area encompassing the five boroughs. Not all homeless persons in New York City lived in the city prior to becoming homeless. In fact, reports indicate that 10.5 percent of the New York City's sheltered homeless were from other states.

na: Not available and/or not applicable.

Source: New York State Department of Social Services (1984) and U.S. Bureau of the Census (1987).

vulnerability are difficult. Even though New York State has facilities for homeless families, there is a pattern of family disintegration among the homeless, resulting in a lower proportion of homeless persons in families (Hagen, 1987b).

Finally, there is a higher proportion of black persons among the sheltered homeless than among the homeless-vulnerable. This indicates that blacks are being disproportionately selected into the homeless sheltered from among the homeless-vulnerable. Housing discrimination may be a factor related to this selection process (cf. Momeni, 1986, 1987). In their study of first-time shelter users in New York City, Hopper, Susser, and Conover (1985) found that selection mechanisms such as landlord preferences for nonminority tenants were important for determining who among the poor community would become homeless. These selection mechanisms were significant because they operate within the city's acute low-income housing shortage. In this environment, landlords can afford to exercise their preferences with assurance that new tenants will quickly appear.

CONCLUSION

Five important generalizations are possible on the basis of the empirical findings reviewed in this chapter. First, homelessness is a condition that disproportionately affects low-income groups in general, and blacks in particular. This is
the case in New York State, and especially in NYC where the proportion of
homeless who are black is more than twice the percentage of black city residents.
While the economic position of blacks is undoubtedly one reason for this finding,
there is some evidence that discrimination is also a factor. Because housing is
a critical resource in a highly urbanized, cold-winter state such as New York,
this finding has obvious implications for social equity.

Second, a substantial percentage of the homeless are members of family units
(persons related by adoption, birth, or marriage living in a common dwelling
unit), including families with children. This finding raises major public policy
challenges in terms of family welfare and the design of shelter facilities. Guar-
anteeing a positive environment for homeless families is not a simple task. New
ideas and programs will be required. Even the term "homeless family" implies
a reality that defies traditional definitions.

Third, the homeless are geographically concentrated in the largest cities of
the state, especially New York City. Homeless persons can be found in every
region of the state, including the rural regions. There appears to be a synergistic
relation between population density and the proportion of homeless—that is,
beyond a certain level of population density, an increment in density would
produce a greater increase in the number of the homeless. But rural, sparsely
populated regions do not contain large numbers of homeless. Providing emergency shelter for thousands of homeless in the large and densely populated cities
across New York has become a major expense; this expense is a major budgetary
item in New York City.

Fourth, a significant number of New Yorkers are vulnerable to homelessness,
and a disproportionate share of the homeless-vulnerable reside in New York
City. This finding implies that the problem is larger than merely sheltering the
existing homeless. Major policy initiatives in the areas of housing and employment opportunities may be necessary to prevent further increases in homelessness
in New York State. State and even federal policymakers need to come to terms
with the larger dimensions of this problem.

And finally, without de-emphasizing the importance and the need for more
affordable housing for poor and low-income groups, the analyses in this chapter
provide some evidence to support the hypothesis that factors other than mere
lack of affordable housing are responsible for the large number of homeless
people in New York (or in the country for that matter). Some of the nonhousing
factors in support of this hypothesis are: (1) family violence and disruptions,
happening among all social classes, account for a significant proportion of homelessness. As long as there are many hourly or daily occurrences of family viol-
ences in the nation, we must expect that there will be a continuous flow of

demand for shelter by the victims of such disruptions. And, (2), despite their minority status, the rate of homelessness is extremely low among the Asian American subgroups possibly in part because of stronger family ties among Asian Americans. Thus, the root cause of homelessness should not and cannot be reduced to the simplistic explanation of lack of affordable housing. There is a definite need for further research in this important area.

NOTES

1. Cuomo and Perales quotations are found in New York State Department of Social Services (1987: Preamble).

2. The regional designations employed here are the same as those employed by the New York State Department of Social Services (1984), which covers the entire state. The divisions are: *Adirondacks*: Jefferson, Lewis, St. Lawrence, Franklin, Clinton, Essex, Hamilton, Herkimer, Fulton, Oneida, Washington, and Warren counties. *Albany*: Montgomery, Saratoga, Schenectady, Albany, and Rensselaer counties. *Buffalo*: Erie and Niagara counties. *Catskills*: Otsego, Delaware, Schoharie, Greene, Columbia, Sullivan, Ulster, and Dutchess counties. *New York City*: the five boroughs—Bronx, Manhattan, Queens, Brooklyn, and Staten Island; *New York City Suburbs*: Suffolk, Nassau, Putnam, Westchester, Orange, and Rockland counties. *Rochester*: Orleans, Monroe, Wayne, Livingston, and Ontario counties. *Southern Tier*: Chautauqua, Cattaraugus, Genesee, Wyoming, Allegany, Steuben, Yates, Schuyler, Chemung, Seneca, Tompkins, Tioga, Cayuga, Cortland, Broome, and Chenango counties. *Syracuse*: Oswego, Onondaga, and Madison counties.

REFERENCES

City of New York. 1985. *Longitudinal Study of Homeless Families: Return to Permanent Housing*. New York: Human Resources Administration. Project Bulletin #85–9.

———. 1986a. *Averting the Need for Emergency Housing: The Feasibility of an Early Warning System for Public Assistance Families*. New York: Human Resources Administration. Project Bulletin #86–3.

———. 1986b. *Homeless Families and Gentrification*. New York: Human Resources Administration. Project Bulletin #86–5.

———. 1986c. *A One-Day "Snapshot" of Homeless Families at the Forbell Street Shelter and Martinque Hotel*. New York: Human Resources Administration.

———. 1986d. *Characteristics and Housing Histories of Families Seeking Shelter from HRA*. New York: Human Resources Administration.

———. 1987. *Toward a Comprehensive Policy on Homelessness*. New York: Mayor's Advisory Task Force on the Homeless.

Council of Community Services of Northeastern New York. 1983. *Research and Program Evaluation Report on the Centralized Emergency Shelter Intake Service*. Albany, N.Y.: Author.

Freeman, Richard B., and Brian Hall. 1987. *Permanent Homelessness in America Today?* Cambridge, Mass.: National Bureau of Economic Research, Working Paper No. 2013.

Goldman, Howard H., and Joseph P. Morrissey. 1985. The Alchemy of Mental Health

Policy: Homelessness and the Fourth Cycle of Reform. *American Journal of Public Health* 75 (7): 727–731.

Hagen, Jan L. 1987a. *The Diversity of the Homeless in New York State*. Albany, N.Y.: Nelson A. Rockefeller Institute of Government. Working Paper No. 30.

———. 1987b. *The Homeless of the Capital District*. Albany, N.Y.: State University of New York–Albany, School of Social Welfare. Mimeo.

Hirschl, Thomas A. 1987. *Finding Shelter in Cortland County: A Local Housing Market Study*. Ithaca, N.Y.: Cornell University, Department of Rural Sociology.

Hoddy, Linda J. 1987. *A Study of Homeless Persons in Schenectady County: March 17– May 30, 1986*. Schenectady, N.Y.: Coalition on the Homeless.

Hopper, Kim, Ezra Susser, and Sarah Conover. 1985. Economies of Market Shift: Deindustrialization and Homelessness in New York City. *Urban Anthropology* 14 (1– 3): 183–236.

Mariano, Ann. 1987. Rising Homelessness Blamed on Budget Cuts. *Washington Post*, December 26: D1, D2.

Momeni, Jamshid A., ed. 1986. *Race, Ethnicity, and Minority Housing in the United States*. Westport, Conn.: Greenwood Press.

———. 1987. *Housing and Racial/Ethnic Minority Status in the United States*. Westport, Conn.: Greenwood Press/Praeger Publishers.

Morrissey, Joseph P., et al. 1985. *The Development and Utilization of the Queens Men's Shelter*. Albany, N.Y.: Bureau of Evaluation Research, New York State Office of Mental Health.

New York State Department of Social Services. 1984. *Homelessness in New York State: A Report to the Governor and the Legislature*. Albany, N.Y.: New York State Department of Social Services.

———. 1986. *Homeless and Housing Assistance Program: Report to the Governor and the Legislature, 1985–86*. Third Quarterly Report. Albany, N.Y.: New York State Department of Social Services.

———. 1987. *Annual Report to the Governor and the Legislature: Homeless Housing and Assistance Program*. Albany, N.Y.

New York State Division of Housing and Community Renewal. 1984. *An Analysis of the Housing Needs of New York State*. New York Urban Systems Research and Engineering.

Rossi, Peter H., et al. 1986. *The Condition of the Homeless of Chicago*. Amherst, Mass., and Chicago: Demographic Research Institute and NORC.

Samuelson, Paul A. 1973. *Economics*, 9th ed. New York: McGraw-Hill.

Struening, Elmer L. 1986. *A Study of Residents of the New York City Shelter System*. New York: New York State Psychiatric Institute.

U.S. Bureau of the Census. 1987. *Money Income and Poverty Status of Families and Persons in the United States*. Current Population Reports, Series P–60, No. 157. Washington, D.C.: Government Printing Office.

U.S. Department of Housing and Urban Development. 1982. *Summary Characteristics for Governmental Units and Standard Metropolitan Statistical Areas: New York*. Washington, D.C.: Government Printing Office. PHC80–3–34, NY.

———. 1984. *A Report to the Secretary on the Homelessness and Emergency Shelters*. Washington, D.C.: HUD, Office of Policy and Development.

Wellington Group. 1984. *A Study of the Homeless Population in Erie County, New York, 1984*. Buffalo, N.Y.: Adult Residential Care Advocates, Inc.

9

Homelessness in Ohio: A Statewide Epidemiological Study

Dee Roth

There is ample evidence that homelessness has existed in the United States since at least the mid-nineteenth century, when there was substantial disruption and dislocation of segments of the population after the Civil War (Bruns, 1980). But it has emerged into the national consciousness as a major social problem in the United States only in the 1980s (Stern, 1984).

The 1980s have also seen a dramatic increase in the amount of literature produced about homelessness. Initially, much of this literature came from the popular media, as print and television journalists discovered the problem and attempted to document it graphically (*Newsweek*, 1982, Alter, 1984; Rouse, 1984). These accounts of homelessness often focused on the most interesting or bizarre case studies—classic "bag ladies," grizzled "street people," or individuals recently released from mental hospitals (Carmody, 1984; *Wall Street Journal*, 1984). While keeping the problem in the public eye, such reports created stereotypical views of homeless people and did not contribute to an understanding of the overall homeless population.

A wide range of research was also begun in the 1980s. Studies were commissioned in a number of cities to give local officials a knowledge base from which to work in planning and developing programs to address the problem (U.S. Conference on Mayors, 1984). In a parallel development, the National Institute of Mental Health funded a number of studies in an attempt to shed more light on the connections between mental illness, the policies of deinstitutionalization, and homelessness (Morrissey and Dennis, 1986). The majority of the research, however, has been limited in both size and scope, for one or more of the following reasons: only a single city was studied; sampling captured only certain types of homeless living conditions, (for example, shelters); sampling was done only in downtown or central city neighborhoods or in major urban areas; or the study focused on only a subset of the homeless population (such as mentally ill individuals or alcoholics).

The Ohio study attempted to reduce many of the methodological limitations of previous research and achieve a more comprehensive picture of homeless people through the inclusion of interviewees from major urban areas as well as rural areas and small cities. In addition, data were collected from individuals in a wide range of homeless conditions, not just in shelters.

Ohio was an excellent setting for this study because the state is, according to 1980 census data, very similar demographically to the rest of the country. Ohio's total 1980 population of 10,797,419, the sixth largest in the nation, was distributed across 88 counties ranging in size from Cuyahoga County with 1,498,295 to Noble County with 11,584. The state is close to the national average on the mix of rural/urban population and in the distribution of race, age, education, and income. Ohio is also undergoing significant changes, both in its economic base and in its population distribution and composition. The state is experiencing firsthand many of the forces and policies that have been purported to be related to the condition of homelessness. The fact that Ohio has a large population and is demographically similar to the rest of the country considerably strengthens the generalizability of study results.

The Ohio study was designed to address some of the existing knowledge gaps about homelessness by examining in depth the characteristics, concerns, and mental health needs of homeless people. The research addressed several areas that have both state and national implications. First, there was an effort to examine many of the major issues surrounding homelessness, such as the demographic characteristics of the population, their mobility patterns, the reasons for their homelessness, their use of social and mental health services, and their level of contact with family and friends. Second, the research looked at the interaction between homelessness and mental health problems and policies from a number of standpoints. The level of mental health problems was assessed in the entire interview population in order to give planners and service providers a data base from which to estimate needs. Special attention was focused on ascertaining the number of homeless people who had had prior mental health service contacts and the nature of those contacts, and the number of individuals who currently needed services.

METHODOLOGY

General Design and Instrumentation

The study contained four different data-collection efforts:

1. A *key informant survey* was done in each of the study counties, in part to ascertain all the physical locations where homeless people could be approached for interviews.

Key informants were persons in positions of authority in their communities in 10 service/agency categories such as public welfare, shelters and soup kitchens, churches, and similar places. In addition to helping the research team establish a sampling frame for homeless persons in their local communities, these individuals were asked about their perceptions and opinions about the characteristics of homeless people in their geographical area, the causes of homelessness, services available, and the like.

2. A *state psychiatric hospital survey* was conducted to identify individuals who were homeless at the time of their admission to adult state psychiatric facilities. All patients admitted from any county in the state during a six-month period were evaluated with regard to their housing status by hospital social workers.

3. A *community mental health agency survey* was designed to identify the individuals discharged from state psychiatric hospitals who had subsequently become homeless for any length of time. Community mental health agencies within the sample counties were asked to identify, from a list of individuals discharged over a two-year period, those who had made contact with their agencies for aftercare services and those who they knew to have been homeless at any time since their discharge.

4. The major effort in this large research project was the *homeless person survey*, in which 979 persons were extensively interviewed by trained field interviewers. The instrument was designed to obtain a wide range of information including demographic characteristics, patterns and causes of homelessness, employment history, mobility, current sources of income, use of social services, physical health problems, social support, drinking behavior, psychiatric hospitalization, and general well-being. In addition, current mental health status of homeless interviewees was assessed using 10 scales of the Psychiatric Status Schedule (Spitzer, Endicott, Fleiss, and Cohen, 1970; Spitzer, Endicott, Cohen, and Nee, 1980). This instrument has been extensively used in psychiatric epidemiological research, and the scales selected measure a wide range of symptoms that represent subjective distress, reality testing disturbance, and behavioral disturbance. In the analysis, the scales were combined into two indices, a Psychiatric Severity Index and a Behavioral Disturbance Index, with scores on the former being indicative of the overall level of psychiatric impairment in the individual.

Sampling Plan for Counties and Homeless Persons

The purpose of the research was to develop descriptive data about the urban and nonurban population of homeless people in Ohio. While it was impossible to use a random sampling plan that was truly representative in the strictest research terms, the investigators attempted to construct a representative sample of the state, as well as solid representation of both nonurban and urban homelessness. Care was taken in designing the sampling plan to assure that individuals throughout the state would be included, and that the sample would contain individuals from both urban and nonurban areas. The first step involved dividing Ohio's 88 counties into five geographic regions. While the five state regions are roughly equivalent in geographic area, they vary considerably in population. Interview quotas were initially established for each region, giving consideration to both the relative proportion of the population and possible regional variability. Within each region, four counties were selected for inclusion in the study. The county containing the major urban center was automatically included, and the other three counties in each region were selected according to the Ohio Department of Health's schema, based on census data, for classifying counties into three categories: urban, mixed, and rural. One county of the mixed type was selected, by using a random numbers table, from all counties of this type in the region. Two counties in the rural category were similarly selected from all rural counties in each region. Hence, the original sample contained 20 counties in Ohio. Homeless people were successfully located and interviewed in 19 of these counties. The one area in which interviewers were not successful in locating and engaging any homeless subjects is an extremely rural community which has one of the largest concentrations of Amish people in the United States.

For sampling purposes, homeless people were stratified according to their homeless condition as defined in the next section. Although the researchers were limited in their ability to use a totally random process, random procedures were used whenever possible, as in the selection of the sampling sites and the selection of individuals within the sites where more than a few homeless people were gathered.

Purposive processes were used to generate the lists of areas where homeless people might be found. In settings like diners, parks, and public buildings, homeless people were selected by encounter and willingness to talk. In these situations, random methods were not feasible. To protect the study from further bias, interviewers kept log sheets of all encounters, documenting the characteristics of those who refused to be interviewed or were incapable of being interviewed. This information was subsequently used to assess whether those refusing to be interviewed were significantly different from those in the sample.

In each urban county, the use of careful purposive methods, the information of key informants, the contact log records, and randomization whenever feasible ensured that the sample drawn was as representative as possible. In the nonurban counties, the project staff tried to interview every identified homeless person, and thus we feel this sample comes close to being the population of homeless individuals in the mixed and rural counties sampled.

Definition of Homelessness

Using the notion that a variety of conditions can constitute "homelessness" and focusing on the physical location component of the definition, homelessness in this study was conceptualized as existing on a continuum. A series of anchor points along this continuum was identified and later critiqued by members of the research team after talking with key informants and pilot testing draft versions of the instrument.

Thus, in this study a person was defined as homeless if he/she sleeps/lives in: (1) limited or no shelter for any length of time (for example, those seeking shelter under bridges, inside door stoops, in cars, in abandoned buildings, in a bus station or all-night cafe, or in any public facility); (2) shelters or missions, run by religious organizations or public agencies for any length of time (facilities that are specifically for homeless people, are run on a drop-in basis, and charge no fee or a minimal fee, including the Salvation Army, Volunteers of America, and Open Shelter of Columbus); (3) cheap hotels or motels when actual length of stay, or the intent to stay, is 45 days or less; and (4) other unique situations that do not fall into the above categories and when the actual length of stay, or the intent to stay, is 45 days or less (for example, staying with family and friends, living in tent cities, or spending a night in jail).

Based on this definition, it was decided that the following kinds of people were not to be considered homeless: battered women living in shelters for battered women; people who had lost their jobs because of cyclical reasons—traditional plant closings—and moved into the homes of relatives or friends for the time that they were unemployed, understanding that their jobs may be regained at some future date; people living in shacks on property that they own; and travelers who, because of lack of money, were forced to accept shelter for the night, but who had come from a permanent home and were going to a permanent home. Further, it was necessary to put a cap on length of stay, or intent to stay, in categories three and four to differentiate between people who move in and out of those settings and those who tended to be there more permanently.

KEY INFORMANT SURVEY RESULTS

A total of 164 key informants were interviewed as representatives of various organizations that had contact with homeless people in the sample counties. More than one quarter of persons interviewed came from religious organizations, including the Salvation Army; other represented agencies included law enforcement, United Way, public welfare, community mental health, and others. Differences were found in the composition of the key informant group in urban and nonurban counties. People who worked with religious organizations made up 40 percent of the group in urban areas, which is probably an indication of more active participation of church-supported shelters, soup kitchens, and food pantries as part of the network of survival services for homeless people in large cities. In contrast, nearly a quarter of key informants in nonurban areas represented public welfare and/or children's services agencies, with less than 20 percent being from religious organizations and 16 percent being from community mental health. In addition, to help establish the lists of potential sampling sites for their areas, key informants were asked to describe the characteristics and service needs of homeless people in their areas and indicate how well they thought local agencies were meeting those needs. Few key informants with whom interviewers spoke were able to identify authoritatively the characteristics of different types of homeless people and their prevalence in the community. In general, urban formal service providers not involved with direct client services to homeless people knew little about the homeless population. Most were surprised that their organizations would be asked about the problem. This was not as frequently the case with those in nonurban systems. Perhaps the large client loads and professional orientations of the urban key informants, as compared with the smaller client loads, fewer homeless people, and the personalized nature of services in the nonurban counties, accounted for urban/nonurban differences.

Overall, responses by key informants to interviewer's questions varied enormously. Those directly involved in services to homeless people tended to focus on a specific kind of problem or characteristic of only some groups, but not all. For example, service providers operating soup kitchens perceived the homeless population to be largely composed of transients, poor people, and an occasional unemployed person "at the end of his rope." They did not tend to depict them as, for example, female single parents who had been abused and/or abandoned by their spouses. Almost no key informants were knowledgeable about the overall homeless population in their counties. Among the responses: (a) One fourth of key informants said they could not estimate the number of homeless people in their area while the others gave figures that ranged from zero to 10,000; (b) Most said the numbers of homeless people are increasing; (c) Over one third said that no homeless people in their area were employed; (d) The most important factors contributing to homelessness were seen as unemployment, family conflict, alcohol and drug abuse, psychological disorder, eviction, and high rents; (e) Key informants estimated that 60 percent of the homeless population had psychological problems, 40 percent had alcohol problems, and 35 percent had chronic health problems; (f) Shelters, housing assistance, and financial aid were seen as the three most needed services, but the three most available services were cited as mental health care, hospital emergency room care, and soup kitchens/food pantries.

In some regions of the state, key informants' descriptions of the causes of homelessness and the problems of homeless people were consistent with the services they indicated were needed. In some regions, they were not. For some regions, there were also inconsistencies between what the key informants told interviewers about the characteristics and problems of the homeless populations in their areas and what was found in the research. It seems clear that key informants and human service systems in local communities could benefit from more specific information about homeless people in their areas in order to address the problems of this population better.

STATE PSYCHIATRIC HOSPITAL SURVEY RESULTS

Almost all adult state hospitals admitted some homeless individuals during the six-month period under study. The two exceptions were long-term care hospitals, which primarily admit patients from other facilities. Overall, 7 percent of hospital admissions were judged by social workers to be homeless at the time of admission.

In addition to determining whether patients were homeless at the time of admission, social workers categorized these individuals into the four levels of homelessness delineated in the initial research design. Most of the homeless patients fell into two of the categories. Level 1 (limited or no shelter) accounted for 37 percent of the homeless admissions; Level 2 (shelter or mission) for 18 percent; Level 3 (cheap motels and hotels) for only 9 percent; and Level 4 (others/with family or friends) accounted for 37 percent of those individuals who were homeless at the time of admission. From the brief unstructured descriptions of the residential status of these patients provided by many of the social workers as supporting data, two distinct patterns of homelessness for hospitalized individuals seemed to emerge: (1) 109 patients (22 percent) had a history of eviction or loss of residence concurrent with the worsening of their psychiatric status, resulting in aggressive or otherwise intolerable behavior (beating up relatives or roommates, being destructive to the apartment, and the like); these patients were more often living with relatives or friends for relatively short periods of time (Level 4) at the time of admission; (2) 96 patients (20 percent) were described as migrants, moving from place to place and, in many instances, from state to state, apparently incapable of settling down; they were generally less severely disabled than those in the previous group and used to living more frequently on the streets (Level 1), in public shelters (Level 2), or in cheap motels for short periods of time (Level 3).

COMMUNITY MENTAL HEALTH AGENCY
SURVEY RESULTS

Among the patients discharged from state psychiatric hospitals to the sample areas during a two-year period, 5,448 (61 percent) were identified in the active files of the community mental health agencies in urban areas, and 597 (71 percent) in those of the community agencies in nonurban areas. A relatively small but significant proportion of the patients discharged were identified as having become homeless by the community mental health agencies at some point after discharge from the hospital.

There were 330 homeless individuals (4 percent of those discharged) identified in urban areas, and 33 (4 percent of those discharged) in nonurban areas. Although the proportion of patients discharged who were found homeless was the same, these individuals were actually more than twice as numerous when compared to the population in urban areas (8.9 per 100,000 population) than in nonurban areas (4.1 per 100,000 population). These findings are with the rates of patients discharged during the study period, which were 242.7 per 100,000 population in urban areas and 105.0 in nonurban areas.

In addition to determining whether individuals in the discharge sample were homeless, community mental health agency personnel were asked to categorize those individuals into the four levels of homelessness delineated in the initial research design. Those patients who became homeless in urban areas were almost equally likely to be living on the streets (Level 1, 33 percent), in shelters (Level 2, 29 percent), or for brief periods with family and friends, or in other unique situations (Level 4, 33 percent). In contrast, nearly half of the patients who became homeless in nonurban areas were in Level 4.

HOMELESS PERSON SURVEY RESULTS

Demographics

As can be seen in Table 9.1, the group of homeless people interviewed was 81 percent male and 19 percent female. This distribution is quite different from that of the overall Ohio population, which was 47 percent male and 53 percent female based on the 1980 census. Minorities accounted for one third of the homeless population; in comparison, according to the 1980 census, the Ohio population consists of 10 percent minorities.

Homeless interviewees spanned a wide age range—from 16 to 83 years old, with the average age being 37 and the median age being 34. In some age groups, such as 40–49 and 50–59, the homeless population is proportionally similar to the overall Ohio population. However, the 30–39 age group and the group over 60 differ in their proportions from Ohio as a whole. A little over half of the homeless group had not graduated from high school, compared to 36 percent in the overall Ohio population. However, 45 percent of the homeless group was made up of high school graduates, and 15 percent had attended or had graduated from college. Nearly half of the homeless respondents had never been married, and another 44 percent were either separated, widowed, or divorced. These figures contrast dramatically with the overall Ohio population, in which 59 percent were married, and only 16 percent were separated, widowed, or divorced. Almost 32 percent of the homeless sample indicated that they were veterans, including 9 percent who said they were Vietnam veterans. In the overall Ohio population aged 16 years and over, 17 percent were veterans. However, some of the contrast between the two groups is a function of the fact that the homeless sample is 81 percent male, and males have a higher likelihood of having served in the military. Of the male homeless population, 39 percent were veterans.

Respondents were asked if they had ever been in jail or prison. Fifty-eight percent indicated that they had. No census data for the overall Ohio population are available for comparison. Homeless people were found in all types of counties (urban, rural, and mixed) in Ohio. Of the 979 interviews completed, 189 (19 percent) were from nonurban areas. Homeless persons in the urban counties differ demographically from homeless persons in the nonurban counties. In terms of age, 32 percent of homeless persons in urban counties were 29 years old or younger, while 39 percent were 40 years or older. Homeless persons in nonurban counties tended to be younger: 48 percent were 29 years old or younger, while only 26 percent were 40 years or older. In the urban counties, homeless persons were more likely to be male than in the nonurban counties (84 as opposed to 68 percent). Not surprisingly, given the general population demographic profile of the different types of counties, homeless persons in the rural and mixed counties

Table 9.1
Demographics of the Homeless Sample, Compared to Ohio Population

Characteristic	Homeless Sample No.	% of Total	1980 Census
Sex			
Male	793	81.0	47.2
Female	186	19.0	52.8
Ethnicity			
White	639	65.3	89.8
Black	292	29.8	9.2
Hispanic	33	3.4	0.9
Other	6	0.6	0.1
Age			
18-29 years	340	34.7	30.0
30-39 years	270	27.6	18.9
40-49 years	164	16.8	14.2
50-59 years	130	13.3	15.2
60 years and over	63	6.4	21.7
Education			
Less than high school graduate	533	54.4	36.1
High school graduate	298	30.4	39.2
At least some college	141	14.4	24.7
Marital Status			
Married, living together	109	11.1	58.8
Separated, widowed, divorced	425	43.4	16.0
Never married	438	44.7	25.2
Veteran Status			
Yes	310	31.7	17.3
Vietnam veteran	83	8.5	4.4
No	665	67.9	82.7
Ever Been in Jail/Prison			
Yes	573	58.5	na
No	398	40.7	na

na: Not available and/or not applicable.

were almost all white (92 percent). In the urban counties, 59 percent of the homeless persons were white, 36 percent were black, 4 percent were Hispanics, and 1 percent identified with other racial groups.

Relatively few urban homeless people were currently married or living with a partner (8 percent). Almost half had never been married. In the nonurban counties, 23 percent were currently married or cohabiting; 38 percent had never married. There were no significant differences among the urban and nonurban counties in terms of the educational attainment of homeless persons. Homeless

persons in the urban counties were slightly more likely to have served in the
military—33 percent versus 24 percent in the nonurban counties.

Length of Homelessness

For most of the individuals interviewed, homelessness was a relatively new
phenomenon. Nearly 75 percent of all respondents reported being homeless for
one year or less; the median was 60 days. However, because of the extreme
scores of some of the respondents (5 percent were homeless longer than eight
years, including nine people who had been homeless for over 30 years), the
mean length of homelessness was found to be 618 days.

Reasons for Homelessness

Respondents gave many reasons, often interrelated, for their homelessness.
When asked to specify the one major reason, economic factors (unemployment,
problems paying rent, eviction, and lack of government support) were cited by
half of the sample. Family problems were cited by 21 percent of the respondents
as the major reason for their homelessness. The idea of homeless people being
on the street by choice is not borne out by the data, since only 6 percent of the
respondents had indicated that they "just like to move around." The following
data show the main reasons and their relative importance as a cause of homelessness. As these data point out, unemployment, lack of affordable housing,
and family problems constituted the three most important reasons for homelessness in Ohio.

Reason	Number	Percent of Total
Unemployment	213	21.7
Problems paying rent	136	13.9
Family conflict	130	13.3
Other reasons	92	9.4
Family dissolution	78	8.0
Alcohol/drug abuse	71	7.3
Just like to move around	60	6.1
Government benefits stopped	27	2.8
Disaster	24	2.5
Deinstitutionalization	24	2.5
Was in jail/prison	16	1.6

Transience

In general, Ohio's homeless people interviewed did not appear as highly mobile
or transient as is typically depicted in the popular press. Slightly less than 60

percent had stayed in two or fewer different places, with slightly less than 85 percent staying in four or fewer different places during the past month. Perhaps a more important finding with implications for local service delivery is that 64 percent of respondents were either long-term (more than one year) or permanent residents of the area where they were interviewed. Thirty-one percent of the respondents were fairly recent arrivals in their counties, having been there six months or less. Nonpermanent residents came to the county where they were interviewed for a variety of reasons. Slightly more than 25 percent came seeking assistance from family and friends, and 28 percent came either to look for a job or to take a job. Only 9 percent came seeking public social support such as shelter accommodations or social services.

Employment History

In response to questions about their work history, 855 homeless respondents (87 percent) indicated that they had had a job at some point in their lives, including 242 people (25 percent) who said they had worked for pay in the past month. A third of those who had worked in the past month had done so as day laborers, but 25 percent had permanent, full-time jobs. Individuals who had worked in the past but who were not now employed were asked in what year they last worked. Over one third reported having last worked in the past 18 months, and about another one third said they last worked between 1978 and 1982. In all, 622 homeless respondents (63 percent) indicated that they had had some income during the past month. Welfare, earnings, or Social Security were the primary sources of income for over 80 percent of those respondents.

Social Services

Respondents were asked whether or not they had used specific kinds of social services within the past month. Of the six social services listed in the questionnaire, community soup kitchens were mentioned most (61 percent). Shelters were the second most used service (56 percent), followed by welfare/general relief (44 percent). Among women, only 12 percent had ever used a shelter for battered women, despite much higher percentages of women indicating family conflict as their major reason for homelessness.

Social Service	Total	Users	Percent of Total
Community kitchens	979	595	60.8
Shelters	979	552	56.4
Welfare/general relief	979	435	44.4
Hospital emergency rooms	979	240	24.5
Shelters for battered women	186	23	12.4
Community mental health centers	979	119	12.2

The interviewers asked homeless persons a number of questions about the degree of their contact with family and friends and the amount of help they were able to get from their social network. The results indicate that they were not, by and large, an isolated group. Eighty percent of respondents had relatives and, of this group, half had had contact with them within the past 14 days and 75 percent had had contact within the past three months. Almost as many homeless people (72 percent) said they had friends, and over 70 percent of this group had had contact with their friends in the past week. Perhaps the more critical issue relates to the extent of material assistance provided by such social support networks.

When asked specifically whether they could count on their family or friends for help, 36 percent of respondents said they could count on their relatives for help, and 41 percent said they could count on friends. Comparative data are available from another study in which these same two questions were asked of a random sample of the general adult population in five rural Ohio counties (Stefl, 1983). In that sample, 92 percent said that they could count on their relatives for help, and 95 percent indicated that they could get help from their friends. This shows that although the homeless population is not completely isolated from family and friends, the extent of their contact with family and friends is significantly less than that among the general population.

Typology of Homeless People

A major concern of this study was to focus on the many varieties of homelessness, not just on street or shelter people, as has been done in numerous other studies. The primary reason for this focus was the assumption that homelessness is a much broader problem than the service needs for those on the street and in shelters would indicate. By casting the net fairly widely, a more comprehensive picture was developed.

Based on study results and key informant consultation, individuals interviewed fell into three groups, which exhibited different homeless life-styles: (1) "Street people" were those who were interviewed on the street or in other open settings and who reported that they had not stayed in shelters for homeless people for at least a month. They tended to be older, less likely to have held a job or have income, and more likely to report alcohol abuse. Nearly 15 percent of the sample fell into this category. (2) "Shelter people" were individuals who were frequent or occasional users of public shelters. These people tended to have been homeless for longer periods of time, and to be users of other social services as well, and they constituted 60 percent of the study group. (3) "Resource people" were individuals who managed to stay off the streets and were able to avoid the shelter system by staying in cheap hotels for short periods of time when money was available or by staying with friends and/or relatives for a few days at a time. These individuals appeared to have more resources, such as part-time work, social support, or welfare payments, which allowed them more choices to maintain themselves while homeless. They tended to be younger than the individuals in the other two groups, have a higher percentage of women, and have fewer serious problems. One-quarter of the sample fell into this category.

Physical and Mental Health Problems

The Ohio study found varying levels of health and mental health problems within the homeless population as noted below:

Problem	Number	Percent of Total
Physical health problems	301	30.7
Problem drinking	204	20.8
Prior psychiatric hospitalization	293	29.9
Psychiatric impairment	301	30.7
Behavioral disturbance	526	53.7

Respondents were asked whether they had any physical health problems that they felt were serious enough to warrant a doctor's attention. Nearly one third said yes and subsequently listed a wide variety of problems, ranging from ill-defined conditions such as headaches, queasiness in the stomach, or pains somewhere in the body, to serious chronic conditions such as heart disease and respiratory problems. Five percent of the respondents had injuries that needed treatment, and nine of the homeless women were pregnant at the time of the interview.

Because of the association between homelessness and alcohol, respondents were also asked about the level of alcohol consumption and alcohol problems. Forty-five percent of the group said they had been drinking "some" during the past month and 19 percent said "a lot." Regardless of their response relative to alcohol consumption, all individuals in the study were asked whether they had at any point in their lives gone to anyone for help about their drinking. A little over one fourth indicated that they had. The study was not designed to yield a clinical diagnosis of alcoholism, but the author worked with researchers at the National Institute for Alcoholism and Alcohol Abuse to construct an index of "problem drinking," which scored those individuals who had previously sought help for a drinking problem but who were still drinking. By this measure, 21 percent of the homeless population can be considered to be likely alcoholics. This group was almost entirely males and differed from the rest of the homeless population in that they were older, had been homeless longer, were more transient, and were more likely to have been in jail.

A major focus of the Ohio study was on the extent to which the population was composed of former psychiatric hospital patients, particularly since this is a constant theme in popular media portrayals of homelessness. Thirty percent of study subjects had had at least one psychiatric hospitalization; 6 percent reported having been in a Veterans' Administration facility, 13 percent had been in a general hospital psychiatric unit, and 18 percent had been treated in a state hospital. The median number of hospitalizations among those who had been in a state hospital was two, and 60 percent of the group indicated that community living arrangements had been made for them when they left the hospital. About half of the group had been released in the 18 months prior to the study, but a quarter of these individuals had been out of the hospital for more than five years.

Examination of the current psychiatric status of the sample showed a lower prevalence of psychiatric impairment than had been reported in some previous studies conducted of shelter residents in major East Coast cities. Thirty-one percent exhibited the presence of at least one symptom on the Psychiatric Severity Index at a sufficiently high level to qualify as impairment. Most individuals scored on only one of the four symptom scales which composed this index: depression/anxiety, suicide/self-mutilation, grandiosity, and suspicion/persecutions/hallucinations. Fewer than 5 percent scored on three or four of the scales. Slightly over half of the group scored on one or more of the five symptom scales that comprise the Behavioral Disturbance Severity Index. Translating these data into statements about the level of mental health needs is very difficult, however, because the scales measure behaviors that can be either symptoms of mental illness or simple reflections of the stresses and difficulties of survival in the homeless life-style. For example, the most prevalent items scored by the sample were a dirty and disheveled appearance and a lowered or flat level of emotion. Hence the Psychiatric Severity Index is considered the best measure of mental health status for the homeless population.

In order to measure homeless people's sense of their own mental health status, interviewees were asked two general well-being items drawn from the Florida Health Study (Schwab, Bell, Warheit, and Schwab, 1979), a large-scale study of psychiatric epidemiology conducted in the early 1970s. The questions have been used widely for mental health needs assessment purposes, including some studies done in Ohio.

When homeless respondents were asked how they would rate their present nerves, spirits, outlook, or mental health, over 40 percent responded with "good" or "excellent," and only 8 percent said "very bad." These results would seem to indicate that a surprisingly large percentage of homeless people are in good spirits despite their circumstances. However, comparative data on these same two items are available from two random probability samples of 2,183 people in five rural southern Ohio counties (Stefl, 1983). These data seem to indicate that the general population rates its spirits and outlook as being substantially higher than the homeless population.

| Response | Homeless | | Stefl/Ohio (%) |
	Number	Percent of Total	(N=2,183)
Excellent	90	9.2	33.0
Good	305	31.2	52.4
Fair	338	34.5	12.6
Poor	152	15.5	1.3
Very bad	77	7.9	0.6

Respondents were also asked how satisfying their lives had been. One third indicated that they had been very satisfying or somewhat satisfying, but 28 percent rated their lives as not very or not at all satisfying. In this instance, comparisons with the Ohio general population sample are even more dramatic, since 87 percent of the latter group said they considered their lives to have been very satisfying or somewhat satisfying.

| Response | Homeless | | Stefl/Ohio (%) |
	Number	Percent of Total	(N=2,183)
Very satisfying	96	9.8	58.3
Somewhat satisfying	232	23.7	28.2
Mixed	360	36.8	11.1
Not very satisfying	196	20.0	1.9
Not at all satisfying	79	8.1	0.6

SERVICE NEEDS

Perhaps the most important findings of the research are that homelessness is a multifaceted issue, that homeless people have a variety of problems, and that there are subtypes within the homeless population that need to be distinguished in order for the phenomenon of homelessness to be more fully understood. However, planners, policymakers, and service providers attempting to develop strategies to ameliorate the condition of homelessness should first consider the overall level of magnitude of various problems within the homeless population. Table 9.2 presents an overview of the relative proportions of the Ohio sample who were experiencing various problems at the time of the study.

The first and most pressing need is for permanent and adequate housing. This may seem obvious when the subject is homelessness, but the lack of permanent housing was the only problem found in 100 percent of the study sample. All of Ohio's major cities have experienced large-scale urban renewal of their downtown areas within the last decade, and these projects have destroyed countless units of very low-income housing, which have not been replaced.

It initially seemed surprising that many of the subjects did have some form of income. As a group, homeless people are not totally without financial re-

Table 9.2
Service Needs Hierarchy of Homeless People in Ohio

Area	Percent Reporting Problems
Housing:	100.0
Employment:	
No work for pay during last month	75.3
Looked, could not find work	29.5
Disabled, could not work	13.0
Do not want to work	3.0
Not job ready	5.0
Social Support:	
No relatives, or cannot count on relatives	64.2
No friends, or cannot count on friends	58.1
Neither friends nor relatives, or cannot	
count on friends or relatives	43.1
Income:	
No income at all during past month	36.6
Welfare as major source of income	23.8
Problems paying rent as major reason for homelessness	13.9
Alcohol/Drug Use:	
Reported alcohol use	64.2
Both alcohol and drug or medication use	39.2
Reported having sought alcohol treatment	26.6
Any type of drug or medication use	32.2
Probable alcoholism	20.8
Mental Health:	
Psychiatric symptom presence requiring service	30.7
Unmet needs for mental health services	24.3
Physical Health:	
Any type of physical health problem	30.7

sources; it is more the case that their meager income is insufficient to purchase/rent permanent housing.

Three quarters of the homeless subjects had not worked for pay in the past month. While some of these individuals indicated that they were disabled and could not work, half of those not currently working said they had looked for work but had been unable to find any. Taken together, these figures suggest a great need for jobs and job-related services to enhance the employment skills of homeless people.

A majority of homeless people said they used alcohol, and nearly one quarter of the population would probably fall into a clinical diagnosis of alcoholism.

Many of these individuals have been homeless for long periods of time and seem to mirror the old "Bowery" image of the alcoholic dropout, living on the fringes of society. Services to these individuals will need to be longer-term and targeted at alcoholism as well as reintegration into the community. Study data on drug use included both prescription and nonprescription drugs, so it is difficult to separate illegal or problematic behaviors in this category. Whether prescribed or not, however, about a third of the homeless group had used drugs, and nearly 40 percent were ingesting both drugs and alcohol. This pattern needs to be taken into account in the provision of both social and health services.

Slightly less than a third of the homeless population showed a need for physical or mental health services. In the area of physical health, homeless people have all of the diseases and problems prevalent in the general population as well as the types of injuries and conditions associated with life on the streets. Likewise, it is difficult and perhaps not even useful to separate, for service purposes, those psychiatric problems that are chronic conditions and occurred prior to homelessness and those that have arisen as a result of a homeless life-style. Regardless of their level or type of psychiatric problem, study results show that most homeless persons who need mental health services are not receiving them (Roth, Bean, and Hyde, 1986). Homeless persons have difficulty fitting into traditional service settings, and community mental health agencies have only rarely attempted the kind of aggressive outreach necessary to engage this population.

Homelessness is clearly a multifaceted problem, for which no one sector of the system is totally or even primarily responsible, and which no one sector of the system will be able to ameliorate on its own. All appropriate service systems must collaborate to address the interrelated needs of homeless individuals. This strategy is difficult and time-consuming, because service systems have not had a great deal of experience working with each other, but it is the strategy that has the best chance to arrive at meaningful and long-term solutions to the problems of homelessness.

SUMMARY

This chapter presents results from a statewide epidemiological study of homeless people in Ohio. The study developed a more comprehensive picture of the overall homeless population than had previously been available through seeking out homeless people in 19 different counties. The counties were randomly selected to include major urban areas, small cities, and rural areas. In addition, the research developed the concept of levels of homelessness. Interview quotas were stratified so that data were collected from individuals in a wide range of homeless conditions, not just in shelters. The research looked at the interaction between homelessness and mental health problems and policies from a number of standpoints. The level of mental health problems was assessed in the entire interview population, in order to give planners and service providers a data base from which to estimate needs. Special attention was focused on ascertaining the proportion of homeless people who had had prior mental health service contacts and the proportion of the overall homeless population who had unmet mental health needs.

The study had four parts: (1) interviews with 130 knowledgeable key inform-ants around the state concerning their perceptions of the problems of homeless-ness in their areas; (2) face-to-face interviews with nearly 1,000 homeless people (including questions about reasons for homelessness, current mental health status, living arrangements, history of psychiatric hospitalization, employment history and income, contact with family and friends, use of social services, medical problems, demographic information, general well-being, and migration patterns); (3) a survey of community mental health agencies in the sample counties to determine how many individuals discharged from state psychiatric hospitals subsequently became homeless; and (4) monitoring of all state psychiatric hos-pital admissions over six months to determine the number of individuals who were homeless at the time of admission.

Perhaps the most important findings of the research are that homelessness is a multifaceted issue, that homeless people have a variety of problems, and that there are subtypes within the homeless population that need to be distinguished in order for the phenomenon of homelessness to be more fully understood. However, after hearing at length from nearly 1,000 homeless people across Ohio, economic factors emerged as a primary theme. For half the group, economic reasons were the major cause of their homelessness, and nearly one quarter cited family problems as the reason for homelessness.

Many of the stereotypes of homeless people in the popular literature were not supported by study findings. The group was less mobile—most had stayed in two or fewer places in the past month—and less transient than might have been expected: 64 percent had either been born in the counties in which they were interviewed or had lived there longer than a year. Most had worked at some point in their lives and a quarter had worked for pay in the past month. Nearly half of those who had been employed in the past but were not working now said they had looked for a job but had been unable to find one. Almost two thirds had some source of income in the past month, primarily from welfare, earnings, or Social Security. The picture that emerged is one of a largely indigenous population who are not totally without funds but whose income is not sufficient to pay for permanent housing.

In addition to their lack of housing, jobs, and resources, homeless people have a variety of other problems. Only a third said they had relatives they could count on, and 41 percent said they had friends they could count on. This seems to indicate that not all homeless people are isolated from social support as has been portrayed in the popular literature. However, comparative data from a needs assessment in five rural southern Ohio counties provides a more realistic contrast. In that study, 92 percent of the general population said they had relatives they could count on, and 95 percent said they had friends. A third of our sample had physical health problems and almost an equal percentage had psychiatric problems. Thirty percent had had a psychiatric hospitalization. Well over half said they had been drinking some or a lot in the past month, and 27 percent indicated they had sought help for a drinking problem at some point in their lives.

ACKNOWLEDGMENT

Research funded by the National Institute of Mental Health, Grant No. 1R18MH38877–01. The authors gratefully acknowledge the assistance of Gerald Bean, Terry Buss, Richard J. First, Harvey Hilbert, Thomas P. Holland, Steven R. Howe, James A. King, Nancy Lust, William A. Muraco, Mary E. Stefl, and Beverly G. Toomey in conducting the study.

REFERENCES

Alter, Jonathan. 1984. Homeless in America. *Newsweek* (January 20): 20–29.

Bruns, Richard. 1980. *Knights of the Road: A Hobo History*. New York: Methaven Press.

Carmody, Dierdre. 1984. The Tangled Life and Mind of Judy whose Home is the Street. *New York Times* (December 17).

Morrissey, Joseph, and Deborah Dennis. 1986. *NIMH-Funded Research Concerning Homeless Mentally Ill Persons: Implications for Policy and Practice*. Rockville, Md.: National Institute of Mental Health, Alcohol, Drug Abuse, and Mental Health Administration, Public Health Service, U.S. Department of Health and Human Services.

Newsweek 1982. Down and Out in America. (March 15): 28–29.

Roth, Dee, Gerald J. Bean, and Pamela S. Hyde. 1986. Homelessness and Mental Health Policy: Developing an Appropriate Role for the 1980s. *Community Mental Health Journal* 22:3 (Fall, 1986): 203–214.

Rouse, Vince. Pittsburgh's Homeless. *Pittsburgh Press Sunday Magazine* (April 8): 10–20.

Schwab, John J., Roger A. Bell, George J. Warheit, and R. B. Schwab. 1979. *Social Order and Mental Health*. New York: Brunner/Mazel.

Spitzer, Robert L., Jean Endicott, Joseph L. Fleiss, and Jacob Cohen. 1970. The Psychiatric Status Schedule: A Technique for Evaluating Psychopathology and Impairment in Role Functioning. *Archives of General Psychiatry* 23: 41–55.

Spitzer, Robert L., Jean Endicott, Jacob Cohen, and John Nee. 1980. The Psychiatric Status Schedule for Epidemiological Research. *Archives of General Psychiatry* 37: 1193–1197.

Stefl, Mary E. 1983. *The Impact of Rapid Social Change on the Mental Health of a Rural Population*. Cincinnati, Ohio: University of Cincinnati; Ohio Department of Mental Health Office of Program Evaluation and Research.

Stern, Mark J. 1984. The Emergence of the Homeless as a Public Problem. *Social Service Review* 58: 291–296.

U.S. Conference of Mayors. 1984. *Homelessness in America's Cities: Ten Case Studies*. Washington, D.C.

Wall Street Journal. 1984. Untouchables. Editorial (May 8).

10

Homelessness in the Pacific Northwest

Gerald F. Blake and Martin L. Abbott

The homeless problem in the northwest region of the United States is concentrated in the metropolitan areas of two major cities, Portland, Oregon (1984 population: 375,000) and Seattle, Washington (1984 population: 490,000). The most recent (1986) estimate of the homeless population in Oregon is 10,000 persons, with over 6,000 homeless persons concentrated in Portland's North Burnside–Old Town district (Banzer, 1987; U.S. Conference of Mayors, 1986a). The state of Washington is estimated to have 5,000 to 7,000 homeless, with between 3,000 to 4,000 homeless persons concentrated in the downtown Seattle area (Washington State Department of Community Development, 1987; Strategy for the Downtown Homeless, 1986).

Estimates of the number of people who are homeless vary, depending on who is conducting the research, how homelessness is defined, and the method used to collect the data (Schwab, 1986). Nationally, estimates of the number of homeless range from a low of 250,000 to 350,000 to between 2 and 4 million persons (Peroff, 1987; Irwin, 1986; Hombs and Snyder, 1982).

Whichever base estimate is used, there remains little doubt that the number of homeless is increasing and the scope of the problem is changing in most major American cities. A recent U.S. Conference of Mayors report (1986a) surveyed 25 U.S. cities in late 1985 and found that the demand for emergency shelter increased by an average of 25 percent in 23 of the 25 cities studied. The report also found that the number of families with children and the number of single young adults who were homeless had grown significantly. For example, the demand for emergency food assistance, especially for families with children, increased by 28 to 30 percent during 1985 alone. Overall, the survey reported that 28 percent of the homeless were families, 12 percent were single women, and 60 percent were single men.

HISTORY OF HOMELESSNESS IN THE NORTHWEST

An understanding of the history of homelessness must include an examination of "skid row," since these areas have developed in order to support large numbers of homeless individuals who otherwise would be without means of survival. Bogue (1963) describes a skid-row district as a natural area in the city containing concentrations of the following institutions: lodging houses and cheap hotels, inexpensive restaurants, secondhand stores and outfitters, homeless male missions, and employment agencies specializing in unskilled labor positions (temporary service jobs and seasonal farm employment).

The skid-row district in Portland was first recognizable as an ecological area as early as 1905 (Sawyer, 1985); skid row in Seattle became evident about 1910. Since Portland's skid row and history of homelessness have received a good deal of research attention, it will serve to illustrate the nature of homelessness as it existed in the Pacific Northwest.

Historically, Portland and Seattle have each had sizable homeless populations and well-established districts within their downtowns where the homeless and other hard-to-house people live. During the 1913–1915 depression, Portland's skid-row district was proportionally the largest in the nation (Sawyer, 1985). During the 1930s' Great Depression, Portland's skid row, like others across the nation, was overwhelmed with an influx of poor, destitute, and homeless people. Studies of homelessness in the 1930s noted with alarm the shift in the hobo population from seasoned middle-aged men to child tramps and females (Minehan, 1934). *The Oregonian* (August 13, 1933: 10) reported, "The Portland tramp of 1934 was likely to be either an aged man, periodically riding boxcars, but usually wandering along little used highways, or a vagrant child."

In 1938, the average age of the homeless was 32 years. Eighty-five percent were unskilled laborers, and 93 percent were single individuals (Sawyer, 1985). In the years after World War II, Portland's skid row declined in size, but still ranked eighth in size nationally (Bogue, 1963).

Portland and Seattle's relatively long experience with homelessness arose from a combination of local and regional circumstances and exogenous economic, political, and social factors. Sawyer (1985: 495–496) specified several determinants of Portland's homeless problem:

1. Portland's foundation as a river-oriented marketing center. The ocean port attracted large numbers of seaman and gamblers, revelers and prostitutes. Portland's skid row emerged from the vice districts surrounding the docks and waterfront areas that housed laborers, transients, and single, older men.

2. Portland was the early regional leader in the hotel trade, catering to both the transient and tourist populations. Portland's explosive growth between 1900 and 1913 exhausted the existing housing market, creating a demand for hotels and other short-term housing. Over time, as the city grew into the suburbs, downtown hotels became underused and thus formed the base for the evolution of the current skid-row district.

3. The transcontinental railroad established Portland as a transportation hub in the region providing new jobs for laborers and railroad workers. This attracted more men to the area and stimulated faster growth of the city.

4. Portland was the contract labor center for the region. Contract labor offices have long been fixtures on skid row, providing temporary, seasonal workers for agriculture and other industries.

The Decline of Portland's Skid Row, 1930–1983

Portland's skid row declined in size and population from the period after the Great Depression through the late 1970s. The transition saw the skid-row district shrink in size from 150 city blocks in 1950 to 16 blocks in 1983, a reduction of nearly 90 percent. Portland experienced a greater rate of shrinkage in its skid row than other U.S. cities, where the average size declined from 37 to 7 city blocks between 1950 and 1979, an average reduction of 80 percent (King, 1982).

Portland's skid row also saw numerous buildings destroyed as various skid-row removal schemes and urban renewal projects were implemented. In all, over 1,900 buildings in the skid-row district were demolished between 1933 and 1953. Skid-row housing was particularly hard hit, suffering a decline in lodging houses from 132 in 1955 to 24 in 1983. In addition, other skid-row institutions disappeared from the district. The number of secondhand clothing shops declined from 44 in 1938 to 6 in 1983. Even the once-thriving casual labor business on skid row was reduced to only three temporary employment agencies by 1983 (Sawyer, 1985).

The skid-row population declined by almost 72 percent over roughly the same period, from a depression-era high of 6,500 persons to 1,825 in 1980. Seattle's skid-row population experienced a similar decline, with the number of homeless decreasing from 8,500 in 1950 to 2,700 in 1970 (Miller, 1982).

Portland's skid-row population was relatively homogeneous during the transformation, being made up of older, single, white men, many of whom were retired seamen and railroad workers living on pensions and residing in single-room occupancy (SRO) hotels. Although containing many chronic, late-stage alcoholics, the population also had a sizeable number of non-alcoholics, with total abstainers making up as much as one third of the residents (*Oregonian*, 1951). By 1970, the skid-row population had become relatively stable, with nearly one half of the men living at the same address for five or more years. Only one in five skid-row residents in the 1970s had lived in Portland for less than one year (Sawyer, 1985).

Slowing the Decline of Skid Row and the Emergence of a Neighborhood

During the 1970s, Portland was in the forefront of the nation's neighborhood activism movement, with organizing and community development activities taking place throughout the city. Portland's skid-row district was the focus of intensive neighborhood organizing by community activists and church groups concerned with public safety, access to social services, and preservation of low-income housing. These efforts, along with a political climate in Portland that favored historic preservation and downtown planning, slowed the destruction of buildings and SRO hotels. In 1979 the city's downtown housing policy was amended to reflect more strongly a desire to maintain and improve low-income and SRO housing stock (Portland Development Commission, 1979).

Several new skid-row organizations emerged during this period to advocate for and provide services to the homeless. One of the first was Burnside Projects, Inc., established in 1970. This nonprofit agency operates a drop-in center, a night shelter, a clean-up center, and several nonprofit enterprises such as a cafe, where the homeless can work for wages, and a cooperative hotel, where residents share housekeeping duties. The organization also provides alcohol and employment counseling to skid-row residents. In 1977, the Burnside Consortium was established by city and county officials to coordinate city and county social service and housing programs in the skid-row district. In 1984, the Burnside Consortium changed its name to Central City Concern, and now manages six downtown SRO hotels and a detoxification program (Lydgate, 1986).

The nonprofit Burnside Community Council (BCC) is a grass-roots community organization that also began in 1977. The BCC operates Baloney Joe's drop-in center as well as night shelters for men and women. In addition, BCC provides a number of services to the homeless including employment assistance, health care, counseling, and referral. The BCC also publishes a quarterly newspaper called *These Homeless Times* (circulation 10,000) and sponsors many community events, including the annual Homeless Parade.

As a result of the organizing efforts on skid row, the rapid increase in homelessness in the 1980s did not bring a return to the full-scale "Hooverville cities" that were seen in Portland in 1932–1933.[1] Skid-row organizations such as the Burnside Community Council and Central City Concern were successful in working with city and county officials to maintain a basic level of social services for skid-row residents. They were also able to establish modest networks of SRO housing and shelter programs that enabled the city to absorb the initial flood of new homeless.

The emergence of skid-row neighborhood organizations in the 1970s slowed but did not stop the destruction of SRO hotels in the downtown area. A March 1986 report by the Portland Bureau of Planning documented a 59 percent decline in SRO units between 1970 and 1986. The number of units decreased from 4,128 to 1,702 over the 16-year period (Bureau of Planning, 1986).

THE HOMELESS EXPLOSION, 1980–1986

Portland's homeless population increased by 200 percent between 1980 and 1986. A 1980 study conducted by the Burnside Consortium (Ille, 1980) estimated the homeless population to be roughly 2,000 persons, with most living in the North Burnside district. This figure is supported by 1980 census tract data (collected earlier in 1980), which reported the skid-row population to be 1,825 residents (U.S. Bureau of Census, 1980). By 1984, the homeless population grew to over 4,500, an increase of 125 percent (Ritzdorf and Sharpe, 1987). In January 1986, the number of homeless in Portland was estimated to have grown to over 6,000 people (U.S. Conference of Mayors, 1986a: 19).

Seattle's homeless population has also grown. As cited earlier, the Strategy for the Downtown Homeless (1986) put King County's homeless population between 3,000 and 4,000 persons. Data from the Emergency Housing Coalition in November 1980–1985 (King County Department of Planning and Community Development, 1986: 40), indicate that total demand for emergency housing (including both demands that were met and those that were turned away) increased from 1,679 in 1980 to 7,716 in 1985, an increase of almost 350 percent. Demand for emergency housing may not, by itself, be an accurate indicator of the size of the homeless population; however, this and other information suggest that homelessness in Seattle has increased in recent years (U.S. Conference of Mayors, 1986a: 27).

What was most evident about the increase in the numbers of homeless during this period was the changing demographic makeup of the population. The older, alcoholic, skid-row male was disappearing from the streets, being replaced by younger, single individuals and, for the first time in many years, entire families. In fact, some observers recognized similarities between the new homeless of the 1980s and the skid-row dwellers of the 1930s (Salerno, Hopper, and Baxter, 1984; Hopper and Hamberg, 1984).

Unemployment and the Local Economy

The economies of Oregon and Washington have been cited frequently as contributors to the homeless problem in both Portland and Seattle. Both cities report that the number of poor people increased in 1985, standing at 13 percent and 11.2 percent, respectively. Unemployment in both cities also increased between 1984 and 1985. In Portland, the jobless rate climbed to 8.3 percent from 7.7 percent, and in Seattle, unemployment jumped from 6.8 percent in 1984 to 7.8 percent in 1985 (U.S. Conference of Mayors, 1986a). A Portland official commented:

Oregon is experiencing an extended recession that is complicated by the fact that its economy is currently undergoing a transformation. Both the timber and agriculture industries which have traditionally been the mainstays of the economy are being reshaped, resulting in a reshaping of the workforce for more low paying jobs. Thus, high unemployment and less revenue for the state from income taxes which could be used to provide services is resulting in continued increases in homelessness. (U.S. Conference of Mayors, 1986a: 25).

A Seattle official added; "Washington State has not yet seen the benefits of the national economic recovery. The homeless are arriving in Seattle from more depressed areas of the state where unemployment is as high as 19 percent" (U.S. Conference of Mayors, 1986a: 11)

Housing and Shelter

Another structural reason for homelessness in the Pacific Northwest, coupled with high unemployment, is the low supply of affordable housing. The Seattle, King County, study (King County Department of Planning and Community Development, 1986: 9) notes that housing availability for low-income households has worsened due to "a decreasing supply of low cost housing, increased costs, and declining Federal subsidies for housing assistance programs." The trend for Seattle, as well as for other cities, is in the direction of increased removal of low-cost central city housing units, which can only exacerbate the conditions for homelessness (Wright and Lam, 1987; Greer, 1986).

One alarming change in Portland's homeless situation in 1983 compared to prior years was the number of persons who reported sleeping outside (under bridges, in alleys, or along the waterfront) as opposed to securing warmer, dryer shelter indoors. A 1973 study (Beall, 1973) found that most of the homeless slept in SRO hotels (55 percent) or in mission facilities (15 percent). By 1983, these figures had changed dramatically, and over half of the homeless were sleeping outside (51 percent), while only 14 percent were sleeping in SRO hotels and 28 percent in skid-row missions (Multnomah County Department of Human Services, 1984: 15).

DEMOGRAPHIC PROFILE OF THE HOMELESS

Aside from the structural factors contributing to the problem of homelessness, it is important to examine the characteristics of the homeless and to comment upon the changes within the group over the last five to ten years. The Seattle, King County, study (King County Department of Planning and Community Development, 1986) is an adequate account of Seattle's homeless problem in the absence of a more comprehensive data base. The study is based upon a survey administered to emergency shelter providers and clients during 1986 and will be used as a source for describing Seattle's homeless in the following sections. A number of studies have been conducted in Portland and will be used to provide information regarding the Portland homeless.

A study of Portland's skid row conducted in 1980 by the Burnside Consortium provides a base line from which to measure the changes in Portland's homeless population (Ille, 1980). In this study residents of SRO hotels were selected at random and interviewed on a range of social characteristics and attitudes toward their living environment.

Two more recent studies conducted by the Multnomah County Department of Human Services document the changes in Portland's homeless population. The first was conducted in October 1983 using an opportunity sample technique to locate 131 homeless persons sleeping in missions and SRO hotels, standing in soup lines, or living under the city's bridges (Multnomah County Department of Human Services, 1984). The second study was done in 1985 and focused on homeless women and children. The researchers located and interviewed 190 women (age range: 18–78 years) who were living in SRO hotels, shelters, and missions, or who were receiving social services (Multnomah County Department of Human Services, 1985).

Age

The Multnomah County studies indicate that Portland's homeless population is considerably younger now than before 1980. The median age has dropped from just under 50 years old in 1980 to 38 years of age in 1983. Moreover, 58 percent were in the 20–40 age group, while only 23 percent were over 50 years of age (Multnomah County Department of Human Services, 1984: 1). In 1985 it was estimated that homeless youth (under 20 years of age) numbered 300–500 in Portland (Donough, 1985). The increase in homelessness among younger people has been documented in studies in several other U.S. cities (Sexton, 1986; Stoner, 1984; Anderson, 1983).

Studies of Seattle's homeless reveal similar age patterns. The Seattle study (King County Department of Planning and Community Development, 1986) shows that 49 percent of the homeless were between the ages of 18 and 44, 20 percent were less than 18 years of age, and only 8 percent were over the age of 60. The age data for both cities stand in marked contrast to the pre–1980 period when generally older men resided on skid row.

Sex

In Portland, the proportion of males among the homeless declined from 90–95 percent before 1980 to 85 percent in 1983, as more females appeared in skid row. The average age of homeless females was 32 years, slightly younger than the age of homeless men. The Seattle data indicate a significantly greater proportion of homeless females than in Portland, with women comprising 48 percent of the homeless. Although this finding may reflect a sampling procedure that favored social service–referred clients, there nevertheless appears to be a significant proportion of women among Seattle's homeless (U.S. Conference of Mayors, 1986a: 16).

Family Status

The majority of homeless persons surveyed in Portland in 1984 were single
(40 percent never married, 41 percent were separated, widowed, or divorced).
However, there also appears to be an increase in the number of families living
on skid row. For example, 68 percent of the women interviewed in the 1985
county study have children (most under the age of six), with 38 percent reporting
that their children were currently living with them (Multnomah County Department of Human Services, 1985: 2). Most of the women with children appear to
be single parents, as the 1984 county study found only 12 percent of the men
living with their families (Multnomah County Department of Human Services,
1984: 11). The Seattle survey reported that 25 percent of the total clients in 1986
were single parents, compared to 18 percent in 1984. Further, about three in
four households with children were headed by single parents, 92 percent of
whom were female (King County Department of Planning and Community Development, 1986: 22).

Multnomah County's 1985 study of homeless women in Portland also found
high rates of abuse, abandonment, and divorce among respondents. Eighty-one
percent indicated that a critical incident (death, divorce, separation) led to their
being homeless. Thirty-one percent reported that abusive relationships were
related to their homeless situation.

Ethnic Minorities

The number of ethnic minorities among Portland's homeless increased dramatically between 1980 and 1983. This was especially the case for American
Indians, but also for blacks and Hispanics. Prior to 1980, the racial composition
of Portland's skid row was almost entirely white, with minorities making up
less than 5–8 percent of the district's population. By 1983, ethnic minorities
made up 23 percent of the homeless with American Indians accounting for 10
percent, blacks 6 percent, and Hispanics 4 percent (Multnomah County Department of Human Services, 1984: 11). Other minorities made up the remaining
3 percent of the homeless.

The Seattle study (King County Department of Planning and Community
Development, 1986: 21) reports that minorities comprise about half (49 percent)
of the homeless. The proportion of whites declined between 1983 and 1985,
with Hispanic shelter clients increasing over the same period. The proportion of
other ethnic minorities remained stable.

Place of Origin

Portland's homeless originate from various other regions of the United States,
a seeming repetition of the migratory patterns of the 1930s. Only 23 percent of

the homeless were natives of Portland or the state of Oregon. Twenty-five percent came from other West Coast cities and towns, 24 percent from southern states, 17 percent from the Midwest, and 6 percent from the East Coast. Although a large proportion of the homeless migrated to Portland in the recent past, once here they became a relatively stable population. Over half of the skid-row dwellers (53 percent) have lived in Portland for five years or more. Approximately one third have lived in the Portland area for less than six months, with roughly 25 percent fitting the traditional transient stereotype of ''just passing through town.'' Seattle's homeless do not reflect as wide a variation in place of origin as the homeless in Portland. Roughly 15 percent of Seattle's homeless are from out of state, while almost 70 percent are from the Seattle area (King County Department of Planning and Community Development, 1986: vi).

Employment, Education, and Income Status

Most of the homeless surveyed in Portland indicated that their main reason for coming to the area was to find employment. Ninety percent of those interviewed were currently unemployed, with over one quarter reporting that they had not worked in over two years. Over 50 percent of the women reported annual incomes of less than $2,000. Nearly one-half of the homeless (44 percent) had worked within the last six months, and 40 percent report supporting themselves by recycling newspaper, cardboard, or bottles, through odd jobs, and by selling plasma. The work history of the homeless is varied, but generally is concentrated in unskilled and semiskilled occupations. Forty-three percent had previously been employed as laborers, 30 percent had worked in service jobs, 10 percent in agriculture, and 7 percent had been employed as operatives (Multnomah County Department of Human Services, 1984: 19).

In terms of educational attainment, over one half of the homeless surveyed in Portland had completed some high school, with 47 percent being high school graduates. In addition, 23 percent have attended college, and 5 percent reported having a college degree (Multnomah County Department of Human Services, 1984: 21).

Alcoholics

The Portland studies revealed that approximately 35 percent of the homeless have chronic alcohol problems, a decrease from 50–60 percent chronic alcoholism rates reported in studies in 1980 and earlier (Ille, 1980). The studies also show that roughly 25 percent of the homeless are abstainers from alcohol. Twenty-five percent of those surveyed indicate that they are chronic drug users, while 75 percent say they do not use street drugs (Multnomah County Department of Human Services, 1984: 23–24). The lower figures for alcohol abuse may reflect the increased numbers of younger persons and families with children, having fewer late-stage alcoholics. By contrast, in Seattle about 16 percent of the homeless are clients in treatment programs for alcohol and/or substance-abuse problems (King County Department of Planning and Community Development, 1986: 18).

Chronically Mentally Ill

At about the same time that the economic crisis of the early 1980s was being felt in the Northwest, there were significant changes in Oregon and Washington state mental health policies, which resulted in deinstitutionalizing and releasing to the community hundreds of chronically mentally ill (CMI) patients from state hospitals. Officials in both Portland and Seattle have pointed to the changes leading to increases in numbers of homeless. Portland officials claim there are more homeless mentally ill individuals in the city "due to decreases in benefit programs with which to provide treatment and shelter to them" (U.S. Conference of Mayors, 1986a: 17). Seattle officials charge that "the state's mental health system has forced many CMI people into communities where they have a difficult time adjusting to an increasingly competitive job market and to stable living conditions" (U.S. Conference of Mayors, 1986a: 21–22).

In 1983, one in five (19 percent) of Portland's homeless had a history of psychiatric hospitalization, with one half of these being under 30 years of age (Multnomah County Department of Human Services, 1984: 27). Twenty-five percent of the women surveyed said that they had attempted suicide and 10 percent were assessed to be chronically mentally ill (Multnomah County Department of Human Services, 1985: 10). Although high, these figures do not approach the 30–50 percent mental illness rates said to exist in other U.S. cities (Snow et al., 1986). However, more recent data indicate that the numbers of mentally ill among Portland's homeless may be increasing (Ritzdorf and Sharpe, 1987). The Seattle study indicates that approximately 11 percent of the city's homeless are chronically mentally ill persons (King County Department of Planning and Community Development, 1986: 18).

THE RESPONSE TO THE HOMELESS PROBLEM

Portland officials designed a response to the homeless problem that focuses on three areas: housing for special needs populations, emergency services, and combating public alcoholism.

Rehabilitation of SRO and Low-Income Housing

A 1986 study, "Status Report on Low Income Single Room Occupancy (SRO) Housing in Downtown Portland" (Bureau of Planning, 1986), estimated that since 1978 the city's SRO housing stock had been declining at an annual rate of 125 units, or roughly 7 percent per year. The study documented a 59 percent decline in SRO units between 1970 and 1986, with the number decreasing from 4,128 to 1,702 units. The dramatic loss of SRO and low-income housing in the nation's central cities has been well documented as a contributing factor to homelessness (Wright and Lam, 1987; Ritzdorf and Sharpe, 1987; Greer, 1986). Until recently there was little that could be done to stop the decline, particularly since cities were prohibited from using federal Section 8 housing funds for SRO rehabilitation.

In 1980, Oregon's congressional delegation, led by Congressman Les AuCoin, sought changes in federal housing regulations so that SRO units would be considered eligible for federal subsidies. SROs have traditionally been defined as substandard housing because each room lacks its own bathroom and kitchen facility and is therefore ineligible for federal housing subsidies. Congressman AuCoin proposed an exemption to the 1936 Housing Act as part of the 1981 Omnibus Budget Reconciliation Act, which redefined adequate housing. The exemption allowed Portland to participate in a HUD-sponsored SRO demonstration effort that rehabilitated 247 SRO units in four downtown hotels.

Since 1980, the Portland Development Commission has renovated an additional 620 SRO units using funds from the Department of Energy, the National Trust for Historic Preservation, and the Federal Emergency Management Agency (U.S. Conference of Mayors, 1986b: 67). Aggressive use of federal funds has also enabled Portland to limit the net loss of non-SRO low-income housing units to 8 percent between 1978 and 1985 (Bureau of Planning, 1986). Section 8 new construction and rehabilitation funds produced and/or refurbished almost 1,000 units of low-income housing during this time, mainly for elderly residents.

The Portland Emergency Basic Needs Committee

In February 1986 the city of Portland and Multnomah County established the city-county Emergency Basic Needs Committee (EBNC). The stated purpose of the committee was "to provide leadership necessary to maximize the ability of the city and county to meet emergency needs" (U.S. Conference of Mayors, 1986b: 65). The committee defined emergency services to include shelter, clean-up, food, clothing, medical help, fuel, transportation, income, and jobs.

The role of the Emergency Basic Needs Committee is to streamline presentations and requests to the city council and the county commission. In addition, the committee is seen as a means of coordinating and involving staff of city bureaus and county departments in its planning efforts. The EBNC carries out its work by using advisory groups comprised of service providers, advocates, and recipients.

Winter Emergency Shelter Network

The Winter Emergency Shelter Network is operated by Burnside Projects, Inc., to insure that the homeless have a warm, dry, and secure place to sleep on winter nights. During cold winter months existing emergency shelters often operate to capacity. This effort provides an additional 455 shelter beds that can be drawn upon when the 350 existing beds become full. As shelter beds fill, Burnside Projects can open a series of back-up shelters around the city to handle the overflow. The additional shelters are staffed by Burnside Projects on a ratio of one attendant to each six persons.

Portland Mayor's Plan for the Homeless

In October 1985, Portland's Mayor J. E. Bud Clark unveiled a comprehensive 12-point plan for the homeless (Mayor's Plan for the Homeless, 1985). The plan proposes local government action in three areas: care and assistance for the homeless, increased law enforcement capability, and the improvement of the business climate in the North Burnside–Old Town district. A major focus of the plan is combating public drunkenness. Specific proposals for increasing treatment for alcoholics, using involuntary commitment proceedings for chronic detox users, and restricting the sale of fortified wines were the result of an earlier Task Force on Public Alcoholism appointed by the mayor prior to the development of the homeless plan (Newton and Duffy, 1987: 64–65). The mayor's plan goes beyond previous efforts by linking skid-row housing rehabilitation with social service delivery systems and by emphasizing planning and coordination among city bureaus and county departments.

Other elements of the mayor's plan call for comprehensive planning, retaining, and expanding of low-income housing, encouraging employment of the homeless at minimum-wage jobs, and establishing a multiservice center in the skid-row district (Mayor's Plan for the Homeless, 1985).

Seattle Mayor's Strategy for the Downtown Homeless

Similar in many respects to Portland's plan for the homeless, Seattle's mayor has developed a strategy that addresses the downtown area (Strategy for the Downtown Homeless, 1986). Based on the findings of the Mayor's Task Force on Street People and the Homeless, the primary intent of the strategy is to "provide initiatives which will better meet the needs of the downtown community as a whole and build stronger downtown neighborhoods for people of all economic levels" (Strategy for the Downtown Homeless, 1986: 1). Thus, the focus of Seattle's plan is on business, visitors, and users of the downtown area as well as upon the homeless.

Concerned primarily with downtown Seattle, the strategy identifies several subpopulations of homeless and proposes specific recommendations for each group. The result of this approach has been the identification of three main groups: "the temporarily displaced"; "chronic alcoholics, drug abusers, and mentally ill"; and "those who are doing harm." The first group is comprised of single individuals and families who are not chronically ill and who are seeking shelter and employment. Proposals for these persons call for housing and employment services through an experimental employment-oriented transitional housing facility. The facility would serve only those "screened by temporary shelters as being job-ready" (Strategy for the Downtown Homeless, 1986: 4). Additional services targeted to the temporarily displaced include expanding temporary shelters, evaluating existing day centers, increasing transitional housing, expanding welfare legislation efforts, and developing family and youth strategies.

The second group of homeless is comprised of substance abusers and is divided into those who are seeking treatment and those who refuse treatment. Proposed activities for persons seeking treatment include revising the diagnostic process and centralizing referrals to diagnostic centers; arranging for "protective payees" to assist with personal money management; increasing the supply of transitional housing linked to services; and using the experimental transition facility for employment services. For homeless alcoholics who are not seeking treatment the plan calls for additional permanent voluntary housing, protective payees, and the establishment of 24-hour sleep-off centers, as an alternative to repeated detox efforts.

The final category of homeless identified in the Seattle strategy is comprised of "those who are doing harm." The effort directed at this group is to strengthen public safety in the downtown area. This includes a review of ordinances pertaining to public safety for citizens (such as restricting aggressive panhandling, disorderly behavior, and so on); deployment of additional police; development of a "homeless fund" as an alternative to panhandling; and additional legislation regarding controlled substances.

As the Seattle strategy states at the outset, the primary focus is to respond to the increasing numbers of homeless and to maintain a safe downtown. Using this criterion, the strategy does speak to some of the central problems confronting the homeless that are "structural" in nature (that is, it addresses the foundational elements that give rise to the problem in the first place). The provision of affordable housing and efforts to increase employment are prominent among these concerns. The strongest feature of the Seattle strategy in this respect is to promote the need for adequate housing. At several points, it is suggested that the size of the homeless population is increasing while affordable housing of various kinds is shrinking. However, the Seattle strategy does not fully develop these initiatives as they relate to the broader context within which the immediate problems of the homeless appear.

In this respect, both the Seattle and Portland plans fall short of a solution that addresses the larger scope of homelessness. This can ultimately compound local issues as piecemeal efforts prove inadequate and fail. A more wide-ranging analysis of homelessness would include more groups of affected people, including single-parent families and youth. While both plans recognize these groups, they chose to focus public policy more on that segment of the homeless who present a more immediate public threat.

Equally important, a more comprehensive strategy would focus public policy more heavily upon employment training and direct job creation, as well as on support services (such as child care and health), which enable the homeless to secure employment and become more self-sufficient. The Seattle strategy proposes an experimental employment-oriented transitional housing facility as a way to address employment needs. However, one facility with the capacity to accommodate 150 persons per year may not be adequate to meet the need.

The Portland plan for the homeless emphasizes employment initiatives even less than the Seattle strategy. The Portland plan calls for public and private sector employers to set aside minimum-wage jobs for the homeless but is relatively silent on employment assistance or job training (Mayor's Plan for the Homeless, 1985). Unfortunately, minimum-wage jobs tend to offer little opportunity for advancement or job security, which are viewed as fundamental necessities for escaping homelessness.

TOWARD A NATIONAL STRATEGY ON HOMELESSNESS

Aside from the specific, emergency responses developed in Portland and Seattle, it should be noted that similar public policy choices confront most major U.S. cities. On the one hand, very little national or local data exist regarding the nature and causes of homelessness. On the other hand, many public and private agencies are poorly equipped to plan and operate services in the highly coordinated environment required by the demographic composition of the new homeless. The lack of data on the homeless prevents a comprehensive understanding of the structural roots of the problem (lack of affordable housing, high unemployment, and inadequate social services), while the fragmentation of state and local governments prevents unified and effective service delivery to homeless individuals and families. Without information and shared action, a "policy balkanization" results.

In many respects, the response to the homeless problem in Portland and Seattle has been more progressive than that in other U.S. cities. Concern for the plight of homeless citizens is evident at all levels of local government and by the networks of private agencies that attempt to meet the needs of people without means for survival. Both cities have active groups and organizations that are taking informed steps to provide better services to the homeless and advocate for change in public policy.

There is a danger, however, that the provincial concerns of metropolitan government will treat the homeless as a population to be "managed" in order to construct a vision of the central city that accommodates only business interests. Often, this results in policies that seek to remove the homeless from sight (as evidenced by recent accounts from across the country of localities razing "tent cities" and more aggressively enforcing vagrancy laws). The problem with these tactics is that they ignore the human cost of homelessness, both to the disaffected individual and to the larger society, which is denied the productive participation of all its members. In addition, and perhaps most important, homeless removal schemes ignore the fact that a growing number of the homeless are women with young children, hardly candidates for police rousts or storefront "drip-lines" put up by merchants to keep the destitute from sitting in front of their businesses.

It is time for a national policy on homelessness that will focus on full employment, including cooperative education and job retraining opportunities; support services for working parents and others, including health services, child care, and early childhood education programs; and on producing affordable housing for families with young children and for special needs populations. It is unrealistic to expect the cities to shoulder the entire responsibility for solving the nation's employment and housing problems, particularly when the roots of both crises lie in the malfunctioning of the national economy.

NOTE

1. In 1932, the Sullivan's Gulch "Hooverville city" on Portland's east side contained a population of over 300 unemployed loggers, aged laborers, and destitute men living in tar-paper shacks. The shantytown had its own elected "mayor" and civil police patrol to maintain public safety. By 1934, the loose-knit community was gone (Johnson, 1940).

REFERENCES

Anderson, George M. 1983. The Homeless. *America* (December 24): 149.

Banzer, Cindy. 1987. The Good, the Bad, the Ugly Times. *These Homeless Times* 2 (Summer): 1, 4.

Beall, Robert. 1973. A Survey of Persons Who Use Social Services on Skid Road. Portland, Ore.: Burnside Projects, Inc.

Bogue, Donald. 1963. Skid Row in American Cities. Chicago: Community and Family Studies Center, University of Chicago.

Bureau of Planning. 1986. Status Report on Low-Income Single Room Occupancy (SRO) Housing in Downtown Portland. Portland, Ore.

Donough, Robert. 1985. Juvenile Prostitution and Street Youth in Portland. Tri-County Youth Services Consortium.

Greer, Nora Richer. 1986. *The Search for Shelter*. Washington, D.C.: The American Institute of Architects.

Hombs, Mary Ellen, and Mitch Snyder. 1982. *Homelessness in America: A Forced March to Nowhere*. Washington, D.C.: The Community for Creative Non-Violence.

Hopper, Kim, and Jill Hamberg. 1984. *The Making of America's Homeless: From Skid Row to New Poor*. New York: Community Service Society.

Ille, Majorie. 1980. Burnside: A Study of Hotel Residents in Portland's Skid Row. Portland, Ore.: Burnside Consortium, Inc.

Irwin, Victoria. 1986. Counting the Homeless. *The Christian Science Monitor* (October 20): 3–4.

Johnson, Harriet. 1940. A Study in Transiency. B.A. thesis, Reed College, Portland, Ore.

King, Larry. 1982. Skid Row: A Geographical Perspective. Ph.D. dissertation, University of Oregon.

King County Department of Planning and Community Development. 1986. *Homelessness Revisited*. Seattle, Wash.

Lydgate, Chris. 1986. Upscale, Downscale: The Other Side of Burnside. *The Free Agent* 1 (November): 14–17.

Mayor's Plan for the Homeless. 1985. Memorandum, Office of J. E. Bud Clark, Mayor, Portland, Ore. (October 31).

Miller, Ronald. 1982. *The Demolition of Skid Row*. Lexington, Mass.: Lexington Books.

Minehan, Thomas. 1934. *Boy and Girl Tramps of America*. Seattle: University of Washington Press.

Multnomah County Department of Human Services. 1984. *The Homeless Poor, 1984*. Portland, Ore.

———. 1985. *Homeless Women, 1985*. Portland, Ore.

Newton, Stephen P., and Charles P. Duffy. 1987. Old Town Portland and an Oldtime Problem. *Alcohol Health and Research World* (Spring): 62–65.

Oregonian. 1933. (August 13): 10.

Oregonian. 1951. (December 10): 19.

Peroff, Kathleen. 1987. Who Are the Homeless and How Many Are There. In *The Homeless in Contemporary Society*, edited by Richard D. Bingham, Roy E. Green, and Sammis B. White. Newbury Park, Calif.: Sage Publications.

Portland Development Commission. 1979. *Downtown Housing Policy and Programs*. Portland, Ore.

Ritzdorf, Marsha, and Sumner M. Sharpe. 1987. Portland, Oregon: A Comprehensive Approach. In *The Homeless in Contemporary Society*, edited by Richard D. Bingham, Roy E. Green, and Sammis B. White. Newbury Park, Calif.: Sage Publications.

Salerno, Dan, Kim Hopper, and Ellen Baxter. 1984. *Hardship in the Heartland: Homelessness in Eight U.S. Cities*. New York: Community Service Society.

Sawyer, Chris. 1985. From Whitechappel to Old Town: The Life and Death of the Skid Row District Portland, Oregon. Ph.D. dissertation, Portland State University.

Schwab, Jim. 1986. Sheltering the Homeless, *Planning* (December): 24–27.

Sexton, Patricia. 1986. Epidemic of Homelessness. *Dissent* (Spring): 137–140.

Snow, David A., et al. 1986. The Myth of Pervasive Mental Illness among the Homeless. *Social Problems* 33: 407–423.

Stoner, Madeleine. 1984. An Analysis of Public and Private Sector Provision for Homeless People. *Urban and Social Change Review* 17: 3–8.

Strategy for the Downtown Homeless. 1986. Office of Charles Royer, Mayor, Seattle, Wash., (December 30).

U.S. Bureau of Census. 1980. Population and Housing: Census Tract, Portland, Ore.

U.S. Conference of Mayors. 1986a. *The Growth of Hunger, Homelessness and Poverty in American Cities in 1985*. Washington, D.C.: United States Conference of Mayors.

———. 1986b. *Responding to Homelessness in American Cities*. Washington, D.C.: United States Conference of Mayors.

Washington State Department of Community Development. 1987. Unpublished Data on the Demographics of Emergency Shelter Users.

Wright, James D., and Julie A. Lam. 1987. Homelessness and the Low Income Housing Supply. *Social Policy* (Spring): 48–53.

11

Homelessness In Tennessee

Barrett A. Lee

Since the publication of McCook's (1893) "Tramp Census" almost a century ago, a vast amount of social scientific literature on homelessness has accumulated. This literature is dominated by studies conducted between 1950 and 1980, during the "Skid-row" generation of homelessness research. From data gathered in New York, Chicago, Philadelphia, Los Angeles, Seattle, and other major cities, much has been learned about virtually every aspect of skid-row life (Bahr, 1970, 1973).

Two demographic generalizations from the scholarly work on skid row are of particular relevance to this chapter. First, as recently as the 1970s, already modest homeless populations were widely reported to be shrinking in size (Lee, 1980; Rubington, 1971; Vander Kooi, 1973). Urban renewal, a declining demand for unskilled labor, and healthy economic conditions had combined to reduce the number of homeless persons, or at least disperse them from their traditional skid-row locations. Even on New York's Bowery, long recognized as the nation's largest skid row, only 4,150 inhabitants remained by 1972 (Bahr and Caplow, 1973: 47).

The second generalization concerns the demographic characteristics of the homeless. All skid-row investigations of note have found urban homeless populations to be homogeneous in composition, consisting disproportionately of single, white, older males with low incomes and transient life-styles (Bahr and Caplow, 1973; Blumberg et al., 1960; Bogue, 1963; Caplow et al., 1958; Wallace, 1965). This profile continues to color public beliefs about the homeless.

Viewed from the 1980s, both skid-row generalizations appear outdated. Though some historic skid-row districts have fallen victim to urban redevelopment, most contributors to the "new homeless" literature argue that homeless individuals are becoming more rather than less numerous (Bassuk, 1984; Erickson and Wilhelm, 1986; Hope and Young, 1986; Redburn and Buss, 1986). Indeed, in the last decade, the United States is thought to have experienced an unprecedented surge in homelessness, with Hombs and Snyder (1982) claiming that 2.2 million people, or roughly 1 percent of the total U.S. population, were homeless as of 1982. At the local level, conservative estimates compiled by the U.S. Department of Housing and Urban Development (1984) put the pool of homeless in cities like New York, Chicago, and Los Angeles at 20,000 or more.

The societal forces presumably behind such numbers—deinstitutionalization, economic displacement, housing shortages, changing welfare policies, and so on—are also held responsible for increasing the demographic diversity of homeless populations. The phrase "new homeless" was originally coined to refer to women, children, blacks, family members, and others who bear little resemblance to the denizens of skid row but who, like them, no longer have a permanent place of residence. According to current reviews (Huth, 1987; Stefl, 1987; U.S. Department of Housing and Urban Development, 1984), these subgroups constitute larger proportions of the homeless than ever before, and their ranks may still be expanding.

In the pages that follow, I examine the demographic dimensions of homelessness in Tennessee against the backdrop of the skid-row and new homeless perspectives. Most post–1980 writing on the topic has embraced the latter perspective and dismissed or ignored the former, but there are good reasons for adopting a more balanced approach. Existing studies, especially those conducted during the latest round of homelessness scholarship, are limited in fundamental ways that leave descriptive conclusions about the most basic demographic facts open to question. The next two sections identify these limitations and discuss how they have been addressed in a series of surveys and enumerations undertaken throughout Tennessee.

PROBLEMS WITH EXISTING RESEARCH

Methodological critiques by Peroff (1987), Rossi et al. (1986), and the U.S. Department of Housing and Urban Development (1984) have identified a variety of technical difficulties that plague recent empirical work, ranging from inconsistencies in how homelessness is conceptualized to weaknesses in sampling and survey design. Rather than attempt an exhaustive treatment of those difficulties here, I restrict my comments to problems associated with the selection of topics, cases, and locations.

Reading the literature, one quickly sees that some aspects of contemporary homelessness are of greater interest than others. When "hot" issues such as mental illness (Fischer et al., 1986; Lamb, 1984; Lipton et al., 1983) or the status of military veterans (Robertson, 1987; Schutt, 1986) receive coverage, they frequently do so at the expense of more mundane questions about the size and composition of homeless populations. Even when demographic questions are asked, the characteristics of women, families, and other new homeless groups tend to be of primary concern, precisely because their homelessness seems to contradict conventional skid-row wisdom (Crystal, 1984; Sullivan and Damrosch, 1987; Watson, 1986). The selective attention given these topics and groups, though understandable, can lead to biased estimates and distorted popular perceptions of both the number and characteristics of homeless people.

Research efforts explicitly intended to provide fuller coverage of the homeless can also yield a misleading demographic picture. Homelessness is a vague, multifaceted, and often temporary condition, making target populations hard to define. Moreover, the members of such populations usually lack the kinds of anchors—residential addresses, telephone numbers, and the like—essential to rigorous sampling or census procedures. Some homeless try to enhance their inaccessibility, hiding from investigators and others who threaten their privacy. As a consequence of these complexities and the normal resource constraints on research, demographic generalizations about a city's homeless population may wind up being based on a survey of persons staying in just one or two shelters, or on statistics kept by service providers. Neither source of data features the systematic selection of cases necessary to insure representative findings.

In fairness, there are several studies from the 1980s that manage to avoid many of the problems just discussed (Brown et al., 1983; Rossi et al., 1986; Roth and Bean, 1986). What is striking about even the better studies—and about the skid-row and new homeless literatures overall—is their lack of geographic generality. To date, few investigations have treated homelessness as a phenomenon that occurs south of the Mason-Dixon line or outside major urban areas. Besides regional and urban biases, existing work on homelessness suffers from what might be labeled geographic atomism. With the exception of HUD's controversial attempt to produce national figures (U.S. Department of Housing and Urban Development, 1984), only rarely has demographic information from local studies been pieced together for geographic entities as large as counties, let alone whole states.

SETTINGS AND DATA SOURCES

Simply by virtue of its southern location, Tennessee represents a strategic state in which to investigate the demographic aspects of homelessness. But the ability to fill a regional hole in the skid-row and new homeless literatures is only one of the state's attractions. Generalizations drawn from both literatures can be subjected to multiple tests because of the great internal variety present: there are five Tennessees rather than one.

The first three Tennessees correspond to the state's "grand divisions," stretching from the mountainous east through the plateaus and hills of the middle section to the low plains and swamplands of the west. These divisions differ in racial composition, population growth, and other aspects of social terrain, not just topography. The last two Tennessees are defined by the urban-rural distinction. Each division contains at least a pair of census-designated metropolitan areas: Memphis and Jackson in the west, Nashville and Clarksville in middle Tennessee, and Knoxville, Chattanooga, and Jackson City–Kingsport–Bristol (the Tri-Cities) in the east. Though a majority of the state's residents are classified as metropolitan by the Census Bureau, roughly two fifths of the population still live in rural settings (U.S. Bureau of the Census, 1982).

Data on homelessness are available for urban and rural areas in every grand division of Tennessee. The most plentiful and trustworthy data come from the state's four largest cities (Memphis, Nashville, Knoxville, and Chattanooga), where perceptions of the growing number and diversity of the homeless have prompted several empirical studies. These studies, typically conducted by advocacy groups, service providers, and government agencies in collaboration with academic researchers, are of two types. One-day *enumerations* or "headcounts" have been undertaken in three of the cities to estimate the size of the local homeless population at a single point in time. In all four places, *surveys* using face-to-face interviews have obtained extensive information on the demographic characteristics of the homeless. More detailed methodological descriptions of the enumerations and surveys can be found elsewhere (Green, 1986; Henniss, 1987; Nooe and Lynch, 1986; Mullins, 1986); the brief overview that follows mentions only their essential features.

The attempts made to count homeless people in Memphis (in November 1985), Knoxville (February 1986), and Nashville (December 1986) have much in common. Enumeration activities in each place were restricted to the early-morning hours, between 4 A.M. and 7 A.M., to minimize the likelihood of double-counting persons as they moved about later in the day. The enumerations were also implemented in cold-weather months, when the homeless tend to congregate in shelters and are easiest to find. Despite this precaution, teams of researchers in each city systematically searched downtown streets and other outdoor sleeping sites in addition to checking the shelters. In Memphis, police officers accompanied the teams involved in the street count, while the Knoxville teams employed homeless individuals as guides. Because of the peripheral locations of several family shelters in Nashville, enumerators there paid more attention to sites outside the downtown area than did their counterparts in Memphis or Knoxville.

Of the four surveys that have been conducted, those in Knoxville (February 1986), Nashville (July 1986), and Chattanooga (February 1987) exhibit the greatest similarities in design. Large numbers of volunteer interviewers were trained and deployed in each city, so that the bulk of the fieldwork could be completed in a two- to three-day period. Interviewers approached homeless respondents on the streets, in shelters, at day service facilities, and in other locations, offering them a monetary incentive to participate. In Nashville, a quota design—informed by enumeration statistics from the previous month—dictated the distribution of respondents across sex, race, age, and family status categories, with a total of 117 (13 percent of the population) finally interviewed.

Knoxville's survey was actually a census; all 258 homeless people who could be found were interviewed, 135 being administered a long form and 123 a short form. The survey sample ($N = 186$) in Chattanooga probably constituted a high percentage of all homeless, too, though lack of enumeration results precludes calculation of the sampling fraction.

Only for Memphis is the representativeness of the survey data questionable. The sample size there ($N = 543$) was larger than in the other cities, but respondents were all drawn from a single site: a men's shelter run by the Salvation Army. During February and March 1986, every individual who spent a night or more at the shelter was interviewed by a staff member as part of the normal registration process. Since no other sites were covered in the survey, it is difficult to rule out the possibility that the persons staying at the shelter may have differed in nonrandom ways from homeless people elsewhere in Memphis at the time. Obviously, women and children were excluded from the men's shelter survey.

With the exception of the Memphis survey, the data-gathering efforts in Tennessee's four major cities avoid many of the weaknesses of recent work noted earlier. Breadth of coverage has not been sacrificed out of concern for special topics or groups, and homeless people have been counted and interviewed in diverse locations. While methodologically sound, the studies are far from perfect. Some hidden homeless—especially those staying temporarily in hotels, doubling up with friends and relatives, or opting for outlying neighborhoods rather than downtown skid-row districts—have undoubtedly been missed. Nevertheless, when taken together, the research efforts in Nashville, Knoxville, Chattanooga, and Memphis provide a fairly clear snapshot of urban homelessness in the state during a one-and-a-half-year period centered on 1986.

The picture of Tennessee's homeless in rural areas and smaller metropolises is less sharply focused. In the same year that the urban homeless were being investigated, staff in the Tennessee Department of Human Services (1986) conducted a study for the legislature on the extent of homelessness in the 91 counties *not* containing any of the four biggest cities. The study was motivated in part by reports of high rural unemployment rates, housing shortages, and a deepening agricultural crisis, all of which would seem to portend significant pockets of homeless people. Administrators of state and local agencies serving the counties acted as knowledgeable informants. They assembled rough estimates of the number of homeless based on a review of shelter and program statistics, police reports, anecdotal material, and other sources. Some of the administrators were more diligent than others in performing this task; a few even described the composition as well as the size of their county's homeless population. None, however, had direct evidence from enumerations or surveys at their disposal.

HOW MANY HOMELESS?

The most elementary demographic question that can be asked about homeless people is, "How many of them are there?" Though the question may seem straightforward, it has been answered in terms of cumulative totals, incidence rates, and many other criteria. Ideally, what one would like is a single figure that indicates the number of homeless within a particular geographic entity at a specific moment in time. To date, the lack of coordination between local research projects—not to mention the complex nature of homelessness itself—has made such a goal impossible to achieve at the state level.

In search of a realistic alternative, I have compiled four kinds of point estimates of Tennessee's homeless population, all representing daily totals from the same general time period (centered on 1986) and broken down for core counties of large and small metropolitan areas and for all other counties (labeled nonmetropolitan). The first two estimates are based on direct evidence, typically from enumerations or surveys, with the *conservative* estimate reflecting the actual number of homeless observed and the *liberal* estimate—which assumes a substantial undercount—doubling the conservative figure. The other two estimates come from expert informants (service providers, officials of advocacy organizations and government agencies, and others) in local or state positions who have reviewed and adjusted available evidence in accordance with their knowledge of data limitations, county circumstances, and so on.[1]

The four different estimates are presented in the second through fifth columns of Table 11.1. To keep the table simple, I have replaced any estimated ranges of population size—often given by local and state informants—with midpoints and have rounded all estimates to the nearest multiple of five. I have also recorded identical numbers in the conservative and local columns (2 and 4) for small metropolitan areas and nonmetropolitan counties. Primary source materials for these two categories of places mixed cumulative counts, service statistics, and informal observations, making the distinction between direct evidence and local informant estimates difficult to preserve. The hybrid estimates shown, derived from my reading of the 91 county reports incorporated in the Department of Human Services study, may err on the conservative side, especially for nonmetropolitan counties.

From a substantive standpoint, what stands out in Table 11.1 is the variability of the estimates and, by implication, the uncertainty about the extent of homelessness in Tennessee. In the bottom row, the estimated state total ranges from a low of 2,135 to a high of 6,500. Even greater contrasts are apparent for individual places: state informants judged the daily number of homeless in Knoxville and Chattanooga to be over four times greater than conservative estimates would suggest, and the local estimate for Memphis is almost six times the conservative figure. In general, the numbers given by state informants appear farthest out of line. These figures might have been inflated by the political purposes for which they were originally produced, or perhaps by their authors' distance from and unfamiliarity with the details of numerous local situations.[2] Whatever the sources of their inaccuracy, they should probably be discounted. That leaves the conservative, data-based estimates in column 2 and those provided

Table 11.1
Size Estimates of Metropolitan and Nonmetropolitan Homeless Populations in Tennessee

Type of Area	Date	Direct Evidence		Expert Estimate		HUD Estimate
		Conserv. Estimate	Liberal Estimate	Local Estimate	State Estimate	
Large metropolitan area (total)		1,860	3,720	5,200	5,625	2,590
Nashville (Davidson Co.)	12/86	900	1,800	1,750	1,750	700
Knoxville (Knox Co.)	2/86	275	550	275	1,250	590
Chattanooga (Hamilton Co.)	2/87	185	370	375	875	340
Memphis (Shelby Co.)	11/85	500	1,000	2,800	1,750	960
Small metropolitan areas (total)		150	300	150		305
Clarksville(Montgomery Co.)	9/86	50[a]	100	50[a]		60
Jackson (Madison Co.)	9/86	20[a]	40	20[a]	875	50
Johnson City (Carter & Washington Cos.)	9/86	45[a]	90	45[a]		95
Kingsport (Sullivan Co.)	9/86	35	70	35		100
Nonmetropolitan counties (total)	9/86	125[a]	250	125[a]		1,385
State total		2,135	4,270	5,475	6,500	4,280

a: Calculated by author from individual county reports summarized in Tennessee Department of Human Services (1986). See text for description of data sources and types of estimates.

by local informants in column 4 as the safest lower and upper bounds, respectively, on the size of the statewide homeless population.

A conclusion that can be more confidently drawn from Table 11.1 concerns the urban character of homelessness. Regardless of which estimates are used, the four largest metropolitan counties contain approximately 9 of every 10 homeless persons in Tennessee but only 4 of every 10 residents. Why homelessness is a big-city phenomenon becomes obvious on contemplation. Memphis, Nashville, Knoxville, and Chattanooga are all economically prosperous and thus are bound to draw some migrants who lack job skills appropriate to the opportunities at hand. The fact that all four cities are easily accessible by interstate highways insures a steady stream of people passing through, as do the tourist attractions at each place. A shortage of affordable housing and the presence of large institutions—colleges, prisons, hospitals, mental health facilities, and the like—are other features these places share that contribute to a local reservoir of potentially homeless individuals. Finally, those individuals already homeless may choose to move to (or stay in) one of the larger Tennessee cities because of the greater range of services available.

In view of the harsh economic conditions outside metropolitan areas, the paucity of rural homelessness requires explanation as well. According to local informants in the nonmetropolitan counties, rural homelessness tends to be a temporary condition, with most individuals able to "get by" with the assistance of family, friends, and church members. Those lacking such a community support system typically head for the nearest major city, or are referred there by rural service providers who are ill equipped to meet the needs of the homeless on a long-term basis. The result of this help-seeking pattern is a steady spatial redistribution of homeless people from outlying areas to the urban centers of the state.

Are the population estimates in Table 11.1 more compatible with the "large and growing" image conveyed by the new homeless literature or with the "small and declining" image from skid-row research? Unfortunately, the estimates by themselves remain meaningless; they can be brought to bear on the new homeless and skid-row perspectives only when examined comparatively. To establish a crude benchmark, I have applied HUD's incidence rates (expressed as the number of homeless per 10,000) for all U.S. metropolitan and nonmetropolitan areas to the corresponding components of Tennessee's population.[3] The resulting estimates, shown in the sixth column of Table 11.1, indicate how many homeless there would be if all counties in the state conformed to the 1984 national averages by size and metropolitan status.

Comparing the HUD estimates with the others in the table, the greatest discrepancies occur for the nonmetropolitan counties; the HUD figures are almost certainly too high. This is due in large measure to the HUD investigators' arbitrary decision to set the rate of rural homelessness equal to that found in small metropolitan areas (6 homeless per 10,000). Even if the liberal estimate in column 3 were doubled to 500, the implied incidence rate in nonmetropolitan Tennessee would barely reach 1 per 10,000.

Although they may slightly undershoot or overshoot in specific instances, the HUD estimates for individual metropolitan areas typically fall within or near the range defined by the conservative and local estimates. The HUD estimate for the state as a whole—4,280—also seems quite reasonable, coinciding with the liberal figure based on direct observations of the homeless. In contrast, the 1 percent incidence rate widely cited in the new homeless literature yields an estimated state homeless population of 47,620 when applied to 1985 data. Obviously, the HUD estimate, which rests on incidence rates frequently criticized as being too low, comes much closer to the mark. If anything, then, the Tennessee findings offer little support for extreme arguments by new homeless researchers about the numerical magnitude of the problem.

Another comparative strategy—and one that sheds more direct light on the new homeless and skid-row perspectives—involves plotting trends in the number of homeless. Rather than juxtaposing different homeless populations, a single population is compared with itself at different points in time; evidence of growth would support the new homeless view, and evidence of decline, the skid-row view. Though the necessary data are not available for the entire state, they do exist for one urban area. The December 1986 enumeration in Nashville described earlier is part of a series of enumerations conducted since 1983. The following results are from six of those enumerations. Only results for the downtown area are shown, since this is the component of the study domain that has remained constant over time.[4]

Enumeration Date	Number	Shelters (%)	Hotels (%)	Streets (%)
December 1983	820	67	26	7
June 1984	689	56	32	12
December 1985	714	84	1	15
June 1986	657	76	0	24
December 1986	741	85	0	15
June 1987	695	69	0	31

A perusal of the first column fails to reveal any clear trend in the number of homeless people counted in downtown Nashville when month is held constant. The December populations are fairly similar to one another in size, as are the June populations. Neither the new homeless nor the skid-row perspective leads one to anticipate such a pattern of stability. Of course, a major surge (or decline) may have taken place prior to the initial enumeration, or changes may have occurred outside the downtown district during the 1983–1987 period.

Another confounding possibility is that Nashville's homeless population has actually been growing, but the growth has been balanced by increasing difficulties in locating the homeless. As can be seen from the data, the percentage of the population in hotels dropped abruptly and the percentage spending the night on the streets (outdoors, in coffee shops, bus stations, and elsewhere) began to climb in December 1985, after the last of the city's downtown SRO facilities were closed or demolished. Simply put, homeless people sleeping outside are more likely to elude detection by enumerators, given the variety of hiding places accessible to them. This principle also helps explain the marked seasonal variation in the counts: the June figures may be consistently lower than the December figures because warmer weather draws the homeless outdoors, not because the local homeless population contracts during the summer.

SEX, RACE, AND AGE

The kinds of problems just noted make it difficult to determine the composition as well as the size of a homeless population with much certainty. Nevertheless, experts seem more confident in describing the basic demographic characteristics of the homeless. With respect to sex, race, and age, the traditional skid-row profile—emphasizing the disproportionate number of older, white males—has largely been discarded. The new homeless of today, asserts the U.S. Department of Housing and Urban Development (1984: 22) "are a much more heterogeneous group consisting of women . . . as well as men, people of all age groups . . . [and] blacks and Hispanics as well as whites." My concern here is with the applicability of this view to Tennessee.

The following 1986–1987 survey and enumeration data are available on sex, race, and age composition:

Sex, Race, and Age	Nashville	Knoxville	Chattanooga	Memphis
Male (%)	85	79	87	90
Black (%)	21	12	36	48
Under 18 years (%)	9	13	14	—
60+ years (%)	7	9	9	4
Median age	35	37	46	34

This information, like that in all subsequent sections of the chapter, is limited to homeless populations in the four major cities of the state, since adequate compositional data do not exist for smaller metropolitan or rural areas. The most striking difference across cities is in the representation of black homeless persons, ranging from a low of 12 percent in Knoxville to a high of 48 percent in Memphis. This racial variation should not be considered a surprise, since the general populations of the cities of their respective grand divisions also differ markedly by race.

There is more consistency from place to place in sex and age composition. Tennessee's urban homeless are predominantly male, and the vast majority fall in the 18–60 age category. A median age in the mid–30s is evident for every city except Chattanooga, where no one under 18 was interviewed.[5] Age break-downs by race and sex (not shown here) suggest that, on the average, homeless blacks and women are somewhat younger than their white and male counterparts.

Overall, these findings provide less than resounding support for the new homeless perspective. While women and young people have clearly joined the ranks of the homeless, their numbers are smaller than many recent studies purport them to be. Proportionally speaking, blacks also remain in the minority. At first glance, then, the urban homeless populations of Tennessee would appear to resemble more closely the skid-row than the new homeless profile.

I consider such a conclusion tentative for two reasons. First, the most recent Nashville enumerations indicate that new homeless groups tend to be concentrated in outlying shelters and other spatial locations beyond traditional skid-row boundaries. Their territorial marginality, in conjunction with a possibly greater propensity to double up with friends or relatives, leaves homeless blacks, women, and the young especially vulnerable to undercounting and to underrepresentation in surveys.

Second, there may be marked temporal variation in the composition of homeless populations. In the Salvation Army's family shelter in Memphis, for example, the percentage of black clients increased from 31.9 percent in 1979–1980 to 57.9 percent in 1985–1986, and the percentage of children rose from 34.5 percent to 56.5 percent over the same period.[6] Due to the lack of citywide longitudinal data, the existence of a parallel trend cannot be firmly established for the Memphis homeless population as a whole. However, the shelter statistics underscore the need to couch generalizations about demographic characteristics in time-specific terms.

FAMILY RELATIONS

According to Caplow et al. (1968: 494), a distinctive feature of skid-row residents has been their *disaffiliation*, defined as a "detachment from society characterized by the absence or attention of the affiliative bonds that link settled persons to a network of interconnected social structures." This condition is dramatically manifested in skid-row residents' lack of family ties. Large-scale surveys conducted in the 1950s and 1960s found that only about half of the homeless had ever been married and that very few stayed in touch with parents, siblings, or other relatives (Bahr, 1973: 89). In contrast, new homeless populations are thought to contain significant—and growing—numbers of people living in or maintaining ties to family units.

Which of these two perspectives best describes Tennessee's urban homeless? Evidence from Nashville's latest enumeration, carried out in June 1987, can be used to address this issue. For the first time, enumerators counted the number of apparent family groupings—childless couples, couples with children, and single-parent families—as well as the number of individuals. Altogether, 48 family units were observed, three-fourths of which included children. Slightly over half (52 percent) of the families had both adults present, and slightly under half (46 percent) were female-headed. Assuming an average of 2.5 persons per family, it appears that as many as 15 percent of Nashville's homeless may be living with immediate family members at any given moment. While this figure is hardly trivial, it pales beside the remaining 85 percent of the population living alone, a pattern that conforms more closely to skid-row than new homeless generalizations.

The survey data on marital status (shown below) would also seem to attest to the continuing accuracy of the skid-row model. In each city investigated, fewer than one out of five respondents reported being currently married. Most, however, had some previous experience with marriage: for three of the four cities, the modal marital status among homeless respondents was divorced or separated. Only for Memphis does the percentage never marrying approach that found in the skid-row studies. The all-male nature of the Memphis sample might account for the high proportion of singles there, since the likelihood of marriage is lower among homeless men than women (Rossi et al., 1986: 67).

Marital Status	Nashville	Knoxville	Chattanooga	Memphis
Married (%)	14	19	7	9
Divorced or separated (%)	45	41	59	30
Widowed (%)	8	6	9	4
Single, never married (%)	34	35	25	57

One legacy of their past and present marriages is that the majority of Tennessee's urban homeless have given birth to or fathered children. In Knoxville 53 percent said they had done so, with the proportion climbing to 62 percent in Nashville. Though few were living with their children at the time they were interviewed, there may still be a substantial amount of familial contact. Over 40 percent of Chattanooga's homeless claimed to have offspring or other relatives in the area, and the percentages are almost as high for Nashville and Knoxville. Moreover, in Nashville half of the respondents with local relatives were in touch with them on a monthly basis, and roughly a third of all homeless persons in Knoxville (90 percent of those with local relatives) had such contact during the course of a year.

The existence of family relations suggests that disaffiliation is not as complete among the homeless as the skid-row literature contends. Indeed, many homeless individuals have networks of local intimates that they can draw upon for information and assistance (Lee, 1987). A measure of the significance of these networks lies in their ability to shape geographic mobility decisions. One-fourth of Nashville's and Knoxville's homeless said that they moved to their current city of residence because they had friends or relatives there, considered it home, or were born there and presumably still felt the pull of interpersonal ties formed during youth.

SOCIOECONOMIC CHARACTERISTICS

While social attachments account for much of the mobility of homeless people, the single most important reason for moving is the desire to work. Depending upon which Tennessee metropolitan area one looks at, the prospect of employment may attract up to 40 percent of the homeless who have moved from other locations. Unfortunately, job opportunities often prove less plentiful than they appeared from a distance. With the exception of Nashville, where three of every ten

survey respondents had worked for pay during the week before they were interviewed, the rate of employment does not exceed 15–16 percent in the state's largest urban homeless populations. This finding is in line with the skid-row and new
homeless perspectives, both of which emphasize the economic marginality of the
homeless.

Those persons who are unemployed hardly fit the public's stereotype of shift-
less bums. Among the homeless interviewed in Nashville and Knoxville, less than
one in 10 voluntarily chose unemployment. The majority still conducted aggressive job searches, checking assorted information sources—newspapers, the "gra-
pevine," friends, day labor offices, work places—at least several times a week
(Campbell, 1987). Given the low ratio of success to effort expended, the frustration felt by homeless individuals over lack of a steady job is quite understandable.
Nashville's homeless pointed to their job situation as the one thing they would like
to change most about their lives, and employment assistance was the biggest service need identified by homeless respondents in Knoxville and Chattanooga.

Why do so few homeless work, especially when the economies of Tennessee's
major cities seem to be thriving? Many are unable to do so because of poor
health, alcoholism, disability, or old age. Also, the jobs most readily available
to homeless people tend to be of short duration. For example, two thirds of the
working homeless in the Nashville survey considered their present positions
temporary rather than permanent, and almost half of the jobs held by Knoxville's
homeless had lasted for less than a week.

Even the types of work for which past employment best qualifies the homeless
offer little security. Data from all four cities on occupational backgrounds reveal
a concentration of experience in the service, construction, and manufacturing
sectors, typically as food preparers, laborers, craftsmen, machine operatives and
the like. Persons in these lines of work have long suffered from seasonal unemployment and sporadic layoffs, and they are now becoming increasingly vulnerable to technological displacement as well.

Both the skid-row and new homeless literatures hold educational deficiencies
partly to blame for the problematic employment situation faced by the homeless.
Yet in each urban homeless population surveyed in Tennessee, the level of educational attainment is quite impressive. As the following data show, a majority of
respondents reported having earned a high school diploma or attended college.
The percentage with high school or college educations ranges from a low of 51
percent in Nashville to a high of 66 percent in Memphis. At the opposite extreme,
some homeless have not gone beyond grade school, but they are the exception
rather than the rule.[7]

Education	Nashville	Knoxville	Chattanooga	Memphis
Grade school (%)	16	24	11	15
Some high school (%)	34	22	25	19
High school graduate (%)	30	33	50	44
Some college or college graduate (%)	21	21	13	22

Educational levels may not correlate well with the incidence of under- and unemployment among the state's homeless, but income levels certainly do. In Nashville, the estimated median monthly income for the entire homeless population is only $100, with 40 percent having an income of $50 or less. For those not working, the financial picture is even bleaker (median monthly income = $77). Despite the high incidence of unemployment, homeless respondents in Nashville and Knoxville cited day labor and the occasional job of longer duration as their major source of income. The second most common source in both cities was giving plasma or blood, followed by contributions from friends and Social Security payments in Nashville, and contributions from relatives and handouts in Knoxville.

GEOGRAPHIC ROOTS

If there is one element of popular opinion that is thought to tap the essence of homelessness, it is the belief that being homeless means extensive geographic mobility. This view reflects the legacy of the hobo life-style and also the desire of local officials to shift the burden of responsibility elsewhere by defining the homeless as nonresidents. The view does not, however, reflect the results from previous skid-row investigations, most of which have discovered high rates of *intra*urban mobility but relatively low rates of *inter*urban mobility in homeless populations (Lee, 1978).

Does the conclusion to be drawn from the skid-row literature—that homeless people are rooted in particular places—apply to the homeless of the 1980s? The following evidence suggests that it does:

Geographic Roots	Nashville	Knoxville	Chattanooga	Memphis
From Tennessee (%)	36	53	60	26
Living in city five years or longer (%)	43	50	50	—
Attached to city (%)	41	67	69	—

Substantial percentages of respondents in each of the state's four major cities were from Tennessee originally, had lived in their respective cities for at least five years, and exhibited some form of attachment or commitment to those cities. Though the table apparently documents sizable differences in rootedness across the four survey locations, much of the variation might be due to the lack of perfect comparability in the measures employed. In the Nashville and Memphis data, for instance, being "from Tennessee" is operationalized as being born there, but a less stringent criterion—"growing up" in the state—has been used for Knoxville and Chattanooga. Similarly, being "attached" to Nashville means considering the city one's "home base"; attachment to Knoxville and Chattanooga is measured by a question about plans to remain in each community in the future.

Despite the appeal of this artifactual explanation, there is reason to believe that at least some of the between-city variation may be real. Of the three cities with complete information, Nashville is the one in which the homeless seem to have sunk the shallowest roots. The greater accessibility of Nashville, along with middle Tennessee's brighter growth and employment picture, might attract more "new blood" and facilitate a higher turnover rate in the homeless population.[8] The city's dual status as state capital and country music capital could further boost the number of homeless who have come from out of state or who are in town on a temporary basis.

Because Nashville provides a setting conducive to transience, the threads of localism found among its homeless citizens are all the more remarkable. Analysis of detailed residential history items from the Nashville survey indicates that many more respondents had previously lived in the South (outside Tennessee) than in other regions of the country, and only 16 percent had lived in all four regions (Northeast, Midwest, West, and South). Indeed, over three fifths were born in Nashville or in Tennessee or another southern state, and 71 percent had most recently moved to Nashville from elsewhere in the state or region. Perhaps most striking is the fact that, on the average, two fifths of the total years lived by Nashville's homeless had been spent in Tennessee, and one fourth of those years were spent in the city.

In summary, the findings in this section refute the stereotypical notion that homeless people are outsiders who move frequently between distant locations. They are locally rooted, more deeply so than most of their fellow urban residents care to admit.

THE HOMELESS AS OUTSIDERS

While Tennessee's homeless may not be geographic outsiders, they are outsiders in the more conventional, sociological sense of the term (Becker, 1963). In each of the urban homeless populations under examination, the serious personal problems labeled deviance by the social scientist are disproportionately represented. Nevertheless, the data below reveal the incidence of these problems to be lower than what recent studies that focused on special new homeless topics and groups would lead one to anticipate.

Type of Problem	Nashville	Knoxville	Chattanooga	Memphis
Alcoholic or drinking problem (%)	32	33	34	28
Hospitalized for mental health problem (%)	22	23	12	12
Spending time in correctional facility (%)	55	44	48	67
Without close friends in city (%)	48	23	—	—
Veteran (%)	42	43	44	46

Alcohol consumption provides a case in point. Contrary to the belief that a majority of homeless individuals are heavy drinkers, the top row of data shows the proportion to be closer to a third. This figure remains fairly constant across the four cities surveyed in Tennessee and corresponds to the findings from skid-row studies conducted in a number of urban areas (Bahr, 1973: 103).[9]

Similarly, less than one fourth of the state's urban homeless have been hospitalized for treatment of mental health problems (see second row above). According to survey results, the percentages hospitalized in the Nashville and Knoxville samples are roughly double the percentages in Chattanooga and Memphis. Given the comparable interview items used and the presence of large mental health facilities in all four places, the explanation of these between-city differences is not readily apparent.

It should be noted that hospitalization is a rather stringent measure of mental illness. In the three cities with additional information available (Nashville, Knoxville, Chattanooga) significant numbers of respondents said they had been treated on an outpatient basis or were suffering from "nerve problems." Overall, however, the incidence of mental problems among the ranks of Tennessee's homeless falls far short of the 90 percent rate claimed by Bassuk (1984) in a study of Boston shelter inhabitants. Other evidence contrary to the Boston findings has been produced by Snow et al. (1986).

An association between homelessness and crime is suggested by the fact that between 40 percent and 70 percent of those interviewed in each Tennessee city had spent time in a correctional facility. The crimes which lead to the incarceration of the homeless are normally of the "nuisance" variety, including public drunkenness, disorderly behavior, and fighting. Unfortunately, what often gets overlooked is that homeless persons are at least as likely to be victims as perpetrators of crime. In Nashville, for example, three fifths of the respondents said they had been victimized, typically within the preceding six months. The high level of fear expressed by these respondents—over 70 percent considered it very dangerous to be out alone at night in the downtown area—further attests to their vulnerability.

The last two rows of data presented above address the social adjustment of the homeless. Veteran's status does this in an admittedly indirect fashion, but the possibility that prior military service may be a disruptive life event with enduring psychological and behavioral implications makes the percentages in the bottom row worthy of mention. Lack of friendships is a more direct adjustment measure. The fact that roughly twice the percentage of homeless in Nashville than Knoxville reported no close friends locally may be a function of the greater transience of the former city. Even among Nashville's homeless, though, long-term residents of the area are frequently enmeshed in interpersonal networks (Lee, 1987). Only about a quarter appear to have truly serious difficulties getting along with other people.

A COMPARATIVE APPROACH

Thus far, the social and demographic characteristics of Tennessee's urban homeless populations have been described in a vacuum, with few standards (other than the skid-row and new homeless perspectives) proposed against which to judge the significance of findings. In this section, as in my earlier discussion of population size, I take a comparative approach, giving the characteristics of the homeless meaning by placing them in broader context.

Perhaps the most valuable type of comparison that can be made is between homeless and settled persons in the same city. This comparison is explicit in the claim, based on skid-row research, that certain groups—singles, whites, males, and so on—are disproportionately likely to be homeless. A similar claim can be found in the new homeless literature, though about different groups (blacks, veterans, and so on). Table 11.2 provides the information needed to check the accuracy of the skid-row and new homeless profiles. For each of the seven compositional variables in the table, survey data on a city's homeless population are presented in the first row, 1980 census data on the city as a whole are presented in the second row, and the ratio of homeless-to-city data is presented in the third row. The ratios are of central interest, with values above or below 1.00 indicating over- or underrepresentation of a particular characteristic in the homeless population relative to the general population of a city.

The easiest results to deal with in Table 11.2 concern sex, marital status, and duration of residence. In every city, the percentage of males among the homeless is almost twice that among all residents, while the percentages married and living in the city at least five years are much smaller in the homeless than general populations. According to the median age ratios, the homeless also tend to be relatively older, although this is attributable to the underrepresentation of children rather than to the overrepresentation of seniors. Finally, the ratios in the bottom row show that veterans constitute a greater proportion of the homeless population than they do of the surrounding city. If anything, the veteran ratios err on the conservative side, since veterans have been calculated as a percentage of all homeless persons but only as a percentage of all males in the settled population.

The results for the remaining variables in Table 11.2 defy easy interpretation. With respect to racial composition, blacks are represented among the homeless at or above their percentages in the general populations of the two cities that are over 30 percent black—Chattanooga and Memphis. High school graduates are slightly overrepresented among the homeless in both of those cities as well. By contrast, Nashville and Knoxville's homeless populations contain relatively few blacks and persons with high school diplomas.

CONCLUSION

While the homeless-to-city ratios for race and education may be difficult to explain, they underscore the need to consider the demographic dimensions of

Table 11.2
Selected Comparisons Between Urban Homeless and General Population in Tennessee

Characteristics	Nashville	Knoxville	Chattanooga	Memphis
% Male				
Homeless	85	79	87	90
City	47	47	47	47
Homeless/City	1.81	1.68	1.85	1.91
% Black				
Homeless	20	12	36	48
City	23	15	32	48
Homeless/City	0.87	0.80	1.12	1.00
Median Age				
Homeless	35	37	46	34
City	30	29	30	28
Homeless/City	1.17	1.28	1.53	1.21
% Married[a]				
Homeless	14	19	7	9
City[b]	52	48	52	49
Homeless/City	0.27	0.40	0.13	0.18
% High School Graduate				
Homeless	51	54	63	66
City[c]	65	61	60	63
Homeless/City	0.78	0.89	1.05	1.05
% Living in City 5 Years or Longer				
Homeless	43	50	50	na
City[d]	77	76	80	86
Homeless/City	0.56	0.66	0.62	na
% Veteran				
Homeless	42	43	44	46
City[e]	33	32	35	32
Homeless/City	1.27	1.34	1.26	1.44

na: Not available and/or not applicable.
a: Excludes married but currently separated.
b: Persons 15 years of age or older.
c: Persons 25 years of age or older.
d: Persons 5 years of age or older.
e: Males 16 years of age or older.

Source: See text for description of data sources and Ns for homeless populations; for general population, see U.S.Bureau of the Census (1983a, 1983b).

homelessness in place-specific terms. Tennessee's four major urban homeless populations differ in size and many aspects of composition, as do its urban and rural areas in the incidence of homelessness. Scanning the chapters of this book, one is likely to detect similar differences at the state level. Such differences can presumably be attributed to variations in economic conditions, housing markets, climate, and other aspects of the geographic settings in which homeless populations are located.

When homelessness is viewed over time rather than across places, a number of continuities in demographic composition become apparent. Like skid-row studies of the past, the surveys and enumerations conducted in Tennessee during the 1980s show the ranks of the homeless to be dominated by unmarried middle-aged men with limited socioeconomic resources and local or regional roots. This is not to deny that certain types of new homeless persons—family members, for example, or those suffering from mental illness—have probably increased in number. There is, however, a tendency to exaggerate the proportional representation and growth of such groups.

Reported increases in the overall number of homeless are often inflated as well. Clearly, the generalization from the skid-row literature no longer applies to Tennessee, if it ever did: homeless populations in the state are hardly shrinking. But one can find little direct evidence that they are expanding as rapidly as proponents of the new homeless perspective might argue, either. Keeping the trends in service-usage statistics in mind, the most reasonable conclusion seems to be that the extent of homelessness in Tennessee has increased substantially but not spectacularly during the past decade.

The fact that many informed observers will regard this conclusion as too conservative raises an important question: What accounts for the discrepancy between perceived and measured demographic properties of homeless populations? While methodological shortcomings cannot be overlooked, I think much of the answer lies in the heightened visibility of the homeless. Redevelopment efforts in downtown areas have combined with the deinstitutionalization movement to push a greater percentage of homeless people—many of whom engage in peculiar, eye-catching behavior—onto the streets and into the public's consciousness. Other homeless individuals, such as women, children, and blacks, are memorable because they fail to fit conventional skid-row categories; the troubling inference is that the forces underlying their situation may be ones to which "normal," settled persons are susceptible. In short, we believe homeless populations are changing dramatically in size and composition because some segments of those populations have become both more and less like us. They are thus harder to forget, distorting our perceptions of the whole.

NOTES

    I am deeply indebted to Ann Henniss (Metropolitan Council for Community Services, Chattanooga), Roger Nooe and Maryanne Lynch (University of Tennessee-Knoxville), Kate Mullins (University of Tennessee-Memphis), Jacqueline Walpole (Salvation Army, Memphis), Barbara Wicks (Memphis Coalition for the Homeless), and Hurston Burkhart and Steven Meinbresse (Tennessee Department of Human Services) for their willingness to share data and insights. Special thanks are also due the members and staff of the

Nashville Coalition for the Homeless and the Task Force on Homelessness of the Metropolitan Development and Housing Agency, who have worked with the author in exploring the demographic dimensions of homelessness in Nashville.

1. Most of the estimates from local informants can be found in the same reports as direct evidence (Green, 1986; Henniss, 1987; Nooe and Lynch, 1986; Tennessee Department of Human Services, 1986). The local informant estimate for Memphis is the midpoint of a large range (600–5,000) given in a two-page demographic profile distributed by the Memphis Coalition for the Homeless. Estimates from state informants are contained in a document issued by the Tennessee Legislative Committee on the Homeless (1987).

2. The authors of the Tennessee Legislative Committee report (1987), from which the estimates have been drawn, were trying to justify funding for a variety of services and programs recommended in the report.

3. Specific HUD incidence rates, as well as the procedures used to calculate them, are described in U.S. Department of Housing and Urban Development (1984: 5–21). I have multiplied the 1984–1985 population of each Rand McNally–defined (Ranally) metropolitan area in Tennessee and of the nonmetropolitan portion of the state by the appropriate incidence rate to arrive at the HUD-based estimates in Table 11.1.

4. Since June 1986, shelters for the homeless located outside the downtown area have been included in the Nashville enumerations.

5. The percentages under 18 and over 60 years of age in Chattanooga were estimated from a combination of survey and shelter use data made available by Ann Henniss.

6. The shelter statistics, which are compiled annually and cover an unduplicated pool of clients, were provided by Jacqueline Boles.

7. The educational data should be interpreted cautiously since they tap the amount of schooling but neglect its quality. The importance of this distinction is underscored by service providers' growing awareness of literacy problems, even among the better-educated homeless.

8. Some indication of the fluidity of Nashville's homeless population comes from a comparison of 1983 client records kept by the two largest shelters in the city. During that year, an estimated 10,000 different homeless individuals spent a night or more in one or both of the shelters.

9. One might expect drinking and other deviant behaviors to be severely underreported by homeless people in face-to-face interviews. However, at least one study that checked the survey responses of the homeless against official records found little evidence of significant inconsistencies (Bahr and Houts, 1971). Because their reputations are already spoiled, homeless persons may have less to lose by answering truthfully than do respectable members of the settled population.

REFERENCES

Bahr, Howard M., ed. 1970. *Disaffiliated Man: Essays and Bibliography on Skid Row, Vagrancy, and Outsiders*. Toronto: University of Toronto Press.
———. 1973. *Skid Row: An Introduction to Disaffiliation*. New York: Oxford University Press.
Bahr, Howard M., and Theodore Caplow. 1973. *Old Men Drunk and Sober*. New York: New York University Press.

Bahr, Howard M., and Kathleen C. Houts. 1971. Can You Trust a Homeless Man? A Comparison of Official Records and Interview Responses by Bowery Men. *Public Opinion Quarterly* 35: 374–382.

Bassuk, Ellen L. 1984. The Homelessness Problem. *Scientific American* 251: 40–45.

Becker, Howard S. 1963. *Outsiders: Studies in the Sociology of Deviance*. Glencoe, Ill.: Free Press.

Blumberg, Leonard U., et al. 1960. *The Men on Skid Row: A Study of Philadelphia's Homeless Man Population*. Philadelphia: Department of Psychiatry, Temple University.

Bogue, Donald J. 1963. *Skid Row in American Cities*. Chicago: Community and Family Study Center, University of Chicago.

Brown, Carl, et al. 1983. *The Homeless of Phoenix: Who Are They and What Should Be Done?* Phoenix: South Community Mental Health Center.

Campbell, Karen E. 1987. Work Experiences of the Homeless. Paper presented at annual meeting of Society for the Study of Social Problems, Chicago.

Caplow, Theodore, et al. 1958. *A General Report on the Problem of Relocating the Population of the Lower Loop Redevelopment Area*. Minneapolis: Minneapolis Housing and Redevelopment Authority.

Caplow, Theodore. 1968. Homelessness. In *International Encyclopedia of the Social Sciences*, Vol. 6, edited by David Stills. New York: Macmillan.

Crystal, Stephen. 1984. Homeless Men and Homeless Women: The Gender Gap. *Urban and Social Change Review* 17: 2–6.

Erickson, Jon, and Charles Wilhelm, eds. 1986. *Housing the Homeless*. New Brunswick, N.J.: Rutgers Center for Urban Policy Research.

Fischer, Pamela J., et al. 1986. Mental Health and Social Characteristics of the Homeless: A Survey of Mission Users. *American Journal of Public Health* 76: 519–524.

Green, Laura L. 1986. *Task Force on Homelessness: Final Report of Findings and Recommendations*. Nashville: Metropolitan Development and Housing Agency.

Henniss, Anne G. 1987. *Chattanooga Survey of the Homeless*. Chattanooga: Metropolitan Council for Community Services.

Hombs, Mary Ellen, and Mitch Snyder. 1982. *Homelessness in America: A Forced March to Nowhere*. Washington, D.C.: Community for Creative Non-Violence.

Hope, Marjorie, and James Young. 1986. *The Faces of Homelessness*. Lexington, Mass.: Lexington Books.

Huth, Mary Jo. 1987. Homelessness in America: Its Nature and Extent. Paper presented at annual meeting of American Sociological Association, Chicago.

Lamb, H. Richard, ed. 1984. *The Homeless Mentally Ill: A Task Force Report of the American Psychiatric Association*. Washington, D.C. American Psychiatric Association.

Lee, Barrett A. 1978. Residential Mobility on Skid Row: Disaffiliation, Powerlessness, and Decision Making. *Demography* 15: 285–300.

———. 1980. The Disappearance of Skid Row: Some Ecological Evidence. *Urban Affairs Quarterly* 16: 81–107.

———. 1987. Homelessness and Community. Paper presented at annual meeting of American Sociological Association, Chicago.

Lipton, Frank R., et al. 1983. Down and Out in the City: The Homeless Mentally Ill. *Hospital and Community Psychiatry* 34: 817–821.

McCook, John J. 1893. A Tramp Census and Its Revelations. *Forum* 15 (August): 753–766.

Mullins, Kate. 1986. *Preliminary Report on Salvation Army Men's Shelter 1986 Study*. Memphis, Tenn.: Salvation Army.

Nooe, Roger M., and Maryanne Lynch. 1986. *Homelessness in Knox County: Report of the Knoxville Coalition for the Homeless*. Knoxville, Tenn.: Knoxville Coalition for the Homeless.

Peroff, Kathleen. 1987. Who Are the Homeless and How Many Are There? In *The Homeless in Contemporary Society*, edited by Richard D. Bingham, et al. Newbury Park, Calif.: Sage.

Redburn, F. Stevens, and Terry F. Buss. 1986. *Responding to America's Homeless: Public Policy Alternatives*. New York: Praeger.

Robertson, Marjorie J. 1987. Homeless Veterans: An Emerging Problem? In *The Homeless in Contemporary Society*, edited by Richard D. Bingham, Roy E. Green, and Sammis B. White. Newbury Park, Calif.: Sage.

Rossi, Peter H., et al. 1986. *The Condition of the Homeless of Chicago*. Amherst, Mass.: Social and Demographic Research Institute, University of Massachusetts.

Roth, Dee, and Gerald J. Bean, Jr. 1986. New Perspectives on Homelessness: Findings from a Statewide Epidemiological Study. *Hospital and Community Psychiatry* 37: 712–719.

Rubington, Earl. 1971. The Changing Skid Row Scene. *Quarterly Journal of Studies on Alcohol* 32: 123–135.

Schutt, Russell K. 1986. *A Short Report on Homeless Veterans: A Supplement to Homeless in Boston in 1985*. Boston: University of Massachusetts.

Snow, Davis A., et al. 1986. The Myth of Pervasive Mental Illness among the Homeless. *Social Problems* 33: 407–423.

Stefl, Mary E. 1987. The New Homeless: A National Perspective. In *The Homeless in Contemporary Society*, edited by Richard D. Bingham, et al. Newbury Park, Calif.: Sage.

Sullivan, Patricia A., and Shirley Damrosch. 1987. Homeless Women and Children. In *The Homeless in Contemporary Society*, edited by Richard D. Bingham, et al. Newbury Park, Calif.: Sage.

Tennessee Department of Human Services. 1986. *Problems of the Homeless in 91 Rural Counties*. Nashville, Tenn.: Tennessee Department of Human Services.

Tennessee Legislative Committee on the Homeless. 1987. *Study of Tennessee's Homeless Problem Report on Findings and Recommendations*. Nashville: Tennessee General Assembly.

U.S. Bureau of the Census. 1982. 1980 Census of Population. Vol. 1, Characteristics of the Population; Chap. A, Number of Inhabitants; Part 44, Tennessee. PC80–1-A44. Washington, D.C.: Government Printing Office.

———. 1983a. 1980 Census of Population. Vol. 1, Characteristics of the Population; Chap. C, General Social and Economic Characteristics; Part 44, Tennessee. PC80–1-C44. Washington, D.C.: Government Printing Office.

———. 1983b. 1980 Census of Population and Housing. Census Tract Reports for Chattanooga, Knoxville, Memphis, and Nashville-Davidson SMSAs. PHC80–2–118, 203, 239, 252. Washington D.C.: Government Printing Office.

U.S. Department of Housing and Urban Development. 1984. *A Report to the Secretary on the Homeless and Emergency Shelters*. Washington, D.C.: Office of Policy

Development and Research, U.S. Department of Housing and Urban Development.

Vander Kooi, Ronald. 1973. The Main Stem: Skid Row Revisited. *Society* 10 (September–October): 64–71.

Wallace, Samuel E. 1965. *Skid Row as a Way of Life*. Totowa, N.J.: Bedminster.

Watson, Sophie. 1986. *Housing and Homelessness: A Feminist Perspective*. London: Routledge and Kegan Paul.

12

Homelessness in Texas: Estimates of Population Size and Demographic Composition

Susan G. Baker and David A. Snow

Like many other socially and economically dispossessed groups, today's homeless have become the object of profound curiosity and intense public policy debates (General Accounting Office, 1985; Hombs and Snyder, 1982; U.S. Department of Housing and Urban Development, 1984; U.S. House Committee on Government Operations, 1985). Regrettably, this concern has rapidly outpaced social science efforts to provide empirically reliable information on the size and composition of the homeless population. This situation underscores one of the central ironies of sociological research: The most important population groups from a policy perspective are often the most difficult to study with orthodox research methods, thus leaving gaps between evidence and sound policy formation.

As with other populous states, Texas has experienced many of the problems emerging from this disjuncture between evidence on homelessness and efforts to address the issue through public and private initiatives. Since 1980 Texas has experienced both a boom in labor migration from the northern United States and Mexico and an ill-timed sharp economic downturn spurred by falling oil prices (Texas Health and Human Service Coordinating Council, 1985). These two factors set the stage for a growing concern about homelessness, as the ranks of unemployed Texas residents swelled and spilled onto the streets. Relief agencies found themselves swamped with requests for services, and the state government found itself pressured to stave off a crisis, but with very little information on the population to which its efforts were to be applied. As a result, in the summer of 1985, the Texas Health and Human Services Coordinating Council responded to a directive issued by Governor Mark White calling for a review of homelessness in Texas. The council convened a meeting of service providers and advocacy groups operating throughout the state. Coalitions from six Texas cities—Austin, Dallas, El Paso, Fort Worth, Houston, and San Antonio—constituted the bulk of the attenders. Drawing on information provided by reports from these coalitions, nationwide attempts to estimate the size of the homeless population, statewide data for Salvation Army clients, and our own longitudinal project examining homelessness in Austin, we attempt in this chapter to provide a reasoned discussion and estimation of the size and demographic composition of the homeless population in Texas. We also briefly discuss some of the recurring problems attendant to the empirical study of homelessness, and the potential for social science research to shed light on the issue of homelessness in ways that would make policy implementation more effective.

While we recognize that the size and characteristics of the homeless population will vary across states, we also assume that the logic underlying our estimation efforts should be appropriate to any region. We begin with an overview of our conceptualization of homelessness.

DEFINING HOMELESSNESS

Homelessness is obviously a broad construct. At its most general level, the term applies not only to the classic image of urban "street people" but also to such undomiciled groups as disaster victims, political refugees, and continually uprooted, poverty-stricken migrant laborers. Since these subgroups can never be clearly delineated, particularly in the face of rapidly changing macrolevel economic circumstances, we focus our analysis on the most conspicuous category of homeless: the urban "street people," whom we conceptualize as individuals living in urban areas whose life-style is characterized by the absence of permanent housing, supportive familial bonds, and consensually defined roles of social utility and moral worth. Our sense is that this subgroup represents the bulk of the homeless population in Texas. It also has been the principal focus of a number of local studies of homelessness in Texas (Snow et al., 1986; Baumann et al., 1985; San Antonio Urban Council, 1984; El Paso Task Force on the Homeless, 1984). Our estimates of the size and composition of the Texas homeless are thus weighted definitionally toward this modal category.

POPULATION SIZE

Given this working definition, we begin our estimation effort by considering preliminary estimates of the homeless population in each of Texas's six largest cities. In 1983, two private foundations—the Robert Wood Johnson Foundation and the Pew Memorial Trust—targeted $19.4 million to be distributed to coalitions on the homeless in 51 of the nation's largest cities for the provision of health care to the homeless. Coalitions from the six Texas cities mentioned above submitted applications for these funds. As part of the application report, each city provided estimates of its homeless population based upon patronage of emergency food and shelter services. These six research projects share the considerable benefit of having been conducted over the same time period, thus controlling in part for intercity mobility among the state's homeless population. These independent estimation attempts provide the following initial size estimates of the homeless population in Texas (Texas Health and Human Services Coordinating Council, 1985).

City	Homeless Population		Range Midpoint
Austin	2,100–4,000	daily	3,050
Dallas	3,000–14,000	daily	8,500
El Paso	921–3,363	daily	2,142
Fort Worth	8,000–10,000	daily	9,000
Houston	6,000–7,000	daily	6,500
San Antonio	12,000–15,000	yearly	13,500

Each of the estimates, with the exception of that for San Antonio, refers to daily rather than yearly numbers. In the case of El Paso, for example, the daily estimate ranges from 921 to 3,363. Comparison of the estimates clearly indicates that they span a range of potential population size. The estimates are also highly discrepant, with several of the cities claiming a larger homeless population than Houston, the nation's fifth largest city. Additionally, these estimates are far greater than would be expected on the basis of traditional census enumeration procedures (Population Today, 1986; Rossi et al., 1987; Wiegard, 1985). Finally, these estimates are rendered somewhat suspect by the tendency for aid-seeking service agencies and coalitions to inflate their estimated constituency in order to make their respective claims and appeals more compelling.

These disclaimers notwithstanding, the figures do provide a point of departure for reaching a more satisfactory estimate of the size of Texas's homeless population. Moreover, there is no way of assaying the accuracy of these estimates without further assessment based on some independent methodology. We thus assess these baseline estimates by comparing them to three nationwide estimates derived from three different estimation logics and procedures.

The first estimate is the most straightforward and controversial. Issued by the Committee for Creative Non-violence (CCNV), a homeless advocacy group headquartered in Washington, D.C., it holds that 1 percent of the U.S. population is homeless at any given time (Hombs and Snyder, 1982). The empirical rationale behind this figure, however, is unclear. The second estimate, generated by the U.S. Department of Housing and Urban Development (1984), is based on an analysis of published estimates of homelessness in U.S. cities (only one of which was in Texas). The analysis yielded a homelessness rate for urban areas of 25 homeless per 10,000 population. The authors of the HUD report characterize this rate as an "outside" estimate. The third estimate, also issued by HUD, is based on an estimation procedure disaggregating local area reports by city size.

Using this technique, large (1 million or more population), medium (250,000 to 1 million population), and small (50,000 to 250,000 population) urban areas demonstrate homelessness rates of 13, 12, and 6.5 persons per 10,000 respectively.

Using these three estimation procedures and Texas's Department of Vital Statistics data on the state's population size for 1986, we generate three independent city and statewide estimates of homelessness.

City/Region	Model 1 (CCNV 1% Estimate)	Model 2 (HUD .25 Rate)	Model 3 (HUD .13, .12, .06 Rates)
Austin	4,925	1,294	621
Dallas	17,133	4,419	2,297
El Paso	5,402	1,402	673
Fort Worth	9,948	2,602	1,353
Houston	27,734	7,261	3,776
San Antonio	10,936	2,824	1,469
Remaining Texas population	79,217	22,081	4,753
Total	155,295	41,883	14,942

These highly disparate estimates serve first to reinforce the lack of consensus evident in policy discussions surrounding homelessness. It makes a considerable difference in budgeting emergency food and shelter programs if the actual demand could ultimately be 10 times the anticipated need. If we extrapolate the Texas estimates to the national level, national estimates range from a high of approximately 2 million to a low of 300,000. We are thus caught in the same trap as policymakers in attempts to zero in on a reliable estimate.

Still, the prospect of deciding on a statewide estimate is not completely bleak. Reliability hinges upon the agreement between independent measures. As we have decided a priori to use the six Texas city coalition reports as our baseline for assessing estimates, we see that Model 2—the HUD rate of 25 per 10,000 population—generates numbers that most closely approximate the range midpoints of these independent estimates. It is also interesting to note that in the case of Austin, the HUD 0.25 estimate matches almost perfectly the city's Task Force on Homelessness recent estimates of 1,300 homeless on any given day (City of Austin, 1986). In light of the considerations, we find the HUD 0.25 percent estimate closer to the mark than either the HUD revised estimates or the CCNV 1 percent estimate.

It is important to note that the HUD report portrays the 0.25 rate as an upwardly biased estimate because it is constructed from published reports by large cities, which are assumed to have a higher proportion of homeless residents than small urban and nonmetropolitan areas. Still, we can identify at least three sources of downward bias that would offset the upward bias in the urban focus of the HUD estimate. First, the HUD estimate excludes from consideration those individuals living in paid shelters—single-room occupancy hotels and for-profit bunkhouses. These individuals avoid the streets only by the slimmest of margins. Second, the estimate ignores those individuals living in temporary protective arrangements—battered spouse shelters, for example. Third, the estimate cannot account for those homeless individuals whose daily orbits do not include the use of emergency food and shelter services. Even if we assumed that each of these subgroups represented only a small proportion of the total homeless population, they would serve nevertheless as possible downward biases in the estimate, and thus provide further reason for accepting the 0.25 rate as a central rather than an upper estimate.

In sum, when comparing the available estimates of homeless population size in Texas cities to the few estimation procedures available in the literature, we find that the HUD estimate of 25 homeless per 10,000 population generates numbers most similar to the Texas estimates. Using this technique, we generate a statewide estimate of approximately 41,000 homeless in Texas in 1986 on any given day.

DEMOGRAPHIC COMPOSITION

While generating an estimate of the number of homeless is an important exercise for policy-making, it does not provide sufficient information on which to base policy decisions. Equally important is the issue of how these 41,000 people are distributed demographically. Using our own sample of 767 homeless adults in Austin, reports generated by other Texas urban areas, and data provided by the state Salvation Army Headquarters in Dallas, we provide a preliminary breakdown of the homeless population in Texas with regard to sex, age, ethnic, and marital and family status.

Since we consider the data generated from our research project on the homeless living in and passing through Austin to be the most systematically derived data set on homelessness in Texas, we begin this section with an overview of the research strategy employed in our project.

We compiled the Austin homeless sample by tracking a random sample of homeless individuals from the street back through the maze of institutions with which they have varying degrees of contact. Four major issues were encountered in this endeavor: construction of a reasonable sampling frame; the securing of identifying information on each case; selection of core institutions with which the homeless could be expected to have contact; and negotiation of access to those institutional records.

Our sampling frame included all homeless men and women who had one or more contacts with the Austin Salvation Army between January 1, 1984, and March 1, 1985. Several considerations justified this decision. Foremost was the fact that the Salvation Army operated Austin's only public shelter for the homeless, whereas most cities of several hundred thousand or more residents have numerous shelters. Moreover, it is also the only facility in Austin that provided free breakfast and dinner. As a consequence, nearly all homeless men and women living in or passing through Austin will have had occasion to use the Salvation Army at least once for food or shelter. The resulting frame for our tracking sample selection based upon these assumptions was the 13,881 homeless men and women who had registered at least once at the Salvation Army during that 14-month period.

The problem of securing identifying information for the purpose of tracking sampled cases through other selected institutions was resolved by the Salvation Army's practice of having all first-time users fill out a small fact sheet that asks for name and Social Security number, if any, as well as some demographic and background information. Upon receiving permission from Salvation Army officials to use this identifying information for tracking purposes, we drew a random sample of 800 names and then negotiated access to the records of six other local and state agencies. These included Austin's city hospital; a local, private agency for the poor and needy called Caritas; the city police department; the Texas Employment Commission; the state Department of Mental Health and Mental Retardation (MHMR); and the local community health center. These agencies were selected because they were central to the lives of the homeless living in or passing through Austin and because each had amassed data that bear directly on much that has been conjectured and hypothesized about today's homeless. Since all but one of the agencies had computerized their records, nearly all of the tracking was computer assisted. When a match was made, all data on that case were coded onto a survey-like instrument that had been constructed on the basis of prior inspection of the record forms of the agencies. Once these data were computerized and cleaned, we were left with a usable tracking sample of 767 cases. For this chapter, we are interested primarily in the original demographic information collected from the Salvation Army records. We will compare this information to that generated in the reports from other Texas cities and the state Salvation Army Headquarters to provide a statewide overview of the demographic composition of the homeless.

Although few local area studies in Texas have generated comprehensive demographic information on the homeless, the evidence that does exist appears to be consistent with the demographic composition of our Austin sample. This is seen clearly in Table 12.1. First, we see that homeless street people in Texas appear to be disproportionately male, with 90 percent or more falling into that category in Austin as well as in San Antonio and El Paso. The homeless in Texas also appear to be a relatively young adult population, with a mean age of around 34. In Austin and El Paso, over 70 percent of the samples fell below age 40, and in San Antonio nearly 30 percent of the sample was under 25, with only 15 percent older than 50. The homeless in the three area local samples are also predominantly white, although we suspect that the representation of blacks and Hispanics increases significantly with an increase in city size. The data also show that most of the homeless in the three cities are single or unattached. Finally, it is interesting to note that there appears to be considerable mobility

Table 12.1
Comparison of Homeless Samples in Texas on Selected Demographic Variables

Demographic Variables	Austin[a] (N=767)	San Antonio[b] (N=139)	El Paso[c] (N=197)
Sex (%)			
Male	90	90	97
Age			
Mean age	35	34	33
Under 40 (%)	73	na	71
Over 60 (%)	1	na	6
Ethnicity (%)			
White	75	60	na
Black	12	15	na
Hispanic	12	25	na
Other	1	na	na
Marital status			
Married	8	15	3
Separated/divorced	28	42	10
Widowed	1	na	na
Single	63	44	88
Residential/Mobility Status			
Local	6	>39	na
From within state	52	na	na
From out of state	42	61	na

na: Not available and/or not applicable.

a: Percent male is based upon the population of men, women, and children registered at least once at the Austin Salvation Army in 1984. Remaining figures are derived from Austin homeless study described in the text.

b: Figures are based on survey conducted in an emergency shelter over a 3-week period in February and March 1984(San Antonio Urban Council, 1984).

c: Figures are based on a survey conducted in an emergency shelter during March and April 1983 (El Paso Task Force on the Homeless, 1984).

among the homeless in Texas, with the vast majority in both the Austin and San Antonio samples claiming residence in other Texas cities or out of state.

A number of these demographic characteristics are quite consistent with the growing literature on the changing face of homelessness in the United States (Bingham et al., 1987; Hope and Young, 1986). Single men, for example, continue to comprise the major demographic subgroup among the homeless. However, we should point out that a substantial "family" file existed at the Austin Salvation Army office, but that we chose not to sample from it for reasons of coding efficiency. It is also worth considering that the low proportion of females in the samples may reflect strategies of survival for homeless women that simply do not include the use of public shelters (Snow et al., 1986; Snow and Anderson, 1987). Yet, it is important not to lose sight of the fact that, throughout the state, counts of homeless are skewed significantly in the direction of males. This is illustrated most dramatically by the statewide Salvation Army data presented in Table 12.2. Here we see that individuals using Salvation Army shelters on one or more occasions in 1986 were predominantly male. While some of the clients were women, children, and families, to be sure, it is clear that they comprised only a small proportion of the homeless who frequented Salvation Army facilities throughout the state in 1986.

The age distribution of the state's homeless also warrants further discussion. The data indicate that not only are today's homeless much younger than the "classic" image of the street person of years ago (Bahr and Caplow, 1973; Bogue, 1963; Wiseman, 1970), but that the vast majority are concentrated in the most productive years of labor force participation. It thus follows that the homeless people today represent a lost contribution to the economic productivity of the state. Indeed, our data provide confirmation of a fairly strong work orientation among the homeless. Eighty-four percent indicated that they came to Austin in search of work. Moreover, slightly more than 45 percent had one or more contacts with the Texas Employment Commission, which exceeded by a considerable margin contacts with any of the other five institutions included in the study. Similarly, the San Antonio project reports that 55 percent of the sample indicated that they were lured to the city in search of work (San Antonio Urban Council, 1984: 8).

In sum, our varigated data set indicates that the homeless in Texas are predominantly male, around 35 years of age, typically white, unmarried, and relatively mobile. The data also suggest that these individuals actively seek employment in the local area, and that migration from one city to another is attributable in part of the search for work.

PATTERNS OF HOMELESSNESS ACROSS TIME

Having examined the size and demographic composition of the homeless population in Texas, we now turn to the question of the temporal stability of that population. Have the ranks of the homeless within the state expanded or contracted since the early 1980s? Or has the state's homeless population remained relatively constant? If Texas's homeless problem is partially attributable to the in migration of many of the victims of the economic downturn that plagued the Midwest and Northeast in the late 1970s and early 1980s, then we might expect the ranks of homeless to have declined somewhat in the last few years as economic conditions have improved in the Northeast. However, if homelessness in Texas is due more to internal factors, such as the decline in oil prices, then we might expect an increase in the size of the state's homeless population during the past

Table 12.2
Percentage Distribution of Salvation Army Clientele Throughout the State by Gender and Family Status in 1986

Family Status, Gender	Austin (10,465)	Dallas (16,588)	Ft. Worth (2,005)	Houston (41,634)	San Antonio (12,211)	Remainder of state (122,700)	Total (205,603)
Unattached							
Males	92	83	70	98	79	88	89
Female	4	5	9	1	9	5	4
Children	2	4	8	1	6	3	3
Families	2	6	13	1	7	4	4

Table 12.3
Change in Size of Client Groups Served by Texas Salvation Army Shelters,
1982–1986

Client Group	1982	1983	1984	1985	1986	% change 1982-1986
Unattached						
Males	143,718	131,833	130,576	123,058	107,567	-25.2
Females	10,180	10,718	11,824	8,875	5,974	-41.3
Children	5,448	5,151	6,5100	5,549	3,908	-28.3
Families	10,459	7,013	7,336	7,206	5,251	-49.8
Total	169,805	154,715	156,246	144,688	122,700	-27.7

several years. We address this issue with trend data provided by the state's Salvation Army Headquarters in Dallas.

Although these data obviously do not provide a full-proof reckoning of the incidence of homelessness across time, they do provide a reasonable reading in that they come from the one frontline agency throughout the state that maintains continuous contact with the homeless. These trend data are presented in Table 12.3. Using 1982 as the base year, we see that the incidence of homelessness in Texas appears to have peaked that year. Since then, there has been an almost steady decline in the total number of homeless, resulting in a 28 percent decrease between 1982 and 1986. As might be expected, the greatest absolute decline has been among unattached males, but the largest percentage decrease has been among homeless families and females.

Insofar as the Salvation Army data provide an accurate picture of the incidence of homelessness in Texas across time, it seems reasonable to conclude that there has been either a decline in the overall number of homeless street people or that they have found other means of survival and have thus ceased to use the Salvation Army as regularly as before. Our suspicion is that the former proposition is closer to the mark. It is consistent with the finding of an increase in homelessness nationwide following the recession of the first third of the 1980s and the subsequent downturn in Texas's economic fortunes. Simply put, it would appear that the pool of marginal or homeless individuals who were attracted to Texas in the early 1980s has either dried up in part or has looked elsewhere in hopes of finding greener economic pastures.

Such observations do not warrant a particularly sanguine attitude regarding the problem of homelessness, however. The ranks of the state's homeless appear to have declined somewhat, to be sure, but the absolute number still remains alarmingly high, thus posing an ongoing, formidable challenge to policymakers and social service agencies.

POLICY ISSUES, IMPLICATIONS, AND CONCLUSIONS

Two glaring problems exist in the research on homelessness in the United States. First, some of the homeless comprise a clandestine population in the sense that the nature of their survival strategies does not make them easy to study using orthodox enumeration techniques. Many are highly mobile, and others seek to conceal themselves from the domiciled population for reasons of personal safety. These characteristics may account for the fact that social scientists and public agencies attempting census-type "street counts" of the homeless in urban areas invariably come up with estimates lower than those of the service providers in those same areas (HUD, 1984; Rossi et al., 1987).

The second problem is that public and private agencies dealing with the homeless within and across geographical areas—cities, states, and regions—demonstrate a profound lack of integration in their attempts to identify the demographic characteristics of the homeless. In Texas, only a few urban areas have generated comprehensive demographic data in any systematic fashion, and the fact that they did so appears to be due more to coincidence than to any concerted effort on the part of research teams in these cities to coordinate their research agendas.

The solutions to these problems are both empirical and political. Repeated attempts to enumerate the homeless suggest the beginnings of a methodological consensus on one point: social scientists cannot assay population size by merely sending out research teams for a few days to beat the bushes looking for street people. As the field research of Baxter and Hopper (1981) and Snow and Anderson (1986, 1987), among others, has revealed, the homeless are far more innovative in their attempts to survive and carve out a safe niche for themselves than the more conventional research strategies assume. A more fruitful empirical approach might be a thorough survey of service provider agencies coupled with longitudinal field data collection in order to measure both the emergency shelter users and the street component of the homeless population.

The issue of comprehensive demographic data collection forces us to confront directly the political issue of responsibility for interagency communication. If states wish to have coordinated information on their homeless populations, state governments must not only convene service providers and advocates but must also construct an explicit outline of basic information these agencies can provide—an information base that can be compiled into a single overview at the statewide level of analysis. This logic applies as well at the city and federal levels of analysis. Before intervention in the issue of homelessness can be at all efficacious, the issue of coordinated information from which to draw a policy plan must be addressed.

In this chapter we have attended in part to these concerns by comparing and integrating a number of different data sets, including our own systematically derived data on the homeless living in or passing through Austin. Our findings suggest that while the incidence of homelessness appears to have declined somewhat since around 1982, the homeless remain a considerable presence in the state, numbering some 41,000 or more. Demographically, we find that they are predominantly white, unattached, young males who are concentrated in the prime ages of labor force participation and who actively seek employment, albeit without much success. The principal implication of such findings is straightforward: Intervention efforts cannot stop with the provision of emergency food and shelter. What is also needed is a concerted effort to integrate these individuals into local and state economics.

ACKNOWLEDGMENT

The research on which this chapter is based was facilitated by the assistance of Carol Frank of the Texas Salvation Army Headquarters in Dallas and by the financial support of the Hogg Foundation for Mental Health.

REFERENCES

Bahr, Howard M., and Theodore Caplow. 1983. *Old Men Drunk and Sober*. New York: New York University Press.

Baumann, Donald J., et al. 1985. *The Austin Homeless: Final Report Provided to the Hogg Foundation Mental Health*. Austin, Texas: Hogg Foundation for Mental Health.

Baxter, Ellen, and Kim Hopper. 1981. *Private Lives/Public Spaces*. New York: Community Service Society.

Bingham, Richard D., et al., eds. 1987. *The Homeless in Contemporary Society*. Newbury Park, Calif.: Sage Publications.

Bogue, Donald J. 1963. *Skid Row in American Cities*. Chicago: Community and Family Study Center, University of Chicago.

City of Austin. 1986. *Final Report: Task Force on the Homeless*. Austin, Texas.

El Paso Task Force on the Homeless. 1984. *Robert Wood Johnson Grant Application: Health Care for the Homeless*. El Paso, Texas: El Paso Task Force on the Homeless.

Hombs, Mary Ellen, and Mitch Snyder. 1982. *Homelessness in America: A Forced March to Nowhere*. Washington, D.C.: Community for Creative Non-Violence.

Hope, Marjorie, and James Young. 1986. *The Facts of Homelessness*. Lexington, Mass.: Lexington Books.

Population Today. 1986. Counting the Uncountable Homeless. 14 (October): 3–8.

Rossi, Peter, et al. 1987. The Urban Homeless: Estimating Composition and Size. *Science* (March).

San Antonio Urban Council. 1984. *Robert Wood Johnson Grant Application: Health Care for the Homeless*. San Antonio, Texas: San Antonio Urban Council.

Snow, David A., and Leon Anderson. 1986. Varieties of Homeless Street People: A Grounded Typology. Unpublished manuscript.

————. 1987. Identity Work among the Homeless: The Verbal Construction and Avowal of Personal Identities. *American Journal of Sociology* 92 (6): 1336–1337.

Snow, David, et al. 1986. The Myth of Pervasive Mental Illness among the Homeless. *Social Problems* 33 (5): 407–423.

Texas Health and Human Service Coordinating Council. 1985. *Final Report on the Homeless in Texas*. Austin, Texas.

U.S. Conference of Mayors. 1985. *Health Care for the Homeless: A 40-City Review*. Washington, D.C.: U.S. Conference of Mayors.

U.S. Department of Housing and Urban Development. 1984. *A Report to the Secretary on the Homeless and Emergency Shelters*. Washington, D.C.: U.S. Department of Housing and Urban Development.

U.S. General Accounting Office. 1985. *Homelessness: A Complex Problem and the Federal Response*. Washington, D.C.: U.S. General Accounting Office.

U.S. House Committee on Government Operations. 1985. *The Federal Response to the Homeless Crisis*. Hearings before a subcommittee of the Committee on Government Operations. House of Representatives, 98th Congress, 2nd Session. Washington, D.C.: U.S. Government Printing Office.

Wiegard, Bruce. 1985. Counting the Homeless. *American Demographics*. December: 34–37.

Wiseman, Jacqueline. 1970. *Stations of the Lost: The Treatment of Skid Row Alcoholics*. Chicago: University of Chicago Press.

13

Homelessness in Utah

Judith T. Maurin and Leslie Russell

The scandal of homelessness in the United States is common knowledge today. Considerable publicity has been given to the problem in large cities, especially those on both coasts. Less in known, however, about the extent of homelessness and the profile of homeless people in America's homeland. Information about the homeless in Utah, a western, intermountain state will be presented in this chapter.

BACKGROUND

Utah is the eleventh largest state in the United States, covering an area of 84,990 square miles. The 1986 census estimates give the state's population at approximately 1,666,000 people, with approximately 77 percent (1,288,500) living in the metropolitan Wasatch Front area of north-central Utah. The major cities along the Wasatch Mountain range are Ogden, Salt Lake City, and Provo. The remainder of Utah's towns and cities are predominantly rural in character, with agriculture and tourism being major industries. Because of their location along major transportation routes, the Wasatch Front cities have become a "Crossroads of the West," attracting many persons from rural areas and neighboring states in search of economic opportunity.

A majority of Utah's people are members of the Mormon Church; however, most other religious denominations are represented among the population as well. According to the 1980 census, 95 percent of Utah's population is Caucasian; 1.5 percent is Hispanic; 1 percent is Native American; .07 percent is black, and the remaining 2.43 percent is composed of other groups such as oriental or Pacific Islander.

According to a recent economic forecast conducted by the Utah State Economic Coordinating Committee (1987), Utah's economic climate has been generally positive until relatively recently. Declines in basic industries such as mining, construction, and manufacturing have resulted in the displacement of workers, although it appears that some industries may make a moderate comeback.

Utah's per capita income is among the lowest in the nation, along with Mississippi and West Virginia, although this may be partially attributable to the large size of Utah's families. Since 1981, Utah's economic growth rate has decreased by 50 percent, due to lower population growth rate and reduction in economic growth. Although Utah's population growth rate is higher than the national rate, from a state perspective, Utah's rate of growth in the 1980s has slowed significantly. Since 1984, more people have left the state than have moved in. Net migration, the measure of in-migration minus out-migration, peaked in 1980 at approximately 24,500 and hit its lowest point in 1986 at −7,400. Because many areas in the state have been impacted by the continuing decline in energy development, the agricultural slump, and mining slowdowns, many persons have left the state, and some rural Utah counties have been reduced to a depression-level economy.

Utah's job creation rate is only one-fifth what it was in 1983; only 6,100 new jobs were created during a recent 12-month period. During the 1980s, Utah's average annual unemployment rate has been approximately one percentage point below the national average; however, the unemployment rate increased during the last half of 1986. Increases have been noted in households earning under $15,000 and over $50,000 annually, without comparable increases in the number of Utah households in the middle-income strata.

Shortages of moderate-income housing have resulted in the displacement of residents. For example, since 1979, over 1,500 low to moderately priced housing units were destroyed, demolished, or converted to other usages in downtown Salt Lake City. All these trends have an impact upon the economy and homelessness in Utah.

INCIDENCE OF HOMELESSNESS

Limited shelter has historically been available for homeless single men at the Salvation Army and the Rescue Mission in both Salt Lake City and Ogden. However, the first large-scale shelter system receiving partial support from public funds was initiated in Salt Lake City in 1982 after three persons froze to death that winter. Since that time, many separate efforts, largely on the part of the private sector but with some help from the public sector, have emerged to provide food and shelter for the homeless in Utah. According to the reports from service providers, homelessness in Utah has escalated dramatically in the past few years, mirroring the national phenomenon. In 1985 service providers in Utah reported an annual increase of as much as 40 percent in the number of persons seeking food and shelter. That same year, Palmer DePaulis, then mayor of Salt Lake City, and two Salt Lake County commissioners, D. Michael Stewart and M. Tom Shimizu, convened a task force to assess the problem of local homeless persons with a mental illness. That task force soon became an intergovernmental task force with support from the governor. Its focus was broadened to include all homeless persons within the state of Utah. Much of the data presented in this chapter comes from expert testimony of knowledgeable persons at task force hearings and from the Utah Homeless Survey conducted for the task force by the authors (Maurin and Russell, 1987).

The same problems that plague national estimates of the number of homeless (Rossi et al., 1987) pertain when trying to estimate the number of homeless in Utah. Despite the inherent limitation of using service-use data to estimate the size of the homeless population in Utah, this was the best available data. Based upon information from service providers, the Utah Homeless Task Force concluded that on a given day in 1986, between 1,000 and 2,400 people were homeless in Utah, with 600 to 1,000 of those being in Salt Lake City. Because of the mobility of a large segment of this population, it was estimated that tens of thousands of homeless people spent some time in Utah in 1986. Because many homeless persons do not contact service providers, there is a good probability that this estimate is an undercount.

Prior to conducting the Utah Homeless Survey, geographic concentrations of homeless persons were identified by conducting a telephone survey of emergency food and shelter providers, social service providers, mental health centers, and law enforcement agencies in Utah. The largest concentrations of homeless persons were reported in cities along the major north-south and east-west transportation routes (highway and rail) in Utah. The number of homeless people in eight Utah cities was sufficient to prompt the development of local shelter programs. The largest numbers of homeless people were reported in the two largest cities, Salt Lake City and Ogden. Listed in Table 13.1 are the emergency food and shelter services that were available to homeless persons in 1986–1987. Emergency food pantries are not included.

THE UTAH HOMELESS SURVEY

The purpose of the Utah Homeless Survey was to obtain information about the homeless in Utah that would help providers and local decision makers assess service needs. The sample was drawn in areas known to contain concentrations of homeless people: emergency shelters, soup kitchens and food banks, temporary employment agencies, churches, parks, and streets. Geographic concentrations of homeless persons had been identified by a telephone survey of service providers and law enforcement agencies in Utah. As a result, five cities were included in the survey. Random sampling was used in settings where there were large numbers of homeless, such as in shelters and soup kitchens; in settings containing only a few people, an attempt was made to interview all homeless persons. For the purpose of the survey, the definition of homelessness used was the respondent's confirmation that he/she was homeless. When the subject was

Table 13.1
Homeless Services in Utah, 1986–1987

City	Population	Service	Meals	Beds
Salt Lake City (includes county)	600,000	Traveler's Aid Emergency Shelters	0	375 men, women, & families
		Salvation Army	300	52 men (Rehab.)
		Rescue Mission	445	75 men, 25 women and children
		Catholic Comm. Services	300	25 women & children
Ogden	69,000	St. Anne's	100 180	65 men, women & families
		Salvation Army	30-40	52 men, women, and families
		Rescue Mission	100	65 men & families
St. George	20,000	Dixie Care and Share	Varies	10
Cedar City	13,000	Cedar City Care and Share	Varies	5-8
Provo	80,000	Utah County Food & Shelter Coalition	Varies	Varies
Helper	2,800	Union Gospel Mission	45	15
Green River	1,200	Highway Angel	Varies	Varies
Myton	560	Salvation Army	Varies	Varies

unsure about calling him or herself homeless, the interviewer probed for adequacy of shelter and whether this was a place where the subject could receive mail.

Data were gathered in interviews conducted over a period of 10 months between January and October 1986. The interviews each lasted approximately one hour and covered the following topics: demographic information, mental health, physical health, substance abuse, employment, social service needs, and history of homelessness. Volunteer interviewers were recruited from agencies serving homeless persons as well as from colleges and universities. Each interviewer received training on the use of the interview schedule and communication strategies, and was initially accompanied by an experienced interviewer. Ongoing supervision was also provided. Each respondent was asked to sign a consent form for the interview, and each respondent completing the interview was given a book of food coupons for their participation. The response rate was 73 percent.

DEMOGRAPHIC CHARACTERISTICS

According to service statistics from Traveler's Aid Society, the largest provider of shelter and services to the homeless in Utah, 63 percent of homeless persons were single men, 12 percent were single women, and 26 percent were families in 1986. Of these persons, approximately 25 percent of single women and 36 percent of families were permanent Utah residents during that same period.

A total of 337 homeless persons were interviewed in five Utah cities. The majority (54 percent) were interviewed at a shelter; 35 percent were questioned while waiting in food lines; 6 percent were interviewed at a social service agency; and 5 percent were interviewed on the street. Seventy-three percent were interviewed in Salt Lake City; 16 percent in Ogden; 5 percent in St. George; 4 percent in Cedar City; and 2 percent in Provo. Seventy-nine percent were men and, while 82 percent were white, minorities were overrepresented compared to Utah's general population. Interviewers asked 183 of the sample about their veteran status; of this number, 41 percent indicated they were veterans, and 59 percent of those were Vietnam veterans.

Consistent with findings from other studies, the homeless population in this study was relatively young; the median age was 33.5 years, with a range of 17 to 71 years. Thirty-three percent reported completing high school, and 23 percent reported education beyond high school. There was no statistically significant difference between men and women in mean age or education.

Respondents to the Utah Homeless Survey reported the following regarding marital status: 34 percent never married; 42 percent were separated, divorced, or widowed; and 24 percent were married. There was a statistically significant difference between men and women in regard to marital status. While only 15.8 percent of the men reported being married, 54 percent of the women reported they were. This difference is statistically significant beyond the .001 level. Eighty percent of those saying they were married (N = 64) reported being homeless with a spouse. Again, women were more likely than men to be homeless with a spouse.

Fifty-six percent of the respondents reported that they had children. However, only 10 percent had one or more of their children with them, and another 18 percent stated that they expected to have their children live with them again one day. Women (28.6 percent) were more likely to have this expectation than men (15 percent). Women were also more likely than men to be homeless with one or more children. Twenty-seven percent of the women interviewed were homeless with a child as compared to only 5 percent of the men. This difference is statistically significant beyond the .001 level. The numbers of children homeless with these respondents ranged from one to six, for a total of 91 homeless children. The children ranged in age from three days to 17 years. Thirty percent were under one year of age; 42.5 percent were between the ages of one and six; and 27.5 percent were six years or older.

Interestingly, 61 percent of the homeless families were two-parent families. This is in marked contrast to the findings of a study done in family shelters in Massachusetts where 94 percent of the families were headed by women (Bassuk et al., 1986). Among the 39 percent homeless single-parent families, half were headed by the male parent, and half by the female parent. Seventy-nine percent of the families reported having been in the Utah city in which they were interviewed for less than six months. This was essentially the same as the sample as a whole. When families were asked where they lived prior to coming to the city in which they were interviewed, 79 percent named neighboring western states.

LENGTH OF HOMELESSNESS AND MOBILITY

For most respondents, homelessness was a relatively new experience. Seventy-two percent reported living at a relatively permanent address one year ago or less; the median length of homelessness was 15.9 weeks. There was considerable mobility among this sample. Respondents reported having been in the city where interviewed for a median length of 3.4 days. Twenty-five percent of the total sample reported having been there six months or more. Mobility appeared to vary seasonally. Of those interviewed during the winter months, 31 percent reported being in the city where interviewed for six months or more as compared to 22 percent of those interviewed during summer months. The mentally ill in this sample appeared to be less mobile than the others. Of those who reported living in the city where interviewed for six months or more, 34 percent were judged by interviewers to exhibit symptoms of mental illness as compared to 18.4 percent of those living in the city less than six months. This difference is statistically significant ($P = 0.004$, using chi-square).

When respondents were asked where they lived prior to coming to the city where interviewed, a large number of states were reported. However, 67 percent reported a neighboring western state, and 12 percent reported Utah. A variety of modes of transportation were used to arrive at the city of interview. Twenty-nine percent came in a private vehicle; 23.3 percent came by freight train; 19.8 percent hitchhiked; and 17 percent came by bus. Eighty-two percent denied being advised by anyone to come to Utah, and only 9 percent reported receiving financial help with travel expenses. The most frequent sources of help were from family, church, or charity.

WORK PATTERNS

Respondents were asked to describe job patterns before becoming homeless. Among the men, 74.6 percent reported that they usually worked; 19.5 percent reported sometimes working; 4.7 percent reported usually not working; and 1.3 percent reported never working. Employment was much less evident among the women: 44.5 percent reported usually working; 20.5 percent reported sometimes working; 18 percent reported usually not working; and 17 percent reported never working.

When respondents were asked to rank needs, the need for a job ranked second. There was no statistically significant difference between men and women in the ranking of this need. Only 19.9 percent of men and 14 percent of women reported they were currently working. However, 73 percent of men and 62 percent of women were reportedly looking for work. When asked about the longest period of employment at one job, the median was 3.1 years. Sixty percent of the total sample had held one job for three or more years.

HEALTH PROBLEMS OF THE HOMELESS

Not surprisingly, many health problems were identified among the homeless in Utah. These problems can be described under the headings of physical health, mental health, and substance abuse.

Physical Health

Forty-four percent of the homeless interviewed reported that they currently had a physical problem that troubled them. Women were more likely than men to report a physical problem, and there was a trend to suggest that physical problems were associated with increased age.

A content analysis of the physical complaints yielded a broad range of physical problems. The most prominent physical problem reported was dental; 51.5 percent reported a problem they believed needed the attention of a dentist. The next three most frequently cited problems were back pain, infections, and other muscular skeletal problems. However, problems such as heart trouble, epilepsy, diabetes, kidney problems, and ulcers were reported as well. In fact, 21.7 percent of respondents reported having a chronic health problem for which they had been instructed to follow a regular medication or treatment regimen. It is surprising that 59 percent of these respondents stated that they were able to follow the prescribed treatment for their chronic condition under their current situation. We made no attempt to evaluate the adequacy of their self-care, however, and feel confident in the conclusion that there were many poorly met physical needs that would go uncared for until they necessitated emergency medical attention. This is as much a result of the design of our health care system as the harsh conditions under which the homeless live. Under the Utah Medical Outreach Program a person can receive care without regard for ability to pay for conditions that are life threatening or infectious. The consequence is that resources are mobilized when a condition has deteriorated to the point that the most costly sophisticated resources are required.

Mental Health

Three methods were used to assess mental health: a score on the National Center for Health Statistics (NCHS) General Well-Being Schedule (Fazio, 1977); judgment of the interviewer as to whether the respondent was currently suffering from a mental illness; and report of having been a patient in a mental health ward or clinic for any personal, emotional, behavioral, or mental problem.

The NCHS General Well-Being Schedule measures emotional health/psychiatric impairment on six dimensions: energy level; relaxed versus tense manner; degree of satisfaction with life; cheerful versus depressed mood; emotional behavioral control; and freedom from worry. A total score is produced on a continuum from distress to positive well-being. Any person whose score fell in the severely distressed range was considered psychiatrically impaired. While this is not equivalent to any specific psychiatric diagnosis, it does indicate that an individual is undergoing severe emotional distress. The NCHS instrument was used because it is reliable and easily administered. Cromback's alpha was the measure used to assess the internal consistency of the data obtained in this sample. An alpha coefficient of 0.83 was obtained, indicating good reliability of the NCHS.

Forty-five percent of respondents scored severely distressed on the NCHS Schedule. The following data show the distribution of scores and compares them

	Severely Distressed (%)	Moderately Distressed (%)	Positive Well-Being (%)
Utah Residents	13	14.7	72.3
Homeless: Total	44.6	15.8	39.6
Men	39.1	17.3	43.6
Women	65.7	10.0	24.3

to scores obtained in a random sample of Utah residents (LeBenta, 1983). The increase in psychological distress among the homeless compared to the general Utah population is striking. Women and those reporting a physical problem were overrepresented among the severely distressed. Sixty-two percent of those who scored severely distressed reported a physical problem that bothered them compared to only 29 percent who scored positive well-being. Using a chi-square, the result was found statistically significant beyond the .001 level. Sixty-six percent of the women compared to 39 percent of the men scored severely distressed, while 24 percent of the women and 40 percent of the men scored positive well-being. A chi-square was statistically significant beyond the .001 level.

Only 22 percent reported having been a mental patient at some time, and one third of those ($N = 25$) reported having been a patient during the past year. Twenty-three percent ($N = 77$) of respondents were judged by the interviewers to have a mental illness. Those judged to have a mental illness tended to score lower on the NCHS Schedule. Fifty-eight percent of those judged to be mentally ill scored severely distressed on the NCHS Schedule. There was no statistically significant relationship between sex and being judged to have a mental illness or reporting having been a mental patient. Because individuals participating in this survey had to have sufficient interpersonal skills to participate in an interview of approximately one hour, we believe that the severely mentally ill in the homeless population of Utah were underrepresented. Those who are suspicious of others are accessible only after repeated patient contact by outreach workers would be unlikely to participate in a study like this.

Substance Abuse

There was considerable discrepancy between the interviewers' judgment and self-report regarding the problem of alcohol and drug abuse. The interviewers judged alcohol or drug abuse to be a problem for 32.4 percent of the respondents. However, only 14 percent moderately or strongly agreed that they needed help with an alcohol problem, and 5 percent moderately agreed to needing help for a drug problem. Slightly more reported having been treated for such problems; 19.6 percent had received treatment for alcohol abuse in the past, and 6.5 percent had been treated for drug abuse.

Being judged to have a substance abuse problem was not associated with the NCHS score. However, it was associated with having been arrested and convicted of a crime during the past year. While only 24.6 percent of the sample reported having been convicted of a crime during the past year, 57.3 percent of those judged to have a substance abuse problem were convicted. A chi-square indicates a statistically significant difference beyond the .001 level between the two groups. This relationship is understandable when one considers the crimes reported. A content analysis revealed that the three most frequent types of crimes for which these respondents reported being convicted included: alcohol-related crimes (public intoxication and drunk driving), assaultive behavior (assault, manslaughter, and attempted murder), and stealing (robbery, burglary, theft, shoplifting). The connection between a substance abuse problem, an alcohol-related crime, and assaultive behavior is not surprising.

SOCIAL SUPPORT SYSTEMS

A majority of respondents (63.6 percent) reported having no family living in Utah. There was no relationship between this variable and age or sex. Forty-seven percent stated they maintained contact with family, although family was a source of interpersonal problems for some. Twenty-six percent reported being separated, 11 percent were divorced, and 20.5 percent had trouble with in-laws during the past year. Two percent experienced death of a spouse, and 19.9 percent experienced the death of a family member in the past year.

Sixty percent reported having a friend with whom they could talk or on whom they could count, but only 41 percent stated that this person was in the same city as the respondent. While the score on the NCHS General Well-Being Schedule was not associated with having contact with family, it was positively associated with having a friend. Likewise, being judged to exhibit symptoms of mental illness was not associated with contact with family, but those judged to be exhibiting symptoms of mental illness were less likely to report having a friend. When asked about friends, many respondents named employees of shelters or soup kitchens as being major sources of social support.

USE OF SOCIAL SERVICES

Respondents were presented with a list of possible needs and asked to express their degree of agreement/disagreement that this need applied to themselves. The scale ranged from 0 (strongly disagree) to 6 (strongly agree). The following data show the rank order of reported needs according to mean score.

Needs	$\bar{X}$
Permanent place to live	5.2
A job	5.0
Financial assistance	4.5
More or better food	4.3
Temporary place to live	4.2
Better medical care	3.5
Job training	3.4
R_x for emotional problems	1.4
R_x for drinking problem	1.1
R_x for drug problem	0.3

As may be noted from the above data, a place to live, a job, and food were high on the list of identified needs. Low on the list of needs was mental health care and treatment of a drinking or drug problem. Even among that part of the sample who scored in the severely distressed range of the NCHS General Well-Being Scale, treatment for mental health problems was not a recognized need. Likewise, although subjects did not perceive treatment for an alcohol or drug problem as a priority need, interviewers judged alcohol or drug abuse to be a problem for 32.4 percent of the respondents.

Fifty-nine percent of respondents reported that they were staying in a shelter; however, this high number reflects the fact that a majority of interviews were conducted in shelters. Only 20.3 percent of individuals interviewed someplace other than a shelter reported that they were staying in a shelter. This pattern did not vary when interviews done during winter months (October through April) were compared to those conducted during summer.

Only 48 percent reported that they were currently looking for a place to live.

However, since the median monthly income reported was $70.50, and 41 percent reported monthly income of $30 or less, there appears to be little point for most to look for a place to live. When asked about sharing living quarters, 59.5 percent reported they would be willing to share a place to live; 14 percent were undecided; and 26.5 percent said no.

Food stamps were the most frequently used service; 55.7 percent reported receiving food stamps within the past year. The second most frequently used service was job placement, used by 52.5 percent of respondents, although only 31.5 percent reported finding a job in this manner. Only 18.9 percent reported receiving public assistance grants: 14.4 percent received Medicaid, and 5.5 percent received SSI during the past year.

Forty-six percent of the sample reported a soup kitchen as the most frequently used place to obtain food. Other sources include grocery stores (12.5 percent), fast-food establishments (6 percent), and a variety of sources (21.7 percent). The mean number of daily meals eaten was 1.69, but 42.6 percent reported eating only one meal per day.

PROBLEMS ASSOCIATED WITH HOMELESSNESS

As shown below, respondents gave many reasons for their homelessness. The total is greater than 100 percent because many respondents cited more than one cause. However, the most frequently cited reasons for homelessness were economic factors, while only 15 percent appeared to choose this life-style because they liked to move around.

Reason	N	%
Lost job/can't find work	150	44.8
Evicted	25	7.5
Live on the streets	33	9.9
Welfare case closed	7	2.1
Drinking	27	8.1
Can't stay with family or friends	49	14.6
Was robbed	15	4.5
Family conflict	39	11.6
Like to move around	51	15.2
Other	96	28.7

Respondents reported experiencing many problems during the past year. Sixty-one percent said they lost something of sentimental value, and 78.9 percent reported their income decreasing during the past year. Twenty-eight percent reported having been physically abused or robbed, 24 percent reported having been evicted, and 15.5 percent reported having had welfare stopped during the past year.

DISCUSSION

The majority of the homeless in Utah were found to be single white men. However, as elsewhere, Utah's homeless also include minorities, women, and homeless families. As a subgroup, the women present special needs. They are more likely to be homeless with child-care responsibilities, to have a physical problem, and to be severely psychologically distressed. The needs of homeless children was not a focus of this study. However, one has to be concerned about the risks these children face in terms of physical, psychosocial, and educational development.

The amount of mobility among this population suggests that ultimately a regional and even national initiative will be needed to address the problem of homelessness as homeless people wander in search of better opportunities. When planning for services, it is well recognized that one must start with what the client perceives as a need. Therefore, it is important to know that the homeless perceive their needs to be very basic: a place to live, a job, income, and food. These are not easy to meet, however, especially in a way that would have any hope of interrupting the cycle in which they find themselves. Forty-four percent of our sample had not completed high school, only 29 percent had a vehicle with which they could get to a job, and 21 percent had some kind of problem on their last job that caused them to be fired. However, 38 percent had job skills that enabled them to hold a job five years or longer in the past. Unfortunately, we do not know what kind of jobs these were or whether they are still readily available in the labor market.

It is also clear that some among the homeless are in need of care for psychological problems and alcohol abuse. This care will have to be offered in conjunction with other needs perceived to be more basic, however, because mental health services received a low priority rating, even among those giving evidence of psychological distress. Such a finding is consistent with other reported studies (Levine & Stockdell, 1986).

Finally, the availability of health care is an obvious need for some. Of special concern is the very high incidence of dental disease, the evidence of serious health problems (such as diabetes and kidney problems) and the data that only half of the individuals with chronic health problems were following the needed regime of care for that problem. Not only does this mean these individuals are at risk for a deteriorated level of health, but it means that society can expect the use of high-cost, crisis medical care in the future.

The data were examined in an attempt to find differences in the sample interviewed in the different cities. However, the only statistically significant difference found was a disproportionate number judged to have a substance abuse problem among the sample in one city. The reader is cautioned, however, that the samples in Provo, Cedar City, and St. George were very small. The most striking finding of this survey was that the homeless in Utah are a diverse group of people. Therefore, a standard approach to meeting their needs will not likely be successful. Rather, an approach that first provides for basic needs and then allows for individual assessment and intervention appears warranted.

REFERENCES

Bassuk, Ellen L., et al. 1986. Characteristics of Sheltered Homeless Families. *American Journal of Public Health* 76 (9): 1097–1101.

Fazio, A. F. 1977. *A Concurrent Validational Study of the NCHS General Well-Being Schedule*. Series 2, No. 73, Hyattsville, Md.: Department of Health, Education and Welfare.

LeBenta, D. 1983. *Incidence and Prevalence of Alcohol, Drug and Mental Disorders*. Salt Lake City, Utah: Utah Division of Alcohol and Drugs.

Levine, I. S., and J. W. Stockdell. 1986. Mentally Ill and Homeless: A National Problem. In *Treating the Homeless: Urban Psychiatry's Challenge*, edited by B. E. Jones. Washington, D.C. : American Psychiatric Press.

Maurin, J., and L. S. Russell. 1987. *Homelessness in Utah: Utah Homeless Survey Final Report*. Salt Lake City, Utah: The Task Force for Appropriate Treatment of the Homeless Mentally Ill (Unpublished report).

Rossi, Peter H., et al. 1987. The Urban Homeless: Estimating Composition and Size. *Science* 235: 1336–1341.

State Economic Coordinating Committee. 1987. *Economic Report to the Governor*. Salt Lake City: State of Utah.

14

Homelessness in Virginia: Dimensions of the Problem and the Public Reaction

David G. Bromley, Daniel M. Johnson,
David W. Hartman, and Alexis L. Ruffin

Homelessness has been a recurrent condition in human societies throughout history. Although homelessness has sometimes been an acceptable or even normative condition for certain segments of the population, it generally has been regarded as problematic by both those who have been without shelter and by members of the society at large. As a problem, homelessness has tended to be associated with periods of social change and dislocation, triggered by events such as political upheaval, wars, plagues, labor shortages and surpluses, migrations, and economic depressions. In U.S. history, for example, increases in the size of the homeless population accompanied the era of rapid industrialization and urban growth during the latter part of the nineteenth century and the depression of the 1930s. Following World War II the number of homeless in the United States declined. The post–World War II images of the homeless have been of the skid-row/alcoholic and vagrant/vagabond populations, both of which were waning. Therefore, the recent sharp increase in the number and diversity of the homeless in the United States was not anticipated by citizenry, public officials, or academicians. The unexpected surge in homelessness across the country has resulted in an outpouring of media attention, research, and policy initiatives designed to address what is clearly a serious and growing social problem.

Despite rapidly escalating concern about homelessness, there is very little accurate information on even the number and characteristics of the homeless (U.S. Department of Health and Human Services, 1984; Redburn and Buss, 1986). The literature depicts a lack of consensus regarding even a definition of the term homeless, which varies from very specific descriptions of living arrangements to more global concepts such as ''disaffiliation'' (Bahr, 1973), with

here are enormous differences in the estimated size of the homeless
aturally, estimates of the homeless population size based on def-
include those moving in with family or friends far exceed those that
viduals living in the streets without any stable source of shelter. In
veral years, not only have various researchers employed different
s, but they have also employed alternative research modalities (for
example, shelter studies, key informant surveys, and street people surveys),
estimated size on the basis of different time periods (single point in time, time
periods of variable duration), and collected information for different objectives.
The result has been that, despite the rapidly growing body of research on homelessness, it is still difficult to generalize about this population with any great
confidence.

CAUSES OF HOMELESSNESS IN THE UNITED STATES

Although the problem of homelessness is complex and multifaceted, there
does appear to be some agreement on factors that have contributed to the recent
growth of the homeless population in the United States. First, the price of housing
has increased rapidly in a number of urban areas, driving individuals and families
into the rental market, which, in turn, has increased the demand for and price
of rental units. As a result, many families are now spending disproportionately
large percentages of their incomes on housing, thereby reducing their ability to
handle other financial problems that might arise. Second, housing renewal and
conversion projects have had the effect of both eliminating low- and moderate-
priced housing and reducing the number of rental units. This trend has led to
the displacement of individuals and families, sometimes even those who have
steady sources of income, as they are unable to afford replacement housing given
rapid price increases. Third, reductions in federally subsidized housing programs
have come at a time when supply has been decreasing and price increasing.
Consequently, some households that maintained their housing through a combination of income and subsidy have been forced out of their homes. Fourth, as
the divorce rate has increased in recent decades, the number of single-parent
households has increased dramatically. Many of the poorer of these households,
most headed by women, do not have sufficient resources to sustain even mini-
mally livable housing. Relatively minor financial problems may be sufficient to
render such families unable to meet rent obligations, which then may lead to
eviction and at least temporary homelessness. Fifth, the deindustrialization of
the economy, resulting in plant closings in smokestack industries, along with
serious economic depression in such industries as oil and agriculture, have led
to substantial numbers of households migrating to new communities in search
of employment opportunities. Such households frequently have expended their
limited resources in the process of migration and therefore find themselves in
intermediate or final destination communities without any resources for housing.
Sixth, the replacement of industrial jobs with service-sector jobs has been ac-

companied by an average wage decline, reflecting the generally lo
in the latter sector. Many families already stretching their incom
their present housing have been displaced by reduced income rat
employment. Seventh, the policy of attempting to deinstitutionali
disabled and criminal offender populations that began in the 1960s h
in releasing several hundred thousand such individuals who must seek
living accommodations. Since these individuals are likely to lack fina ... resources, credit histories, and employment opportunities, they may be unable to
obtain or maintain living quarters. Finally, the increased number of abused
spouses and youthful runaways seeking shelter has added another significant
component to the homeless population. The result of these various developments
is that the homeless population is larger and more variegated than at any time
in the last several decades and that it possesses few common characteristics
except the condition of homelessness and its attendant effects.

OBJECTIVE, DATA, AND METHOD

This chapter attempts to provide some baseline data on homelessness in Virginia through an exploration of two issues. First, we summarize the limited
information available from local studies and reports on homelessness in Virginia
and through key informants attempt to estimate the size of the homeless population in the state's largest cities. Second, we examine public perceptions of
homelessness in the state capital, Richmond. Although data on the size and
composition of the homeless are fragmentary, even less is known about the
extent to which public awareness has kept pace with the growth of the problem
itself and what the nature of the public reaction has been. Therefore, we have
used survey data collected in 1984 and 1987 to assess the public's perception
of the seriousness, change, causes, and preferred government line of action with
respect to homelessness.

The estimates of temporary and chronic homeless population size reported in
this paper were obtained through identifying key informants in each Virginia
city with a population of 100,000 or more. There is one city in Virginia with a
population of over 300,000 (Virginia Beach), two have between 200,000 and
300,000 (Norfolk and Richmond), and five between 100,000 and 200,000 (Alexandria, Hampton, Newport News, Portsmouth, and Roanoke). Most of the
larger cities are located in the coastal region of eastern Virginia (Hampton,
Newport News, Norfolk, Portsmouth, and Virginia Beach) with one city each
in the central region (Richmond), the northern region (Alexandria), and the
western region (Roanoke). Between June and August 1987 the mayor's office
in each city was asked to identify the agency or individual in the municipal
government responsible for administering municipal programs or agencies dealing with the problem of homelessness and coordinating with nongovernmental
entities providing services to the homeless. The estimate of homelessness provided by key informants is based on the following questions: "What is the total

number of individuals in your city who over the last year experienced temporary or short-term (chronic or long-term) homelessness?'' It should be noted that the key informants in virtually every jurisdiction emphasized that the estimates they provided us were simply projections based on whatever data they had available and their observations derived from coordinating various community efforts to address the homelessness problem. Most of these communities have some type of assessment of homelessness underway but as yet have no accurate count or profile of the homeless.

The data on public perceptions of homelessness were gathered in two telephone surveys of adult residents of Richmond, Virginia; the first was conducted in March 1984 and the second was taken in August 1987. The sample was drawn by a commercial sampling organization using a random digit dialing probability procedure. The survey was conducted by the Survey Research Laboratory at Virginia Commonwealth University. The 1984 and 1987 sample sizes were 602 and 404 respondents, respectively. Both surveys contained questions on a variety of social issues and included the following four questions on homelessness:

1. Please tell me if you think homelessness in Richmond is a very serious, fairly serious, or not very serious problem.
2. Over the past five years, do you think the problem of homelessness in Richmond has increased, decreased, or remained about the same?
3. Do you think local government should do more, about the same, or do less to help reduce the problem of homelessness in Richmond?
4. What do you think is the single most important cause of homelessness: emotional or mental disturbance, family problems, alcohol or drug abuse, long-term unemployment, recent unemployment, or something else?

In addition, information was collected on the age, sex, race, education, income, and homeownership status of each respondent.

DIMENSIONS OF HOMELESSNESS IN VIRGINIA

As the following data show, the key informant estimates of the size of the homeless population (long- and short-term) in Virginia cities with populations of 100,000 or more yields a total of 14,836 for Virginia's eight largest cities.

City	Long-term Population		Short-term Population		Total	Percent of Population
	Percent/Number		*Percent/Number*			
Alexandria	20.0	332	80.0	1,326	1,658	1.55
Hampton	9.1	20	90.9	200	220	0.17
Newport News	12.5	50	89.5	350	400	0.26
Norfolk	27.3	450	72.7	1,200	1,650	0.59
Portsmouth	14.6	23	85.4	135	158	0.15
Richmond	27.3	1,200	72.7	3,200	4,400	2.01
Roanoke	28.6	100	71.4	250	350	0.35
Virginia Beach	20.0	1,200	80.0	4,800	6,000	1.94
Total		3,375		11,461	14,836	

These data show that just over three quarters of the homeless in these cities are homeless for a short term (77.3 percent) and the remainder (22.7 percent) are long-term homeless. There is substantial variation in these two broad categories, however. For individual cities, the percentage of short-term homeless ranges between 70 and 90 percent, with the percentage of long-term homeless ranging between 10 and 30 percent of the total homeless population. In general, there is a strong relationship between the size of the short- and long-term homeless populations, and the size of the short-term is at least several times the size of the long-term population. Further, the size of the homeless population relative to the total population of these cities varies considerably. The homeless population in Richmond, for example, comprises 2.01 percent of the total city population compared with Portsmouth where the homeless comprise only 0.15 percent of the population. For most of the cities we surveyed, the homeless population is well under 1 percent of the population; in only three cities did the percentage exceed this (Richmond, 2.01; Virginia Beach, 1.94; Alexandria, 1.55). For these eight cities overall, the homeless rate is 1.1 percent. If this percentage is applied to the remainder of the Virginia population, the projected number of homeless would equal 64,592. There is reason to believe that such an estimate might be too high, as the state contains a considerable rural population for which the homelessness rate is in all probability considerably lower. At the same time, there are several large urban counties which were not surveyed in this study where the rate of homelessness is comparable to those reported here. Further, it seems likely that the estimates provided to us by key informants are conservative; an accurate census of the homeless would probably yield higher numbers than those reported in this study. From this perspective, then, a statewide estimate of 64,592 may not be unrealistic.

CAUSES AND PROFILE OF HOMELESSNESS IN VIRGINIA CITIES

Given the paucity of data on homelessness nationally, it is not surprising that there is relatively little detailed information about the size and composition of the homeless population and the causes of homelessness in Virginia. To date there has been no statewide assessment of the homeless problem although the issue has received some limited attention in the context of other problems such as hunger (Commonwealth of Virginia, 1985). However, in recent years several cities and counties, including both municipalities for which we did and did not gather homeless population size estimates, have issued reports containing rudimentary information on various aspects of the problem and, in some cases, have included recommendations for new policy and program initiatives. Reports from individual cities present all of the problems so frequently noted in reviews of existing research: definitions of homelessness vary, data have been collected by various combinations of public and private agencies, very different methods of estimating homeless population size have been employed, estimates are for different time periods, and different categorizations of the homeless are used.

Although these diverse sources of data are not directly comparable, the reports do generally confirm the broad outlines of the findings reported elsewhere by local, state, and federal agencies. Among the highlights of local report findings are the following:

Northern Virginia

In northern Virginia, a major contributor to the dimension of homelessness is the severe shortage of housing stock. A study of housing conducted by the Fairfax–Falls Church United Way (1984: 4–5), for example, reported that only a tiny minority of rental units are in low- and moderate-price categories; that rents are rising more rapidly than inflation; that rents are rising most sharply for low-cost units; that many middle- and upper-income households are being priced out of the home-purchase market and thus competing with low-income households for available rental property; and that almost half of the households cannot afford even the least expensive housing being produced anywhere in the country. In addition, there has been a large amount of replacement of low-cost housing units with more expensive ones either through renewal or conversion projects, with a resulting displacement of households unable to find replacement living quarters (Arlington United Way, 1985).

Western Virginia

Lack of affordable housing is also cited as a major problem in the city of Roanoke and surrounding areas. The Roanoke City Manager's Task Force (1987: 36; see also Roanoke Valley Council of Community Services, 1984, 1982) reports that, based on current rental prices, individuals in Roanoke earning the minimum wage would spend 62 percent of their incomes on housing. About $5.50 per hour would be necessary to pay for unsubsidized housing. The very limited supply of subsidized housing and the lack of medical and retirement plans for many workers (particularly part-time employees) place such individuals at considerable risk (1987: 29). Indeed, the task force estimates that as many as 10,104 households risk homelessness because of the high proportion of income they must commit to housing.

Particularly endangered groups include individuals working part time or for minimum wage, female heads of households with dependent children, disabled persons, individuals released from mental health or correctional facilities, and the elderly. For example, AFDC payments do not even meet poverty-level income standards, and hence unexpected expenses may place families in rent arrears; deinstitutionalized populations frequently lack money and credit histories, leaving them in a disadvantaged position when trying to obtain housing; the elderly may literally wear out housing in which they have lived for long periods; and disabled individuals may require subsidized housing with support services. Although the liabilities of these various populations differ, the result in each case is that they are precariously balanced and may easily be pushed over the brink into homelessness.

Southeastern Virginia

The extent of homelessness in the southeastern region of Virginia varies considerably between municipalities. One study of households requiring emergency housing services was conducted among 21 regional agencies in 1984 in Chesapeake, Norfolk, Portsmouth, and Virginia Beach. This study recorded 388 cases during the 90-day survey period. More than half (55 percent) of the cases were located in Norfolk, with 26 percent from Virginia Beach, and the remainder from Chesapeake, Portsmouth, or other surrounding areas. Of these cases, 40 percent were single spouses, predominantly female, with children. Another 26 percent involved families, all but a few of which also included children. Fully 41 percent of these individuals or families sought shelter because they were being evicted, and another 27 percent had been living with friends or family. The remainder were in temporary shelter, had no shelter, or were new to the area.

In Virginia Beach, which is the largest city in Virginia and also reports the largest number of homeless, several factors contribute to the recent growth of the homeless population. One result of the centrality of the resort industry to the city's economic base is that housing is extremely expensive. Further, a relatively small proportion of the housing stock is in the low to moderate price range, which has tended to inflate prices in the lower segment of the housing market. There is also considerable seasonal fluctuation in housing costs and availability. As a result, individuals arriving in Virginia Beach out of the primary vacation months may be able to obtain housing that they cannot sustain during the summer months when demand for housing surges. Finally, there is considerable migration into the area by individuals who had previously been visitors or served at the nearby military base and who are now seeking employment. Although the unemployment rate is indeed low, there is no surplus of year-round jobs to accommodate these newcomers.

Central Virginia

The problem of homelessness in Richmond is substantial. The available studies and reports point to a variety of factors as causes of the high rate of homelessness in the city and surrounding areas (Richmond Landlord-Tenant Resource Committee, n.d.; United Way of Greater Richmond, 1984, 1982; Koenig, 1984). These various reports document a large and diverse homeless population in Richmond that includes many of the groups identified in current research on homelessness: migrants in search of employment, deinstitutionalized populations, long-term homeless street people, and displaced low-income families. First, Richmond is located on the north-south and east-west interstate highway network and hence has become a collection point for those migrating in search of work, particularly between New York and Florida. According to local officials, a significant number of these individuals become stranded in Richmond, remain in the city, and ultimately seek various types of social services. Second, Richmond's widely publicized low unemployment rate has attracted migrants in search of job opportunities. Since the supply of jobs is not as great as the city's reputation for employment opportunities and jobs do not necessarily match migrant qualifications, some households have migrated to Richmond only to fail to locate work. Third, Richmond is known throughout the state for having more extensive support resources; indeed, one report (United Way of Greater Richmond, 1982: 5) found that Richmond accounted for one quarter of all the general relief funds expended in the state. As a result, deinstitutionalized populations from other regions of the state have tended to gravitate toward Richmond. Finally, both in downtown and in some surrounding areas, there have been major redevelopment and revitalization projects, which have eliminated substantial numbers of low-cost housing units or upgraded them, thus displacing low-income households. Since more than half of the residential units in the city are tenant occupied and these households tend to have lower incomes than owner-occupied units, the competition for scarce low- to moderate-priced housing has grown.

PUBLIC PERCEPTIONS OF HOMELESSNESS IN RICHMOND

One way of assessing the public reaction to the homelessness problem is to compare evaluations of the seriousness of homelessness with other problems confronting the local community. In the Richmond survey we asked respondents to assess the seriousness of a range of urban social problems: crime, drug abuse, unemployment, homelessness, traffic congestion, race relations, and dirty streets. The data (table not presented) make it clear that the problems of crime and drug abuse dominate public consciousness and that concern has been growing. In 1984, 94.5 percent of those interviewed evaluated crime as very or fairly serious; by 1987, fully 81.8 percent regarded crime as a very serious problem and 98.0 percent termed it either very or fairly serious. Drug abuse ranked second in this list of problems with 92.2 and 93.6 percent of survey respondents evaluating it as fairly or very serious in 1984 and 1987, respectively. The public alarm over crime and drug abuse may derive in part from the extremely high homicide rate in Richmond in recent years. Many of these offenses reportedly were linked to drug use and trafficking, which has made Richmond one of the national leaders in homicide.

Homelessness, unemployment, and traffic congestions occupy the middle range in this list of urban problems. Between 1984 and 1987, the percent of respondents defining unemployment as fairly or very serious declined from 77.4 to 60.5 percent, and there was a comparable decline in concern about traffic congestion from 71.0 to 68.0 percent. By contrast, as we have already reported,

Table 14.1
Citizen Assessment of Seriousness, Change, Preferred Local Government
Response, and Causes of Homelessness, 1984 and 1987

Assessment Categories	1984		1987	
	%	N	%	N
Seriousness of Homelessness:				
Very serious	33.2	163	46.1	165
Fairly serious	41.5	204	36.6	131
Not very serious	25.3	124	17.3	62
Change in Homelessness:				
Increased	54.2	252	66.3	213
Remained the same	40.6	189	26.2	84
Decreased	5.2	24	7.5	24
Local Help for the Homeless:				
Do more	76.3	392	80.4	282
Do the same	17.1	88	16.5	58
Do less	6.6	34	3.1	11
Causes of Homelessness:				
Emotional/mental	9.4	49	19.0	73
Family problems	13.7	72	9.1	35
Alcohol/drugs	24.4	128	21.1	81
Unemployment	39.9	209	29.4	113
Recent unemployment	3.8	20	4.2	16
Other	8.8	46	17.2	66

the percent of respondents assessing homelessness as fairly or very serious increased from 74.7 to 82.7 percent.

Race relations and dirty streets are perceived as the least serious municipal problems. Over the three-year period, the percentage of respondents regarding dirty streets as fairly or very serious increased from 48.6 to 53.7 while there was a slight decline in the comparable percentages for race relations from 56.0 to 52.5. These data make it clear that homelessness is regarded by the citizens of Richmond as a moderately serious local problem when compared with other problems commonly facing local communities; in addition, there is a trend toward evaluating homelessness as increasingly serious.

The data indicate that there is an increased awareness and concern with the problem of homelessness. As Table 14.1 shows, in 1984, one-third of survey respondents (33.2 percent) rated the homeless problem as very serious; by 1987, nearly half (46.1 percent) of those interviewed assessed homelessness as very serious. This increase was the result of a drop both in the percentage of respondents regarding homelessness as a fairly serious problem, from 41.5 percent to 36.6 percent, and in those regarding homelessness as not a very serious problem, from 25.3 percent to 17.3 percent. Thus, by 1987, a substantial plurality of Richmonders (82.7 percent) regarded homelessness as either fairly or very serious.

It might be expected that our respondents also would view the problem of homelessness as increasing, and indeed, they did. Whereas in 1984 more than 54 percent of respondents estimated that the problem was increasing, by 1987, the percentage had risen to 66.3. It is interesting to note that, while the proportion of citizens regarding homelessness as very serious is high and growing, support for local government action has risen only slightly during the last three years (76.3 percent versus 80.4 percent). It may well be that the proportion of citizens who will advocate doing more to help the homeless is unlikely to rise further as a result either of competing concerns about other local and national problems or of components of the population staunchly committed to limited governmental involvement in solving any social problems.

The change in the perceptions regarding the causes of homelessness is revealing. In both 1984 and 1987, unemployment was perceived as the most important cause of homelessness (43.7 percent and 33.6 percent, respectively). It may well be that the highly publicized recent fall in national unemployment indicators has led to the impression that lack of jobs is no longer a major contributor to the creation of homelessness. Yet there has also been a substantial decrease in the proportion of individuals identifying unemployment as well as family problems as major causes for homelessness (from 13.7 percent to 9.1 percent) over the three-year period while the proportion of those selecting emotional and mental problems increased significantly (from 9.4 to 19.0 percent) as did those identifying a variety of factors not listed on the survey instruments (from 8.8 to 17.2 percent). The change in perceived cause of homelessness away from unemployment toward emotional and mental problems is significant, of course, since the latter are more highly stigmatized, are more likely to be regarded as personal than structural, and elicit a greater sense of obligatory public assistance. This shift toward explanations traditionally associated with personal responsibility may be another reason why the percentage of individuals supporting greater governmental action has not increased.

Table 14.2 presents data on the perceived seriousness of homelessness by selected social characteristics of respondents. It is evident from these data that those segments of the population most likely to be impacted by homelessness are most likely to view it as a serious problem. This pattern is most pronounced for the 1984 data. Thus respondents 60 and older are more likely than 18 to 34-year-olds to view homelessness as a very or fairly serious problem (83.8 versus 74.1 percent), as are females than males (79.5 versus 67.3 percent), blacks than whites (80.8 versus 71.7 percent), those with some high school education than college graduates (63.4 versus 81.9 percent), those with family incomes under $10,000 than those with incomes over $30,000 (83.3 versus 67.2 percent), and those who rent versus those who own their homes (79.2 versus 70.6). Education and income appear to be the most strongly related to the perception of homelessness as very serious, as nearly 60 percent (59.7 and 56.7, respectively) of

Table 14.2
Seriousness of Homelessness by Selected Social Characteristics of Respondents, 1984 and 1987

Respondent Characteristics	Seriousness of Homelessness: Very 1984	Very 1987	Fairly 1984	Fairly 1987	Not Very 1984	Not Very 1987	N 1984	N 1987
Age:								
18-34	31.4	41.7	42.7	40.4	25.9	17.9	220	151
35-59	30.1	48.9	42.3	33.8	27.6	17.3	196	133
60+	47.0	53.5	36.8	29.3	16.2	17.2	68	58
Sex:								
Female	38.2	52.9	41.3	33.0	20.5	14.1	288	206
Male	26.6	36.7	40.7	41.5	32.7	21.8	199	147
Race:								
Black	49.7	54.8	31.1	33.6	19.2	11.6	151	146
White	25.5	37.9	46.2	40.0	28.3	22.1	321	190
Education:								
Some H.S.	59.7	55.2	22.2	27.6	18.1	17.2	72	58
H.S. grad.	37.4	51.5	40.3	33.0	22.3	15.5	139	97
Some Coll.	32.5	43.5	48.8	42.4	18.7	14.1	123	85
Coll. grad.	18.3	37.5	45.1	40.2	36.6	22.3	153	112
Income ($000):								
<10	56.6	52.0	26.7	26.0	16.7	22.0	60	50
10-19	37.7	50.0	45.3	38.6	17.0	11.4	106	88
20-29	29.9	33.8	41.6	45.1	28.5	21.1	137	71
30+	21.4	47.4	45.8	34.3	32.8	18.3	131	99
Own Home:								
Yes	27.1	43.5	43.5	36.9	29.4	19.6	255	179
No	39.8	48.6	39.4	36.8	20.8	14.6	231	171

those in the lowest categories on these variables made this assessment while in the highest categories, the comparable percentages for education and income were 18.3 and 21.4 percent. Correspondingly, about one third of those in the highest education and income categories (36.6 and 32.8 percent, respectively) regarded homelessness as not a very serious problem.

The various respondent characteristics are still related to assessments of homelessness in the 1987 data but there is a general reduction in the size of differences. In 1987, 82.8 percent of the 60 and older age group and 82.1 of the 18–34 group regarded homelessness as a fairly or very serious problem. In assessments of seriousness, females were still higher than males (85.9 versus 78.2 percent), as were blacks than whites (88.4 versus 77.9), lowest education than highest education (82.8 versus 77.7), and renters than homeowners (85.4 versus 80.4). This narrowing of differences was most apparent on the education and income variables where they were greatest in 1984; by 1987 these differences had closed substantially for education and reversed slightly for income (78.0 versus 81.8 percent). This reduction in patterning by social characteristics is partly a function of the general increase in the perception of homelessness as a serious problem. In virtually every social category, the assessment of homelessness as a serious problem increased substantially between 1984 and 1987.

Data on perceived change in the homelessness problem (table not presented) are generally consistent with the findings in Table 14.2. Older individuals, women, and blacks are more likely to view homelessness as an increasingly serious problem. These differences are evident for both the 1984 and 1987 data. In 1987, for example, 71.2 percent of respondents 60 years old and over regarded homelessness as increasing compared with 61.8 of those between 18 and 34. Similarly, in 1987, females were more likely than males to perceive homelessness as increasing (69.4 versus 62.8 percent), as were blacks than whites (67.9 versus 65.2 percent). Furthermore, in virtually every category, respondents were more likely in 1987 than in 1984 to perceive homelessness as increasing. Likewise, the proportion who regard homelessness as increasing exceeds those who regard the problem as serious, which suggests that evaluations of homelessness as a very serious problem may well continue.

Tables 14.3 and 14.4 contain percentage distributions on causes of homelessness by the various respondents' characteristics. As Table 14.1 revealed, unemployment is perceived to be the most important cause of homelessness, but there has been a decline in the proportion of respondents identifying this factor as well as family problems while the proportion of respondents identifying emotional and mental problems has increased. In contrast to the rather consistent relationship between social characteristics and degree of seriousness attributed to the homelessness problem (Table 14.2), there is much less consensus on perceptions of its causes. For the 1984 data (Table 14.3), there appeared to be a tendency for whites to perceive emotional and mental problems and drug and alcohol problems as causes of homelessness (11.8 versus 4.0 percent and 27.7 versus 17.3 percent, respectively), while blacks were more likely to cite unemployment (50.7 versus 35.6 percent and 56.0 versus 39.0 percent if the two employment categories were combined).

In the 1987 data (Table 14.4), the tendency of whites to identify emotional and mental problems more frequently (22.9 percent versus 14.5 percent) and of blacks to identify unemployment problems (35.2 versus 25.3 percent and 39.9 versus 29.0 percent when the categories are combined) continued, but the difference in citing alcohol or drugs largely disappeared (whites at 21.5 percent and blacks at 22.1 percent). There appeared to be a slight tendency for homeowners to favor emotional and mental explanations and for renters to favor unemployment explanations (20.1 versus 17.7 and 35.4 versus 31.5 percent, respectively). However, it is striking that, in contrast to the pattern of seriousness assessments by social characteristics, there was no comparable pattern with respect to perceived causes. The pattern that does occur may reflect a tendency by those most vulnerable to homelessness to attribute its causes to structural factors, while those least impacted attribute it to personal factors.

Table 14.5 examines the relationship between perceived seriousness and pre-

Table 14.3
Causes of Homelessness by Selected Social Characteristics, 1984

Respondent Characteristics	Causes of Homelessness						
	Emotional, Mental	Family	Alcohol, Drugs	Unemployment	Recent Unemployment	Other	N
Age:							
18-34	11.8	14.5	17.6	46.2	2.7	7.2	221
35-59	6.1	13.6	29.6	35.2	4.7	10.0	213
60+	11.3	12.5	25.0	37.4	5.0	8.0	80
Sex:							
Female	9.6	14.4	22.4	40.8	5.1	7.7	313
Male	9.1	13.0	26.9	38.5	1.9	10.6	208
Race:							
Black	4.0	12.7	17.3	50.7	5.3	10.0	150
White	11.8	13.4	27.7	35.6	3.4	8.1	357
Education:							
Some H.S.	9.1	9.1	29.9	36.3	5.2	10.4	77
H.S. grad.	6.7	15.4	20.8	43.0	4.0	10.1	149
Some Coll.	10.1	15.2	24.6	40.7	5.1	4.3	138
Coll. grad.	11.4	13.3	24.1	38.5	1.9	10.8	158
Income ($000):							
<10	10.6	10.6	22.7	39.5	3.0	13.6	66
10-19	7.9	11.4	19.3	51.7	4.4	5.3	114
20-29	9.0	13.8	27.6	37.9	3.4	8.3	145
30+	11.4	15.7	22.1	36.5	4.3	10.0	140
Own Home:							
Yes	9.5	13.4	25.8	36.1	4.6	10.6	283
No	9.2	13.9	22.7	44.6	2.9	6.7	238

Table 14.4
Causes of Homelessness by Selected Social Characteristics, 1987

Respondent Characteristics	Emotional, Mental	Family	Alcohol, Drugs	Unemployment	Recent Unemployment	Other	N
Age:							
18-34	16.8	10.6	21.1	29.1	5.0	17.4	161
35-59	22.2	8.1	14.8	37.2	4.4	13.3	135
60+	14.1	5.6	36.7	16.9	2.8	23.9	71
Sex:							
Female	18.8	8.5	20.2	31.9	4.0	16.6	223
Male	19.6	8.5	23.5	26.2	4.6	17.6	153
Race:							
Black	14.5	6.9	22.1	35.2	4.7	16.6	145
White	22.9	8.4	21.5	25.3	3.7	18.2	214
Education:							
Some H.S.	11.7	8.3	35.0	21.7	3.3	20.0	60
H.S. grad.	18.4	15.5	25.3	21.4	2.9	16.5	103
Some Coll.	18.9	5.6	20.0	36.6	2.2	16.7	90
Coll. grad.	22.8	6.5	13.0	34.1	7.3	16.3	123
Income ($000):							
<10	20.4	4.1	30.6	30.7	2.0	12.2	49
10-19	17.4	12.0	21.7	27.2	5.4	16.3	92
20-29	18.2	5.2	20.8	37.6	5.2	13.0	77
30+	21.9	8.6	17.1	30.5	3.8	18.1	105
Own Home:							
Yes	20.1	8.8	21.6	29.4	2.1	18.0	194
No	17.7	9.9	21.0	29.3	6.1	16.0	181

Causes of Homelessness

Table 14.5
Preferred Local Government Response to Homelessness by Seriousness, Change, and Causes of Homelessness, 1984 and 1987

Assessment Category	Local Government Should Do							
	More		Same		Less		N	
	1984	1987	1984	1987	1984	1987	1984	1987
Seriousness:								
Very	88.6	89.0	8.9	9.1	2.5	1.9	157	154
Fairly	75.5	77.6	19.6	20.7	4.9	1.7	184	116
Not very	60.9	62.5	28.6	28.6	10.5	8.9	105	56
Change:								
Increased	86.3	85.9	9.4	11.0	4.3	3.1	235	191
Decreased	60.9	68.2	39.1	27.3	0.0	4.5	23	22
Same	68.3	69.5	21.5	27.8	10.2	2.5	177	79
Cause:								
Emotional/mental	73.3	78.5	17.8	21.5	8.9	0.0	45	65
Family	79.1	93.4	14.9	3.3	6.0	3.3	67	30
Alcohol/drugs	63.2	68.2	26.3	27.5	10.5	4.3	114	69
Unemployment	87.0	84.4	11.4	12.8	1.6	2.8	193	109
Recent unemployment	75.0	93.3	25.0	6.7	0.0	0.0	20	15
Other	59.0	76.0	23.1	16.0	17.9	8.0	39	50

ferred social actions for local government. The data in Table 14.1 revealed that substantial majorities of those interviewed perceive homelessness to be a fairly serious or very serious problem, that this proportion increased between 1984 and 1987, and that large majorities are in favor of local government taking more action in response to this problem. The data in Table 14.5 indicate that support for further local government action was extraordinarily high among those who regarded the problem as very serious (88.6 percent in 1984 and 89.0 percent in 1987). Indeed, by 1987, it was virtually unanimous that the government should do at least as much as it had done in recent years, which is reflected in the very small minorities (always less than 10 percent) in favor of less governmental assistance. Even among those who regarded the problem as not very serious, there was considerable support (over 60 percent in both years) for additional government action.

A similar pattern was evident among those who viewed the problem as growing more serious. There was also a solid majority support for more governmental action irrespective of the perceived cause of homelessness. In general, support for additional governmental action increased over the three-year period, with the sharpest increase where family problems (79.1 percent in 1984 and 93.4 percent in 1987) or recent unemployment (75.0 percent in 1984 versus 93.3 percent in 1987) were identified as the primary cause of homelessness. It is clear that the greatest support for doing more comes from those who attribute homelessness to family and unemployment problems, and the least support where homelessness is thought to be rooted in emotional and mental or alcohol or drug problems.

Nevertheless, in the 1987 data even where emotional and mental or alcohol or drugs were identified as primary causes, at least two thirds of those interviewed supported additional governmental action (78.5 and 68.2 percent, respectively), and most of the remainder (21.5 and 27.5 percent respectively) favored the same level of governmental support.

Finally, data on the preferred role for local government action by respondent social characteristics (table not presented) are not nearly as predictive of preferences for the role of local government as they are in the analysis of seriousness. There was a strong tendency for blacks to favor more government action than whites in both 1984 (87.5 percent versus 70.2 percent) and in 1987 (86.8 versus 73.7). The strong relationship between sex and homeownership status and assessments of seriousness was not evident in this analysis for either 1984 or 1987. There appears to be a weak inverse relationship between income and education and preference for governmental initiative; for example, the highest education group had the lowest support for more government assistance to the homeless in both years (70.0 and 75.0 percent, respectively) as did the highest income group (74.1 and 78.5 percent, respectively).

In light of the strong direct relationship between age and the perceived seriousness of homelessness, it is puzzling that, for the 1987 data in this analysis, age appeared to be inversely related to support for local government action. Indeed, only in the 60 and older age group and among whites was the support in any category below 75 percent (66.6 percent and 73.7, respectively). It is important to emphasize, however, that support for local government action is strong across all social groups, and that it increased in almost every category between 1984 and 1987. Thus, perceptions that the homelessness problem is serious and growing are being accompanied by broad-based support for additional government assistance in this area.

SUMMARY AND CONCLUSIONS

Over the last decade both the seriousness and the visibility of homelessness have grown in the United States. The roots of the problem are in changes in the economic structure and the resulting housing market, which have increased the cost and reduced the supply of low- and moderate-priced units; the shift from an industrial to a service-based economy, which has produced economic dislocations and lower wage scales; changes in family structure, which have created more single-parent households with weaker purchasing power; redefinition of public-sector priorities at the federal level, which has reduced housing subsidies; and the new philosophical directions in the management of marginal populations, which has led to the deinstitutionalization movement. As our review of reports from local communities around Virginia has demonstrated, conditions in this state reflect in microcosm the problems being experienced by cities throughout the country. The extent and character of the homelessness problem of individual cities in Virginia depends on such factors as the structure of the local economy and housing market, the geographical location, and the capacity to respond to the needs of homeless populations. There is little doubt from our survey of the largest cities in Virginia that the problem of homelessness is substantial and growing and that local communities are just beginning to assess its dimensions and implications.

The data on citizen awareness and assessment of the homeless problem in Richmond indicate that this problem has significantly penetrated the public consciousness. While there is a greater public concern with problems such as crime and drug abuse, obviously our respondents perceive homelessness to be a significant problem, and that perception is growing. Unemployment continues to be regarded as the most important cause of homelessness, but there has been an erosion of support for this explanation in favor of emotional and mental problems. This shift may be significant to the extent that this constitutes a trend toward attributing homelessness to personal rather than social structural factors. Not surprisingly, those segments of the population most vulnerable to homelessness (elderly, women, blacks, low-income and low-education groups, and renters) are most likely to regard homelessness as a serious problem. However, there has been considerable reduction in the strength of these relationships over the last three years as general public awareness and concern about homelessness has grown. There is also a tendency by those vulnerable to homelessness to perceive its causes in structural terms while those less vulnerable are more likely to see it as a product of personal responsibility. These data leave no question that there is substantial public support for increased governmental initiative in addressing the problem of homelessness. This support is strongest where respondents view the problem as very serious and where it is viewed as a result of conditions traditionally thought to be beyond individual control, such as unemployment. However, perhaps the most striking finding of this survey is that public support across social categories, irrespective of the perceived cause of homelessness, is extremely strong and growing.

These findings suggest several important directions for future research. First, at present the mere estimates of the size and demographic composition of the homeless population are rough and speculative. It is clear that a more detailed profile or description of the homeless and further surveys are needed for a better understanding of this serious social problem. Further, given the plethora of public and private agencies involved in providing some type of services to the homeless, it is imperative that some mechanism for yielding a more accurate count be developed. Second, the geographic scope of research on homelessness should be expanded. To date much of the research has focused on urban populations, but the nature and severity of the problem in rural areas are equally significant in human terms even if the number of individuals and families involved may be smaller. Third, it is clear that migration may be both a cause and a product of homelessness. Numerous communities are finding their resources for responding to the homeless overwhelmed by migrating individuals and families searching for employment and housing. Other communities surely are experiencing out-migration of homeless or at-risk populations, but there are virtually no data on this phenomenon. Research on mobility patterns of the homeless is essential, because it helps to create more effective distribution of economic support resources among local communities. Finally, there is a need for new governmental initiatives to combat the root causes of homelessness. Such broadly based policy initiatives would need to include industrial, housing, family, and tax components. It would be difficult not to interpret the public opinion data presented in this paper as a mandate for such public action.

REFERENCES

Arlington United Way. 1985. *Homelessness in Arlington: December, 1985.* Arlington, Va.: United Way of the National Capital Area.

Bahr, Howard M. 1973. *Skid Row: An Introduction to Disaffiliation.* New York: Oxford University Press.

Commonwealth of Virginia. 1985. *Report of the Joint Subcommittee Studying Hunger and Malnutrition in the Commonwealth to the Governor and the General Assembly of Virginia.* Senate Document No. 13. Richmond, Va.: Commonwealth of Virginia Senate.

Falls Church United Way. 1984. *Housing.* Annandale, Va.: Social Needs Planning Committee, Falls Church United Way.

Koenig, Alice. 1983. *Street People Survey.* Richmond, Va.: Department of Public Welfare and Virginia Commonwealth University School of Social Work.

Redburn, F. Stevens, and Terry F. Buss. 1986. *Responding to America's Homeless: Public Policy Alternatives.* New York: Praeger Publishers.

Richmond Landlord-Tenant Resource Committee. n.d. *Renting in Richmond: The Need for an Independent Landlord and Tenant Commission.* Richmond, Va.: Richmond Landlord-Tenant Commission.

Roanoke City Manager's Task Force. 1987. *No Place to Call Home: A Study of Housing and Homelessness in Roanoke, Virginia.* Roanoke, Va.: Task Force on Housing and Homelessness.

Roanoke Valley Council of Community Services. 1984. *Demonstration Project Client Tracking of Non-Medical Emergency Services: February-March, 1984.* Roanoke, Va.: Roanoke Valley Council of Community Services.

————. 1982. *Study of Emergency Services in the Roanoke Valley.* Roanoke, Va.: Roanoke Valley Council of Community Services.

Southeastern Virginia Planning District Commission. 1984. *Emergency Housing Survey.* Chesapeake, Va.: Southeastern Virginia Planning District Commission.

United Way of Greater Richmond. 1984. *Emergency Services: Developments in the Richmond Area: 1982–1984.* Richmond, Va.: United Way of Greater Richmond.

————. 1982. *Emergency Services Report.* Richmond, Va.: United Way of Greater Richmond.

U.S. Department of Health and Human Services. 1984. *A Report to the Secretary on the Homeless and Emergency Shelters.* Washington, D.C.: Office of Policy Development and Research.

Index

About the Contributors

MARTIN L. ABBOTT is an associate professor of sociology at Seattle Pacific University. He teaches and conducts research in applied sociology. Currently, Dr. Abbott is working on manuscripts that address youth homelessness and youth services policy. He has coauthored (with Gerald F. Blake) several publications in the fields of education and employment policy.

SUSAN G. BAKER is a Ph.D. candidate in sociology at the University of Texas at Austin. She specializes in demography and has done research on undocumented laborers in the United States and on the demography of homelessness in Texas.

GERALD F. BLAKE is a professor of urban studies and planning at Portland State University. His teaching and research are in the areas of community development, juvenile delinquency, and public policy. In October 1986, Dr. Blake was awarded special recognition for his work by the U.S. Department of Housing and Urban Development in conjunction with the United Nations International Year of Shelter for the Homeless.

DAVID G. BROMLEY is a professor of sociology and senior project director at the Survey Research Laboratory, Virginia Commonwealth University. His most recent book, edited with Phillip Hammond, is entitled *The Future of New Religious Movements*.

GERALD R. GARRETT is a professor of sociology at the University of Massachusetts, Boston. He currently holds a joint appointment at the university's Criminal Justice Center. He has written extensively in the field of homelessness and alcohol studies. In 1987, he coproduced (with Russell K. Schutt) a video-based training program entitled "Working with the Homeless."

GERALD R. GIOGLIO is a researcher for the New Jersey Department of Human Services, Division of Youth and Family Services. He is also an adjunct assistant professor of sociology at Rider College and an adjunct instructor at Trenton State College. He is the senior author of a statewide report (1986) on homelessness in New Jersey.

DAVID W. HARTMAN is an associate professor of anthropology and special assistant to the vice provost at Virginia Commonwealth University. He is the editor of *Immigrants and Migrants: The Detroit Ethnic Experience*.

THOMAS HIRSCHL is an assistant professor of rural sociology at Cornell University.

DANIEL M. JOHNSON is a professor of sociology and director of the Survey Research Laboratory at Virginia Commonwealth University. He is the author of *Black Migration in America*.

PETER KIVISTO is an assistant professor at Augustana College. He is the author of *Immigrant Socialists in the United States*. His most recent publications include "A Historical Review of Changes in Public Housing Policies and Their Impacts on Minorities," in *Race, Ethnicity, and Minority Housing in the United States*, edited by Jamshid A. Momeni (Greenwood Press, 1986).

J. DAVID KNOTTNERUS is an associate professor of sociology at the University of Tampa. His most recent publications include "Status Attainment Research and Its Image of Society" in the *American Sociological Review* and "Emile Durkheim: His Methodology and Uses of History" in *The Journal of the History of the Behavioral Sciences*.

JULIA S. KUNZ is a research consultant and was a member of the Missouri Task Force on Survival. Her most recent publications include *Low Income Housing in Missouri: A Report of the Low Income Housing Task Force*, published by the Missouri Association for Social Welfare in 1987.

MARK LA GORY is an associate professor of sociology, University of Alabama at Birmingham. His most recent book, co-authored with Russell Ward and Susan Sherman, is entitled *The Contexts for Aging*.

BARRETT A. LEE is an associate professor of sociology at Vanderbilt University. His current research on homelessness addresses many issues—community ties, residential mobility, and neighborhood change—that have been of general interest to urban sociologists as well as demographers.

JUDITH T. MAURIN is a professor and associate dean for academic affairs at the College of Nursing, University of Utah, Salt Lake City. She was research consultant to the Intergovernmental Task Force in Utah, formed to explore the needs and problems of homelessness in Utah. Her major research interests and publications fall in the area of psychiatric nursing.

JAMSHID A. MOMENI is an associate professor at the Graduate School of Arts and Sciences, Howard University. His most recent books include *Race, Ethnicity, and Minority Housing in the United States* (Greenwood Press, 1986) and *Housing and Racial/Ethnic Minority Status in the United States* (Greenwood Press, 1987). The twelfth edition of *Men of Achievement* is dedicated to Dr. Momeni for his outstanding contribution to the "study of low-income and minority groups in the U.S., and study of the family in the Islamic culture."

HAZEL A. MORROW-JONES is a geographer in the Department of City and Regional Planning at the Ohio State University. Her research focuses on housing and residential mobility with an emphasis on housing changes over an individual's life. Two of her recent publications are "Neighborhood Change and the Federal Housing Administration: Some Theoretical and Empirical Issues," in *Urban Studies*; and "Housing Life Cycle and the Transition from Renting to Owning a Home in the U.S," in *Environment and Planning A* (in press).

JEFFREY MULLIS is a graduate student in the Department of Sociology, University of Alabama at Birmingham. His M.S. thesis deals with homelessness in Birmingham.

TIMOTHY O'DONOGHUE is a Ph.D. candidate in the Department of Sociology, Ohio State University at Columbus. His M.S. thesis research deals with homelessness in Birmingham, Alabama.

FERRIS J. RITCHEY is an associate professor of sociology, University of Alabama at Birmingham. He has published extensively on the health professions in such journals as the *American Journal of Public Health, Human Organization*, and *Social Science and Medicine*. He is currently working on a book dealing with the history of health and medicine in Birmingham, Alabama.

DEE ROTH is chief of the Office of Program Evaluation and Research, Ohio Department of Mental Health. She was the principal investigator of a statewide epidemiological study of homeless persons in Ohio, which was funded by the National Institute of Health. Her must recent publication is "New Perspectives on the Homelessness: Findings from a Statewide Epidemiological Study'' in *Hospital and Community Psychiatry*.

ALEXIS L. RUFFIN is a graduate research assistant in the Department of Sociology and Anthropology at Virginia Commonwealth University.

LESLIE RUSSELL is a social worker with the Travelers' Aid in Salt Lake City, Utah. She coordinated the survey of homelessness in Utah under the direction of the Intergovernmental Task Force to address the needs of the homeless in Utah.

RUSSELL K. SCHUTT is an associate professor and graduate program director in the Department of Sociology at the University of Massachusetts, Boston. He is the author of *Organization in a Changing Environment* and numerous articles in the areas of homelessness, the sociology of organizations, and law.

DAVID A. SNOW is a professor of sociology at the University of Arizona. He has authored numerous articles on collective action and social movements, qualitative field work, and the current wave of homelessness in America. He and Leon Anderson are currently working on a monograph based on their field study of homelessness.

DOUG A. TIMMER is an associate professor of sociology at North Central College. His most recent publications include *Crime in the Streets and Crime in the Suites* (with D. Stanley Eitzan).

WILLEM VAN VLIET— is a sociologist in the College of Environmental Design and a research associate in the Institute of Behavioral Science at the University of Colorado, Boulder. His interests include the political-economic context of planning and the housing and community requirements of special population groups. Among his publications are several edited books, including *Housing Markets and Policies under Fiscal Austerity* (Greenwood Press, 1987), the *International Handbook of Housing Policies and Practices* (Greenwood Press, 1988), and *Women, Housing and Community*.